STAR TRUCK

A FAMILY'S JOURNEY

JOHN R. MORRISON

Trafford
PUBLISHING

Order this book online at www.trafford.com/08-0990
or email orders@trafford.com

Most Trafford titles are also available at major online book retailers.

Edited by Sheryl A. Morrison
Cover Design by Mathew Calfas

Note for Librarians: A cataloguing record for this book is available from Library
and Archives Canada at www.collectionscanada.ca/amicus/index-e.html

Printed in Victoria, BC, Canada.

ISBN: 978-1-4251-8464-3

*We at Trafford believe that it is the responsibility of us all, as both individuals
and corporations, to make choices that are environmentally and socially sound.
You, in turn, are supporting this responsible conduct each time you purchase a
Trafford book, or make use of our publishing services. To find out how you are
helping, please visit www.trafford.com/responsiblepublishing.html*

*Our mission is to efficiently provide the world's finest, most comprehensive
book publishing service, enabling every author to experience success.
To find out how to publish your book, your way, and have it available
worldwide, visit us online at www.trafford.com/10510*

www.trafford.com

North America & international
toll-free: 1 888 232 4444 (USA & Canada)
phone: 250 383 6864 ♦ fax: 250 383 6804
email: info@trafford.com

The United Kingdom & Europe
phone: +44 (0)1865 487 395 ♦ local rate: 0845 230 9601
facsimile: +44 (0)1865 481 507 ♦ email: info.uk@trafford.com

10 9 8 7 6 5 4 3 2 1

This book is dedicated to the love of my life, Sheryl, and the result of that love, Adam and Katie.

Everything happens for a reason. Who would have thought when my ancestors came across the ocean with all their worldly goods in the form of bundles of silk, anticipating the new adventure of owning a general store, that subsequent generations would spend their lives throwing papers? This is the story of my family, beginning with events in my journey, looking back at my parent's struggles, and ending with my children, finally loosening the stranglehold of the paper route.

Although every event mentioned in the book actually happened, I have adjusted some timings, locations, details and names to make more sense and flow better for my readers. The stories are taken from my perspective of what I saw, what I felt and believed. Others may not remember the events as I do. Any grammatical mistakes are mine and are not the responsibility of the diligent efforts of my English teachers. My editor probably pointed them out, but I overruled her.

RAGING WATERS KILL 18

IT WAS A DARK AND STORMY NIGHT. No, it really was a DARK and STORMY night. Check the almanac, September 12, 1977. Power was out to a large portion of the Kansas City area. Street lights that normally illuminated the neighborhoods were extinguished. The only source of light came from the nearly constant lightning, which was accompanied by the resounding clap of thunder. It was as if we were standing in a large metal building and a huge bowling ball was dropped on the roof. The rumble continued as the ball rolled to the edge, just as another ball rolled in the opposite direction up the roof. The rare occasions of silence were quickly broken by the next round of rumbling, rolling reports. Activity in the metropolitan area had ground to a halt. The main source of movement was finding protection from the onslaught wherever possible. Even though most people hibernated in the safety and warmth of their homes, a few brave souls ventured out to find food or entertainment.

The Royals tried to extend their winning streak to 13 games, but so far the only thing that could beat the Royals was the weather. They had just completed a road trip in Minnesota on Sunday with their twelfth win in a row. It had been raining in the Kansas City area since early Sunday and showed no signs of slowing down. In spite of the near torrential downfall, about 15,000 fans showed up to cheer the Royals to another certain Division title. However, in the bottom of the first inning when the good guys were just starting their rally, the skies opened up and everyone headed for cover.

Normally, the second deck overhang protected the fans sitting on the first level, but on this night, there was no protection. The rain came straight in over the left field fence and traveled horizontally until each piercing drop impaled an innocent fan. The drops were more like arrows that stung on impact. A few hardy people waited the hour rain delay before the game was officially called, but not many. Most surrendered to the storm and headed to the dry comfort of their vehicle. After sloshing through ankle-deep water, it was indeed a comfort to close the car door to the rain.

As the fans struggled to head home, they were constantly bombarded by the torrential rain. Hundreds of cars were left abandoned on normally quiet neighborhood streets as the flooding engulfed the low lying areas. For those who did not attend the game, but chose to spend a quiet evening on the Plaza, their night was shortened by warnings of high water and potential Brush Creek flooding. Most escaped the Plaza before Brush Creek charged over the banks onto the streets, but many were forced to leave their flooded cars and headed to higher ground. The newscasters said Kansas City had received over eleven inches of rain in the past twenty-four hours. This was being touted as the wettest day in Kansas City history.

My wife, Pat, and I listened to the Royals' game in the comfort of my parents' home. We were usually invited to their home every Monday evening for supper. Mother fixed my favorite, salmon croquettes and macaroni with cheese, almost every week. Pat refused to make the croquettes at home, because they were too messy and the smell of the salmon was more than she could bear. After finishing supper and clearing the table, Mother always wanted to play pinochle. We turned on the radio and listened to the ball game while we played cards. Dad shared my enthusiasm for baseball and we were thrilled to finally have a successful team in Kansas City. We would have preferred to watch the game on television, but the Royal's organization rarely televised home games. I guess they were afraid if the fans could watch the game from the comfort of their own home, no one would visit the stadium. The main source of revenue for professional baseball was still derived from ticket sales and concessions. That was the reason the Athletics left town; not many fans chose to spend their hard-earned money just to watch the home team lose another game. Charlie Finley did everything he could to make the ball park experience more exciting and enjoyable, but even green sheep grazing on the hill behind the right field fence became boring after a few minutes. We managed to play three games of pinochle by the time the Royal's game was called. It was time to get home to make sure our house hadn't floated away.

From my parents' house to our house was a short three mile trek south on Crysler. Normally, it would be an uneventful ten minute trip. However, at the bottom of the long gradual hill near 30th street, there was a very inconspicuous culvert that carried a beginning branch of Rock Creek from the east to the west. About two blocks further south, another branch rambled from the south, ran parallel to Crysler, joining the other branch to head north and west to meet up with the Little Blue. With the extreme amount of rain that had fallen in such a short time, neither bank could hold Rock Creek. It spilled out of its confines onto all of the surrounding streets and into the basements of any available home. Crysler had become impassable. I lived my whole life in Independence, yet I still spent nearly an hour navigating around creeks and low spots. At last, we arrived home, happy to see our house was still there, but disgusted to find our basement flooded. As we pulled in the driveway and opened the garage door, water came pouring out. A hundred years ago, the area where our house was built was a wooded area and a creek ran directly through our property. During extremely heavy downpours, the water table bubbled up through cracks in the basement floor, filled the basement area, and searched for any means of escape. Leaving the garage door open a couple of inches, allowed the water to just pass through. The sump pump normally eliminated the water, but the power was off and our whole neighborhood was dark.

"Are you going to work?" Pat asked the question, but already knew the answer.

"I wish I had a choice." I was not looking forward to spending three or four hours getting soaked.

In every community, there are people who are considered 'essential personnel'. Doctors, police, firemen, clergy, emergency rescue people, radio personnel, television personnel, hospital personnel, and their various support staff would certainly be considered essential. I'm not a doctor, even though

I have saved lives. I'm not a policeman, but I have caught robbers. I'm not a fireman, but I have carried people out of burning buildings. I'm definitely not a preacher, but I've done my share of preaching. I'm not a radio or television personality, but I have something to do with the media. I'm the paperboy. That certainly doesn't sound like a notable profession and I don't consider myself to be important, but the Star demands, and the customers expect, the newspaper be delivered.

Don't believe all of the hullabaloo about the mailman. If there is too much snow or ice or rain, you can expect to find an empty mailbox. If you happen to have a vicious sounding dog in your neighborhood, don't expect the mailman to venture down your street. If the roads are being resurfaced, you must go to the post office to get your mail. It doesn't take much out of the ordinary to 'stay the postman from his appointed rounds'. However, there is absolutely nothing that will allow the paperboy to shorten his route. I have driven through knee-deep snow and even pulled snow plows out of the ditch. I wasn't just being a Good Samaritan. He was in my way and I needed to get on with the route. Once in an ice storm, my truck couldn't make it to the top of the hill and it started to slide backwards. I put the transmission in Park. The wheels were not turning, but the truck was slowly sliding down the hill. On the driver's side of the street there were no cars, but the other side had cars parked all along the curb. I got out of the truck and slid around to the passenger's side. I put myself between my truck and the parked cars and manually pushed my truck away from the parked cars down to the bottom of the hill where it mercifully slowed to a stop. Even that couldn't keep me from delivering my papers to customers. In areas where it was too slick for the truck, I delivered them on foot.

When the city decided to resurface about two miles of 35th Street, they didn't just resurface it, they replaced it. The workers removed the entire existing paved surface and left nothing but a wide, deep dirt trench. When it rained, the dirt path became an impassable mud pit. The entire process from paved surface to dirt and back to paved surface took about three months. Everyone who lived on that street trudged to the post office to get their mail. They carried their trash bags to the nearest intersection for trash pick up. Those people who were unfortunate enough to live on 35th Street could not even drive to their own home. They parked their cars at the nearest intersection. Short trips to the store became a little less frequent because each trip started with a hike just to get to their car, followed by another hike carrying bags when they returned. With all of this inconvenience, the one thing that remained constant was their newspaper delivery. The paper was in every subscriber's yard every day. I parked my truck at an intersection, hiked the necessary distance to deliver to my customers, and then returned to my truck. I got plenty of exercise during those three months.

Yes, I wish I had a choice but I gave that up when I signed the contract. I agreed to deliver the papers to the subscribers every day, no matter what. You might think death would be the one thing to prevent the delivery, but it doesn't; it only delays it long enough to get someone else out to finish the route. I'm not exactly certain who decides what is essential and what is not. I just know that every day for over 100 years, the newspaper carriers in this part of the country have successfully delivered their newspapers to their appointed subscribers without exception. That may sound like a bunch of really dedicated individuals, but I believe there is a fine line between dedication and stupidity and I crossed that line a long time ago.

"It's just stupid to go out in this downpour and throw papers out in peoples' yards!" Pat wasn't letting it go. "You know how absorbent newsprint is. By the time the customers get out to pick up their papers, they'll be so soaked that they're too heavy to carry. Some of the papers will probably just float away."

"I'm not defending the intelligence of the system. I just know if I don't get out there and do the job, the Star will find someone else and I will be without income." The Star was especially demanding. If a person was unable, for any reason, to accomplish the assignment, he would be replaced. Even though I had been delivering the papers for many years, and was extremely loyal to the job, I felt no loyalty from the company in return. Whether a carrier had been delivering his route for three weeks or three decades, the Star's expectation was the same. Every paper must be delivered on time every day or that carrier would be replaced. By contract, each carrier was allowed a few complaints from customers, but not many. Every route had a different number of allowable misses but even the minimum requirement was one miss in one thousand deliveries. I was allowed one miss in fifteen hundred deliveries. More than that, and someone from the Star's corporate offices in downtown Kansas City called me to ask for an explanation. If the problem continued, I would be replaced.

The overwhelming majority of customers understood. They didn't expect miracles. When it rained as hard as it did that night, most people realized the newspaper might be a little wet. However, there were some people who expected perfection. If their neighborhood was flooded and water was standing up to their doorstep, they expected their paper to be hanging on the doorknob. Most customers thought they wanted their paper delivered on the driveway. When they picked it up, they didn't want to get their shoes wet. In order to keep the paper as dry as possible, I put it in a plastic bag. The end of the bag was open, but the bag was usually about six to eight inches longer than the paper, so it didn't gap open. When the bagged paper hit in the grass, it generally stayed relatively dry. When the bagged paper hit on the driveway, the hard surface tore tiny holes in the bag and water soaked through the holes like a sponge. Therefore, I endeavored to place each paper in the grass, but less than three feet from the driveway or sidewalk so the customer could retrieve a dry paper without getting wet shoes. If the subscriber demanded their paper on the driveway, I tried to hit the grass and slide or roll it onto the driveway. My purpose was to keep the subscriber happy. As long as they received a relatively dry paper as early as possible, they usually didn't complain.

"The power is off, so how are you going to wake up?" Pat was resigned to the fact that I would be working, but still trying to find excuses not to.

"I'll just use my old wind-up alarm clock, but I doubt if I will be getting much sleep. With the constant thunder, water in the basement, and the threat of oversleeping, I'll be happy if I get a short nap." Sleeping before the route was a luxury, not a necessity. I usually tried to get a couple of hours of sleep before the route and then passed out when I got home. Once the job was done, I could totally relax and sleep like a baby.

It seemed like only seconds until the alarm blasted. I was accustomed to waking up to the radio, so I nearly jumped out of bed when the old-fashioned bell alarm went off. I sat up on the edge of the bed, but I didn't want to say anything in case Pat managed to sleep through the din of the abnormal alarm.

"Be careful." She was awake.

"Sorry about that alarm, I forgot it was so loud."

"If I didn't have to go to work today, I'd go with you. I probably won't sleep much and I'll worry til you get home." We had already been discussing divorce, but she still did care about my safety.

"I'll be fine. It's just a little rain. Do you want me to set this alarm for you to get up? I may not be home before you leave."

"Yeah, I guess, but call me at work when you get home." She rolled over and I could hear her snoring before I went out the back door.

The rain wasn't falling when I went out to get in the truck; it was being propelled to earth as if it were shot from a gun. The raindrops were bouncing at least a foot in the air after hitting the ground. The wind was blowing so hard that the rain, at times, appeared to be moving horizontally. Water was literally coming from every direction; propelled down, bounced up, and wind-blown side to side. When I jumped in the truck, the sound was deafening. Full-size Chevy vans had no insulation in the ceiling, so there was nothing to lessen the roar of the rain. At least, for the moment, I was dry. That wouldn't last long though. I could stay dry while I picked up my helpers and even while we loaded the papers, but as soon as I started throwing papers, I would be soaked. General Motors probably spent millions of dollars on technological advancements each year, but for some reason they decided to place a gutter all around the roof of the full-size vans. The gutters had two downspouts; one, right above the driver's window and one, right above the passenger's window. I realize most people aren't foolish enough to drive around in the rain with their window open, but it's impossible to get the papers out of the truck without some sort of opening. Just having the window down, obviously, causes the driver to get wet, but whenever a corner turns to the right, all of the water on the roof pours through the downspout right in the driver's window. At that point, I might as well be driving a convertible.

I checked to make sure I had a supply of towels. I tried to always keep at least two bath towels in the truck just in case it rained. I generally folded one of the towels in fourths and placed it on my left leg to absorb as much water as possible. I used the other one to dry my face and arm. On a day like this, the towels would be saturated in the first few minutes. From then on, I would just have to deal with the discomfort of being drenched.

At about 2:00 a.m. on a cloudy night, the main source of illumination is supplied by street lights. From an airplane, it is easy to identify cities by the number of lights along streets and highways. The glow from the lights in Kansas City is normally visible for miles. During a strong storm like this one, most of the electrical substations experience trouble and lose power to the lights. With the moon hidden and most of the street lights out, the Kansas City area probably looked similar to the way it must have looked to Lewis and Clark when they explored the area. As I turned on Blue Ridge, which was a common trail for the explorers, I had an unobstructed view to the East and the West. I noticed one small area to the Southwest that still had lights and one area to the East over by Noland Road was still illuminated. Noland Road was the retail hotspot in Independence and nearly every business offered large parking lots with plenty of artificial light. The natural light was not provided by the moon on this night; it was provided by the nearly constant flashes of lightning.

"Whoa! That was too close!" Lightning struck a tree off to my left just as I passed. As the tree fell, some of the branches extended into the road behind me. Then another strike occurred just ahead of me and to the north. I felt as if I was driving a tank down a deserted road and being used as target practice. As I turned onto 40 Highway, the rain slacked up a little. There were still numerous lightning strikes, but the thunder was delayed, so I knew the current storm was moving away.

As I headed west to pick up my helpers, Rick and Charles, I recollected the problems I had getting home a few hours earlier and tried to plan ahead. Where would the low-lying areas be that might cause trouble? The first problem would certainly be Manchester. That area always had problems with flooding. Blue Ridge Cut-Off and Raytown Road might be a problem also. I could only do my job and deal with issues as I encountered them.

As I pulled up in Rick's driveway, I honked my horn. Normally he would flick the light off and on to let me know he was up, but it occurred to me, after a quick look at his darkened street light, he probably didn't have any electricity. I waited patiently because he was very good about getting ready quickly. Rick was only 15 years old, and he was very small, but strong. Frequently he wore weights around his wrists and ankles to build up his strength. He knew he couldn't do much about his height, but he wouldn't even entertain the thought of being weak. The rain had nearly stopped when he came out the front door. He was too cool to be bothered by the rain, so he didn't hurry.

"Mornin." He never did say much.

"Good morning! Isn't this a beautiful day?" I hoped to get a smile out of him.

"You're weird. I'm just glad I don't have to run the apartments." Even though he didn't say a lot, he usually was thinking. I had forgotten about the apartments. I had two sets of apartments on my route. One of them was pretty short and only took about 15 minutes to deliver about 40 papers. The set he was referring to, took about an hour to deliver about 100 papers. Rick and Charles took turns delivering the apartments. While one was out of the truck delivering the apartments, the other one would go with me to deliver papers to about 200 customers.

"I hope Charles remembers he'll be out of the truck in the rain." I never really knew what to expect from Charles. He was a 15-year-old Barney Fife without a gun. He was definitely a geek and certainly not strong. He may have possessed average intelligence, but lacked common sense.

"We're talkin' about Charles here. We'll be lucky if he remembers to wear shoes." Rick loved to make fun of Charles but in truth, they were good friends.

Charles lived just a couple of blocks from Rick. His house was on the corner and he slept right in front of the window. He usually left the curtains open so the headlights from the truck would wake him up. I turned around at the corner and stopped so the lights were shining right in the window.

"Looks like you'll have to honk." Rick said with a slight smirk on his face. He enjoyed seeing Charles react to the horn.

I hit the horn and it was as if I had set off an explosion in his mattress. Sheets went flying and Charles was launched out of bed.

Rick and I could not control the laughter. Charles went to the light switch and could not figure out why the lights didn't work.

"What a dork!" Rick said with a grin.

Charles managed to find his clothes and disappear out of his room. It was several minutes before he came out the front door.

"What a dork!" Rick said again as Charles appeared wearing a rain coat, a rain hat, and boots. His mother was standing at the door behind him. "Looks like his mom dressed him."

"Our lights don't work!" Charles said as he got in the truck, possibly giving an excuse why it took him so long to get ready.

Before I had a chance to say anything, Rick blurted out, "Everybody's lights are out, idiot." Rick constantly made fun of Charles. "You plannin' on goin' swimmin'?"

"It's my turn to run the long apartments and I don't want to get soaked." Charles said, with an air of superiority, as if he knew something Rick didn't.

"With all of that stuff on, you wouldn't get wet if you fell in a lake." Rick just had to get the last word.

"Can we split the apartments?" Charles just ignored Rick and was hoping I would give him a little break. Sometimes, when the weather was particularly nasty, I would let one helper out at the first apartment building and the other one out at the last building, while I drove around by myself and threw a short section that only took about 20 minutes.

"No, with this weather, I want someone in the truck with me just in case of any trouble." I didn't tell Charles what he wanted to hear.

"What do you mean 'trouble'?" Rick sounded like he might wish he was running the long apartments instead of going with me.

"I don't know. You just never know what problems might come up in these weather conditions." I didn't expect any problems, but I was telling the truth: you never know.

"Hey Cricket, are you on your way? This is Scoreboard. Over." The CB radio surprised all of us. I had forgotten it was on. Don was another carrier who picked up his papers at the same location I did. He lived just across the interstate from the Royals' scoreboard, thus the handle. I could do a weird sound with my tongue people said sounded like a cricket, thus my handle.

"This is Cricket. I'll be there in a couple of minutes. Are the papers there yet? Over."

"Yeah. I guess they ran early because of the weather. Over."

I pulled into the gas station and backed up under the canopy as close as I could get to the Star truck. Rick and Charles already had the back door open and were starting to load the papers. They knew I was in a hurry.

"How many do I get, Chuck?" I walked up to the driver and he handed me a small stack of loose papers.

"You get 17 bundles and here's your odd. What do you want me to do with Charlie's papers?" Chuck didn't want to set anyone's papers on the ground because there wasn't a dry place, even under the canopy.

"Did you hear that, Rick, 17?" I looked in the back door and quickly counted the bundles. Rick was already in his chair and starting to roll the papers. He had counted correctly. I handed the odd to Charles. I was supposed to receive 1036 papers. There were 60 papers in a bundle and I trusted Chuck to count the additional 16 loose papers.

Charlie didn't have a CB in his truck but I knew he was on his way. He probably had trouble waking up his helpers.

"Do you want me to put his papers in my truck?" I was hoping Chuck would say no but I had to offer because we want to keep our truck driver happy and I knew his job was not done. After giving us our papers, he still had to drive out to Blue Springs and take papers to another eight carriers.

"No, I'll wait a little longer." He knew I didn't want to deal with anything extra on a night like this.

"Here he comes. I'd better get out of the way." Charlie was moving pretty fast toward us on 40 Highway. I pulled around to the other side of the gas pumps and waited for Charlie to start loading his papers. Sometimes he had messages for me from customers who either wanted to start or stop their service. I didn't own this route. It belonged to Charlie's dad, Raymond. Since most of the customers had been given Raymond's phone number, they preferred to call him for any change in their service.

"Got any messages for me?" I asked Charlie, after he had all of his papers loaded.

"No, just try to keep dry and look out for standing water." I imagined that was the same advice Raymond gave Charlie before he left to go on his route. Raymond had finally retired after spending about 40 years running his route. Raymond's dad was one of the first newspaper carriers in the area. When Raymond, Sr. started delivering papers, he was responsible for most of the area east of Kansas City.

"Not much of a chance keeping dry, but I'll try to get around without giving the truck a belly-bath. If there are any areas I can't get to because of high water, I'll call Raymond and let him know." Even though Raymond had quit driving a route, he still was up and awake doing something while we were out delivering and available if we needed help. That's why I invested in a CB radio. In case of emergency, I could call on the radio and ask for someone with a land-line to make a call for me. It had already come in handy a couple of times.

My route began as soon as I left the gas station. Some carriers have to drive for several miles before they start actually delivering to subscribers. I thought back to all of the routes I had delivered and realized I had been fortunate. The longest distance I ever drove before I started to throw to customers was about a mile.

It didn't take very long to throw all of the papers in the area south of 40 Highway. Then I stopped in to drop off the papers at the Sheraton-Royal Hotel. I left one stack of papers at the front desk. Those papers went to special guests who requested the morning paper with their breakfast. When a visiting baseball team stayed at the Sheraton, the number of papers at the front desk was always a lot larger. I left another stack of papers at the Gift Shop for sale to other guests.

From the Sheraton I headed straight to the Sports Complex to deliver the area west of Blue Ridge Cut-Off and south of 40 Highway. With the long driveways and parking lots at the Complex, it was a long distance to drive and a lot of trouble to deliver a very small number of papers. The Royals wanted four papers delivered to the main door of their stadium. The Jackson County Sports Authority wanted six papers delivered on the south side of Arrowhead Stadium, up a long sidewalk, and over a 10 foot tall fence. I guess the Chiefs couldn't read, because they didn't subscribe to the paper. From the Sports Complex, I headed out the west exit and down the hill to Manchester, where I encountered my first battle with the flooding. The Little Blue had backed up over its banks and flooded the intersection of Manchester and Stadium Drive. It was impossible for me to get through, so I turned around and went back up Stadium Drive to 40 Highway. It was a little more back-tracking than usual, but we made it easily during the rest of the north section. The rain slacked up while Rick delivered the short apartments. Just about the time I headed south on Sterling and crossed under I-70, it started to pour again. By the time I pulled into the apartment complex, Charles was in full battle gear. The only part of his body left exposed was his nose.

"Look out for the Bogey Man!" Rick warned Charles as he was getting ready to get out. "With all of this rain, he could be waiting for you inside any building." Charles wouldn't admit it, but he was scared to run the apartments by himself. Rick took full advantage of his fear by saying anything that might make Charles worry. Rick loved to hurry around and finish our deliveries before Charles completed his, so he could try to scare him. As we pulled out of the apartment complex, Rick was urging me to hurry so he could scare Charles.

We made it down 43rd Street and through the loop just east of Blue Ridge Cut-Off, but when I turned south on the Cut-Off, I could see I wasn't going to get to the trailer court. The intersection with Raytown Road was flooded. Rick wanted to get a close look at it, so I drove down as close as I felt was safe. As I turned around, my headlights hit something reflective.

"What's the matter?" Rick asked as I stopped my u-turn and backed up.

"Something's down there. Can you see how my lights are reflecting off of something?" Just then a bright flash of lightning helped both of us to see the tail of a car sticking up out of the ditch.

"I hope there's no one in it!" I said as I began to get out of the truck.

"Where are you going? Are you going to leave me here alone?" There was definitely apprehension in his voice.

"Get on the CB and ask for help. Tell someone you need the police and an ambulance sent to the intersection of Blue Ridge Cut-Off and Raytown Road. Be sure to tell them to come in from the north." I was glad I had Rick with me instead of Charles. Rick's nature was more calm and he was more likely to get the instructions correct than Charles. I heard him calling on the CB as I ran toward the wrecked car.

The water level had been higher and the car may have been totally submerged at one time, but now the back half was sticking up out of the ditch. It had probably been washed down the ditch and had come to rest against a tree. Before I realized it, I was walking in water about six inches deep. I thought about Charlie's warning; so much for staying dry. Once I reached the car, I held on to it for stability. I tried to see if there was anyone in the car, but it was too dark. Just then, "Thank you God", another bright flash of lightning illuminated the whole area. Someone was inside the car. I couldn't tell much, but he or she was not moving. I hoped the police would be arriving soon but I still hadn't heard any sirens. What if the person was still alive? I felt I needed to do whatever I could to get this person out of this car. I wondered why the car was not full of water and then I realized when water impaled the car on the tree, a window busted out. I slowly maneuvered my way around the car and reached the open window. Now I could see the occupant was a woman who apparently had her seat belt on and was still behind the steering wheel. The door was too badly crushed to open, so I leaned in through the open window. As I put my weight on the car, it shifted and I could just envision myself and the car being swept away by the current. I could hear the distant wail of a siren. Maybe I should just get out of this thing and let the pros handle it, but what if she was still alive? I had to get her out. As I tried to reach for the seat belt release, the car moved again. At this point I was committed to the retrieval. We were either getting out of this car together or we were going to go for a ride down the river together. Once I released the seat belt, her body slumped toward the open window. Her body felt lifeless, but I knew it was possible to be under water for a while and still be revived. I pushed on her stomach and water came out of her mouth. I know that should probably tell me something, but at the time I just wanted to help. I pushed again and when no water came out, I put my mouth over hers and blew into it. I knew how to do mouth-to-mouth resuscitation and I knew time was of the essence. Between breaths, I moved her closer to the window. After one last breath, I pulled her out of the car. The water was moving rapidly and it was difficult for me to move. I pinned her against the car and gave her another breath.

"Hold on! We'll help you!" I was never so happy to hear a stranger's voice. In just a few seconds, there were 3 or 4 men holding on to me.

"I'm fine, but I don't know about her." I said as I handed her off to one of the firemen. One man helped me cross the street and get up on the hill. He wrapped a blanket around me and I realized I was freezing.

"Is she alive?" I asked but no one answered.

Several paramedics were working on her as they loaded her into an ambulance. After it pulled away, one of the policemen came over to me. When he got close, I realized it was Don. Don was not only a policeman, but a friend I had known for several years. In fact, we coached a little league baseball team together. Physically, he was the consummate police officer. He was a little over 6 feet tall and over 200 pounds. He had a very kind disposition and rarely gave out tickets.

"They're doing everything they can to revive her but I think it's too late. Did you see the car get swept away?" He asked, as he pulled out his pad of paper.

"No, I didn't see it get swept away. I just saw it as I turned around to head back up the hill. I didn't know how long it had been there." I wished I could have been more help.

"She could have been there for a long time." He said as he put his pad of paper away. "I know who you are and how to get in touch with you, so you can get back to work if you want." Don knew the paperman routine. One of the firemen handed me a cup of hot coffee.

"Thanks, I feel a lot better now, but I'm only about half done with the route, so I'd better get back to work. I don't suppose you guys have some dry clothes do you?" I was not really expecting them to supply me with dry clothes, but, as it turned out, was glad I asked.

"Hey John, I keep a spare pair of sweats in the trunk of my car. You can wear those if you want." As we reached Don's patrol car, he said, "Here's the sweats but I don't have a towel."

"That's okay; I have a towel in the truck." I took off all of the wet clothes, dried off, and put on the dry sweats.

"Thanks a lot, Don. I was gonna run home and get some dry clothes. That would have added about an hour to the route. I'll bring the sweats by your house later today."

"No rush, it's not my only pair." He said as he got in his car.

"I'd like to stay and chat but I left a helper in the apartments and I need to pick him up. Do you have to stay here?" I was still talking to him as I turned the truck around.

"Yeah, I have to stay and write up the report and wait for a tow truck to come pull the car out of the ditch. I don't suppose you have any extra papers, do you?" I was a little embarrassed he had to ask. I tried to always offer a paper to policemen whenever I saw them, because they frequently had to spend a lot of time just sitting around waiting to receive a call. I had to carry a lot of extra papers to supply the hotels and news racks, so I always had extra papers.

"Here you go." I said as I tossed him a paper. "Thanks again for the dry clothes."

"That was cool of him to let you have his sweats." Rick said as we started heading back to the north. He hadn't said much but he was observing everything that took place. He was a teenager and to him cops were seen as the enemy, not the friend.

"Most cops are just guys like you and me." I wanted to be very careful how I worded my next statement. I didn't want it to sound fake but I wanted him to remember it. "Cops are kind of like preachers, they receive a calling. They become cops because they want to help and protect people. The only trouble is sometimes in the process of doing their job they have to arrest people or give out tickets, so they are seen as bad guys. As long as you stay on the right side of the law, you will find that cops are your friends."

He didn't say anything but I could tell he was thinking it over. I needed to change the subject because I didn't want this to become a discussion about the good and bad points of being a policeman. Don had made a very positive impression by helping me and I wanted to leave it at that.

"I wonder if Charles is done with the apartments." I was trying to lighten the conversation.

"Was she dead?" Rick had observed a lot of things happening and he was still trying to process all he had seen.

"I don't know. Don said she wasn't breathing when they put her in the ambulance but the paramedics were still trying to revive her." I was trying to stick to the facts and not express my opinions.

"You took a big chance wading out in the water and climbing in to pull her out of that car. Why'd you do it? You didn't know her, did you?" The questions had been bottled up and now they were coming out.

"I didn't know her and I did it because it needed to be done. Someone was in trouble and I was in a position to help. I would hope you would do the same thing if you were in my place. She is someone's daughter and maybe someone's mother. What if it was your mother, wouldn't you want someone to help, even if he was a stranger?"

"Of course, I'd want someone to help my mom." He hesitated for a long while and then he said something that made the whole ordeal of getting soaked and frozen and nearly drowned all worthwhile. "Thanks." A tear came to my eye. That one word couldn't have meant any more to me if it had come from the woman's only son.

We didn't say any more about the subject. We pulled in to the apartments and Charles came running out. He had a story to tell about the exciting events that happened to him while he was delivering the papers in the apartments.

"You won't believe what happened!" He was so excited.

I looked in the rear view mirror just as Rick looked up at me. He smiled and I nodded my head and smiled back.

"There was some guy sleeping down under the stairs in the building down by the freeway. I guess he came in to get out of the rain and fell asleep. It scared me when I first saw him and then I realized he was asleep." The story didn't have the impact that Charles was hoping for.

"Maybe he was dead." Rick was trying to help Charles make his story more exciting.

"I thought he was at first, but then I heard him snoring." Charles realized his story was not quite as scary as he had hoped. "What took you guys so long?"

Before I could say anything, Rick said, "John waded out into a river and pulled a dead woman out of a car."

"Yeah, right. I'm sure THAT happened." Charles thought Rick was just making up a story to beat his.

"He's telling the truth Charles, but we're not sure if she is dead. I hope not." That's about all I got to say about the events that transpired. Rick took over and spent the rest of the route telling Charles every exciting tidbit, making certain to point out I was wearing different clothes.

After we finished the route and were on our way back to their houses, Charles asked, "Is that the most exciting thing that ever happened to you?"

I thought for a moment and said, "No, it's not the MOST exciting, but it's probably in the top ten.

"I want to hear about the other nine." Rick said.

"Me, too!" Charles chimed in, instantly.

"We don't have time now." I said as I turned down their street.

"Will you tell us the other nine this afternoon?" Charles was excited about the possibility of hearing some thrilling stories.

"Maybe I can tell you one or two." I let them out of the truck and headed home.

With all of the time I spent on the route, my wife was going to be gone to work by the time I got home. I called her and told her the exciting tale.

After our conversation, I laid down to try to sleep. My mind wandered as I considered my current situation. I was a paperboy. Why hadn't I become a lawyer? What stopped me from becoming a preacher or teacher, like Grandma Parrish hoped for? Why was I facing divorce? At critical times in my past, I had to choose one path and avoid the other. If I could do it all over, would I choose the same path?

My life has been a journey. As I grew older, I developed likes and dislikes. I became interested in some things and steered away from others. I imagine there are times when a person chooses a particular path and there are probably times when the path chooses the person. Some people choose labor, some choose professional work, some choose parenthood, and some just wander aimlessly looking for direction. What were the other nine exciting events in my life? How did this whole thing get started? At 30 years old, why was I still a paperboy?

MORRISON-PARRISH NUPTIALS

MY NEWSPAPER DELIVERY JOURNEY BEGAN WITH THE DEATH OF ABIGAIL JONES. I never met her, but her death affected my parents' lives, and ultimately my own. Anyone who shares this account is also influenced by her death. It's strange how seemingly innocuous events can sometimes change the course of history. The majority of people seem to be walking down one path. It is the chosen path because it is the shortest and most direct way of moving from one place to another. Then one day, someone decides to step off of the path and journey up the hill. Even though my life has not been constantly down the chosen path, I have tried to stay close enough to return to it, if necessary. On a few of those occasions when I have strayed off of the beaten path, I have experienced remarkable events. On other occasions, I have experienced heart-wrenching catastrophes. Sometimes, even the busiest roadways become impassable and it is necessary to take a detour. Those detours may have been dead ends, or they may have been beautiful passageways. Everyone must make their own choices and follow their own path.

I should start at the beginning. My parents met at a time when most travel was done on foot or on horse-back and the boundary of their world was the distance that could be covered in a single day. Since they were both from a rural area, the number of potential marriage partners was very limited. Religion was very important in each of their families, so it is not surprising they met at a church function. Dorothy was a wiry tomboy who loved to climb trees and didn't mind getting dirty. She would tell you she lived in the city, but Norborne only had about 200 occupants and that sounds rural to me. Her family, the Parrishes, attended the Methodist Church. She never missed attending Delphian League, which was the youth group meeting. Bill was a wiry little guy, but he didn't have time to climb any trees. He didn't mind getting dirty. He was a farmer. He made his living in the dirt. The Morrisons were very devout Presbyterians and never missed a Sunday service.

Two of Dorothy's close friends, Henry and Allen Brenneman, had decided to earn some extra money during the summer by helping out on one of the local farms. As chance would have it, they chose the Morrison farm. There, they became close friends with the youngest Morrison boy, Bill. After a week of hard labor on the farm, they invited Bill to attend Delphian League with them on Sunday afternoon. However, Bill, the Presbyterian, didn't have any idea what a Delphian could possibly be.

Once he found out girls attended this activity, he didn't have to be asked twice. Dorothy had several friends, but her closest were those who also attended her church. Georgia Marie and Marjorie Thomas were her best girl friends and Leon Beck was her best male friend. Most people in Norborne thought Dorothy and Leon would probably get married some day. They lived next door to each other, attended the same class in school, and worshipped at the same church. They actually may have gotten married some day if Bill hadn't chosen to take the 'other' path and went to a Methodist Church function. Dorothy loved to laugh and Bill was funny. When Leon asked Dorothy to walk home with him from Church, Bill asked her to go with him and the Brenneman boys and the Thomas girls to Richmond to get some ice cream. She loved ice cream and wanted to spend some more time with Bill, so she chose to stray from the well-worn path with Leon and venture down the unknown path with Bill. From that time forward, Leon never had a chance. It took Bill about three months to get up enough courage to kiss Dorothy, but by then, they knew they had a special bond.

Bill had graduated from high school when he met Dorothy and he became her constant escort to all school, church, and community activities. To his parents' chagrin, he attended the Methodist Church every Sunday. He couldn't tell the difference between what the Presbyterian preacher said and what the Methodist preacher said. Dorothy was at the Methodist Church, so choosing a pew on Sunday morning was an easy decision. They didn't totally abandon the Presbyterian church. Dorothy knew the Morrisons were quite active in their own church and, since she didn't want to cause any potential problems with Bill's family, they occasionally attended Presbyterian church activities.

Over the next year, Bill spent a great deal of time in Norborne. Almost every Sunday, Bill went to the Parrish house for dinner. While Dorothy helped her mother in the kitchen, Bill visited with Mr. Parrish in the parlor. During those times, Mr. Parrish talked to Bill about the future and his plans and dreams. Bill wanted to follow in his dad's footsteps and make a living working on the farm. Mr. Parrish told him being a farmer was hard work and there were no days off. Someday he hoped one of his children might take over the Parrish family store.

During the summer, after Dorothy graduated from high school, Bill spent more and more time in Norborne with her and her family. Dorothy worked at her dad's store and sometimes didn't get home until late. Bill patiently waited for her and then they would go for a ride in his car. Sometimes they went to Richmond. Sometimes they went to Carrollton. Sometimes they just rode around in Norborne. It didn't really matter where they went or what they did, as long as they could do it together. On one of those warm evenings, as they sat on Dorothy's front porch, Bill seemed more serious than usual. After a particularly long quiet time, he said, "I really do like you."

Dorothy was very quick to respond, "Oh, Bill, I really like you, too. When I'm not with you, I look forward to the time I will see you and when I'm with you, I dread thinking of the time when you have to leave."

Bill tried to figure out what to say. "I've liked lots of people, but it's not the same with you. 'Like' isn't quite strong enough. I'm not real sure what love is, but I know when I'm with you, I feel happy and when I'm not with you, I feel like I forgot to do something or something's missing. I care a great deal about you and it hurts me when something bad happens to you. I like it when you laugh because I feel like I'm making you happy."

Dorothy interrupted, "You really do make me happy."

Bill continued, "I would like to make you happy for the rest of your life. I've seen the way my parents care about each other and I know they love each other. I've read in the Bible about love and…" There was a long pause as Bill reached to the depths of his soul. His face was very serious and, as they held hands, Dorothy looked at him with anticipation. "I do love you!"

Dorothy couldn't hold back the tears any longer. "I do love you, too, Bill!"

"Why are you crying? I thought you'd be happy." Bill was confused.

"Oh, Bill, I am happier than I've ever been in my whole life. These are tears of joy."

They continued to take short trips to the surrounding area over the next couple of months. They enjoyed their time together and took a great deal of joy in experiencing new places together for the first time. In August, Bill asked Dorothy if she would walk down another new path with him. He told her he didn't know where the path might lead or what they might encounter along the way, but whatever life brought, he wanted to share with her. She had no idea what the future had in store for her, but she had come to trust Bill, and she knew he would take care of her. Even when things felt hopeless, Bill would find a way to make her laugh and fix the problem.

"Even if our house burns down, we still need to feed the livestock and milk the cows. When that's done, we can rebuild a bigger house." His phi- losophy sounded very simple, but I think that's what made him strong. He didn't question why things had to be done, he just did them. His time on the farm prepared him for other work. He'd love to be able to take a day off and relax, but 'the cows don't know if it's Sunday or Wednesday, they still need to be milked.'

Bill's oldest brother, Kirk, was an ordained minister for the Presbyterian Church and served as a missionary to Africa. Although Kirk and his family lived in the Belgian Congo for most of the year, he was given an opportunity to return home to the church that sponsored him about once a year to report to the church about the year's events in the Congo. Kirk and his wife, Eleanor, were to return to Missouri around Christmas and stay there about a month. It was Bill's hope that he and Dorothy could be married by Kirk while he was home. There wasn't a lot of time for wedding preparation and Dorothy had hoped for a Spring wedding, but their only chance to have Kirk perform the service would mean a wedding in the first weekend of January.

Winter was tough in Missouri. The temperature could reach 60 between December 1 and February 1, but it was truly a rare event. The daily high temperature was normally in the thirties and the overnight low could easily drop below zero. I would like to say God blessed Bill and Dorothy with a 60 degree beautiful day, but He didn't. The weather was just another rough spot in the road. They worked around it. The temperature dropped into the twenties overnight, but at least it hadn't snowed. Then, in mid morning, the freezing rain started to fall. Luckily, Kirk had spent the night on the Morrison farm. It would have been difficult for him to travel from Richmond in the inclement weather. Dorothy was not only concerned about keeping her wedding dress dry, but now, with ice forming on the ground, falling was also a concern. After lunch, the freezing rain subsided and the temperature warmed up a little. However, the rain continued to fall. She was afraid the bad weather would prevent people from attending her wedding. It would be very unlikely Grandpa and Grandma Fidler would be able to make the trip from Meadville. Dorothy loved her grandparents very much and she wanted them to witness this special day.

Considering the dreadful weather conditions, Bill and Dorothy were pleasantly surprised with the large number of people who attended the ceremony. Since Dorothy's father owned the local dry goods store, most people in town and even in surrounding areas knew the family. The Morrisons and the Parrishes were very active in their respective churches, so many church members braved the elements. Both families were well represented. Dorothy and Bill were married in the living room of the Parrish home. There were about 75 people in attendance. Bill's brother, S.B., was the best man and Dorothy's sister-in-law, Helen, was the matron-of-honor. Dorothy's little sister, Carolyn was the flower girl. The wedding service was lovely and Kirk tied a knot that would never be broken.

There was a small reception after the service and the newlyweds left for a honeymoon in Kansas City. The rain stopped, but the roads were still slick and dangerous. The new couple traveled in Bill's 1930 Dodge and made the 70 mile trip in about three hours. Even though they thoroughly enjoyed staying at the new Aladdin Hotel and were awed by the many new inventions in the big city, they still longed to be home. After a short 4 day stay in Kansas City, they returned home to Norborne. Before they settled down to life on the farm, they took a trip to Meadville to visit Dorothy's grandparents. Dorothy was very close to her mother's parents. She loved to sit and listen to her grandfather tell stories of the old days and Grandmother Fidler always had a plethora of helpful hints for making a happy home. Bill listened intently to Grandfather Fidler's advice and was astonished to find this old man was still so strong and so vibrant. The weather began to turn bad again, so the young couple decided they should head for home. When they returned to Cowgill, they settled into the Morrison farm, sharing the house with Bill's parents. Dorothy was a willing student, as Mother Morrison taught her how to cook, clean, sew, and do farm chores. Her goal was to keep her new husband happy.

HELP WANTED: RETAIL

THE YOUNG COUPLE WORKED DILIGENTLY AND MADE A GREAT EFFORT TO SURVIVE ON THE FARM, BUT EVENTUALLY, THEY HAD TO MOVE INTO TOWN. With a growing family and greater needs, Bill realized he must work harder to take care of his wife and children. Robert, their first-born, was born a year and nine months after their marriage. Barbara came along about five years later. When the war broke out, Bill wanted to serve in the military. Even though he had two children at home, he went to Kansas City with some friends to enlist in the army. During the physical examination, the doctors discovered his flat feet and he was not accepted in any branch of the military. He was very disappointed and embarrassed that he could not pass the physical to get into the army. He wanted to do his part in fighting the war. The enlistment officer told him if he wanted to help out, he could apply for a job at Lake City Ammunition Plant. Bill was familiar with Lake City, so he stopped by there on his way back to Norborne. The enlistment officer was right; Lake City was in need of people to work all shifts. Bill was happy working in support of the military and Dorothy was happy he didn't have to go overseas. Their third child, Billy, was born on the same day the atomic bomb was dropped on

Hiroshima, Japan -- August 6, 1945. Billy's birthday signaled an end to World War II, but it also signaled an end to Bill's job.

For most of the next year, Bill floundered around looking for work. He and Dorothy both helped out at Grandpa Parrish's store and he took whatever work he could find to bring home some money. Grandpa Parrish continued to remind Bill and Dorothy their best chance to succeed would be if they could run their own business. Dorothy's brother Carlton worked in Kansas City and he said he saw an advertisement in the Star for someone to open a clothing store in Windsor, Missouri. Carlton, Bill, and Grandpa Parrish went to look at the community. There was already a clothing store there, but they all agreed the area should be able to support another one. They went to the other store and discovered it was lacking in many areas of supplies. Grandpa Parrish told Bill he would help him with ordering goods and giving him advice on volume of stock to keep on hand. Carlton said he would be available to help out financially, if he was needed. Bill needed about $2000.00 to get the store stocked and open. When the young couple discussed their options, they didn't know if Windsor was taking them further off the path or bringing them back to the path. Bill still felt he would be more comfortable depending on the soil to meet his needs, but with a wife and family to provide for, he followed the advice of his father-in-law. After selling their home in Norborne, the family made the 100 mile move south to Windsor. It was a summer move, so Dorothy registered Robert and Barbara for their new school. Bill ordered clothing similar to what was in the Parrish store in Norborne, but soon found out he had over-stocked. Residents of the community were loyal to the old store and making enough sales proved to be difficult.

Bill and Dorothy struggled to make enough money to meet the needs of their young family, but they both felt they were on a dead end. With three children at home and another one on the way, Dorothy was not able to help much at the store. Bill put in long hours and great effort to succeed, but this path wasn't meant to be. He contacted family members to see if anyone knew of any potential job openings. He didn't want to move his family until after the new baby arrived. In July of 1947, I was born. I was the only one of my mother's children born in a hospital and held the record for being the biggest baby in the hospital nursery. For my short stay in the hospital, I was nicknamed Butch by the nursing staff. Thankfully, when I came home with my parents, I left the moniker in the nursery.

Mother received a great deal of help from her neighbor, Genevieve Nine, but with the store barely making a profit, and another mouth to feed, Dad knew it was time to choose another path. He had signed a two-year lease on the store building and was renting a small house on a month-to-month basis. When the store owner contacted Dad with the option to sign another lease, my parents agreed it was time to leave town. Dad had relatives who worked in Kansas City and they told him he could get a job at Montgomery Wards. After closing the store in Windsor, Dad took a trip to the Kansas City area to locate a job and a place to live. Dad's cousin invited the Morrison clan to live with them until a suitable residence could be found. My parents packed up all of the clothes from the store and moved our family again. This time the path led us to Independence.

My parents looked diligently for a house they felt they could afford. Dad's cousin worked with a woman whose father had recently passed away. The old man's house was in deplorable condition, but the price was affordable. When Mother first walked in the front door, she nearly fainted from the stench. In addition to chewing tobacco, the old man had not completely accepted the concept of indoor plumbing and was totally against laundering clothes. Mother recognized making the house livable was an immense chore, but attainable. She also realized the prospect of finding another house as large as this one, for a comparable price, was very unlikely. It was a large two story house with two bedrooms upstairs, a living room, dining room, bedroom, kitchen, and bathroom on the first floor, and a full basement. Probably the biggest selling point for Dad was it had a large vacant lot attached to it. Dad saw the lot as a perfect garden place. He could use his farming skills to grow food for the family. Dad worked at many jobs, sometimes 2 or 3 at a time. While working at Wards, he also worked at a garage, where he pumped gas and did some light mechanic work. We certainly were not rich, but there was always food on the table, clean clothes to wear, and presents under the tree on Christmas morning.

Grandpa Parrish knew our family was having a hard time financially, so when Robert finished the seventh grade, he gave him ten dollars with the understanding, "I don't want you to go out and spend all of that money on candy and soda pop. You have to promise me you will use the money to buy a lawn mower so you can make some extra money." As soon as he could, Robert rode his bicycle up to the Western Auto store just a block from the Square in uptown Independence and looked at lawn mowers. The cheapest one was $19.50. When he returned home, he told Dad he wasn't going to be able to buy a lawn mower yet, because he didn't have enough money. Dad told him he couldn't afford to give him $10.00, but he would loan it to him. Robert agreed to give Dad $2.00 each week until he had paid back the entire $10.00. The next day Robert went to Western Auto and put down the ten dollar bill he got from Grandpa Parrish. The following week, when Dad got his paycheck, Robert was able to pay the other $10.00 and bring home the mower. He started out mowing a couple of lawns on our street, but soon some of the church members wanted him to mow their yards. He built up his business and before long he had twenty-two customers and walked as far as 2 miles between jobs. Even after Robert had paid back the $10.00 loan to Dad, he continued to give him half of whatever he made.

One day when Robert was mowing a lawn on Noland Road, a man across the street asked him if he would like a drink of water. As they sat in the shade, the man introduced himself as Myron Johnson and told Robert he delivered the Kansas City Star in the Independence area. Myron asked where he lived, and Robert told him his family lived just south of 23rd Street on Pleasant. Myron was familiar with the location because he delivered papers on that street. Realizing Robert was facing a 2-mile hike home, pushing a lawn mower, on a ninety degree day, Myron offered to take him home. Myron said he always needed good helpers and asked Robert if he would like to earn some additional money working on the paper route. Myron paid his help two dollars per trip. Robert would have helped on the paper route just to get the ride home, but he was certainly not going to turn down the additional cash. Mother was a little surprised when Robert showed up later than expected in some stranger's truck. She went out to the truck to talk to Mr. Johnson and agreed to allow Robert to work for him on a part-time basis. Robert worked nearly every morning and afternoon on the paper route and still continued to mow lawns. Myron realized the Morrison family could use the financial assistance and he always looked for good responsible help, so he was happy to allow Robert to work as much as he wanted.

Occasionally, when Myron brought Robert home after the paper route, Dad or Mother would go out and talk to him. Myron and his wife, Margaret, became good friends with Dad and Mother. Even though Dad was working at two jobs, nights at the steel mill and days driving the city bus, Myron asked him if he would be interested in driving the paper route so he could take a few days off. Newspaper carriers rarely had the opportunity to take days off because the paper had to be delivered seven days a week. It was extremely difficult to find drivers who understood the importance of dependability. Myron offered to pay Bill $50.00 to run the route for seven days. In addition, he would pay Robert $2.50 a trip plus $5.00 on Sunday. Together, they could make $85.00. Bill couldn't pass up the opportunity to put that much money in his family's account.

Dad went along on the route with Myron for two morning trips and two afternoon trips to understand the responsibilities. It was pretty easy to figure out. Leave home by 2:00 a.m., pick up the help, go up to Truman Road (which just happened to pass by Harry's house) to meet the Star truck that brought the papers out from Kansas City, be sure to get the right amount of papers, put wax paper around the newspapers if it was calling for rain, and take a set number of papers into the stores for resale. The routine was about the same in the afternoon, except he left home at about 2:30 p.m. and the boys met him at the gas station where they met the Star truck. The boys, Robert and Dee, knew which houses were supposed to receive the paper, so Dad just had to make sure they were both awake and doing their job. Dee had a tendency to doze off once in a while in the morning so Dad or Robert talked to him to try to keep him awake. Myron filled the truck up with gas on Saturday before he left town, and he gave Dad a $5.00 bill to fill it up again on Wednesday. Saturday evening, Dad went out to the truck to change the string for Sunday. The boys used a tying machine to tie a string around each paper. During the week, they used a thin 6-ply string, but on Sunday the paper was bigger, so they had to use a heavier 8-ply string.

I went out to the truck with Dad because the whole idea was very exciting to me. This was a new country to be explored. I had that excited feeling of curiosity any great explorer would have as he spied a far-off island or topped a mountain for the first time. What wonderful adventures lurked behind the door in the back of that big green truck? As Dad opened the back door, I inhaled the unmistakable aroma of ink.

"What's that smell?" I asked.

Dad leaned in and inhaled deeply. "It's just the smell of the paper truck," he said. "You'll get used to it."

I climbed up into the back of the truck and Dad asked me to push the trash back to the back so he could put it in the barrel. Each bundle of papers that came out from the Star had a piece of old paper on the top and the bottom to protect that day's paper, and each bundle was secured with a wire. The boys had a pair of wire cutters. They cut each bundle wire, removed the scrap paper, rolled all of the papers in the bundle and then removed the bottom piece of scrap paper and the wire. The boys knew Myron expected them to put the scrap paper beside their chair in a stack, but sometimes they got lazy and tossed it into the back of the truck. All of the wires were put in a bucket by the back door. Each boy sat in the same place every day – in one of the two old chairs in the back of the truck. One chair was directly behind the driver's seat and the other one was on the passenger's side. Right in the middle of the truck, were two funny looking black machines, each turned slightly toward one of the chairs. A large cone of string sat on a plate behind each machine and was threaded straight up and through a hole in a bent piece of metal. The hole had a screw down through it and there was a spring on the screw.

Dad had moved to the front seat and he could see I was investigating the machine, so he offered an explanation. "That's how you increase the tension."

"What do you mean, 'tension'?" I had no idea what he was talking about.

"The string has to be real tight so the machine can tie a good knot." He could probably tell by the look on my face that I didn't understand any of what he was saying.

"Here let me show you," he said as he climbed into the chair next to me. He took a piece of the scrap paper, folded a couple of times, put it in the machine, turned the crank, and showed me the pretty bow knot tied around the paper.

"Wow! That's cool! Can I do it?" It was like magic. Somehow, just by turning the crank, a string had been securely tied around the paper and it had a neat little bow knot with two loops.

"Yeah, but when you get done, you're going to have to untie all the papers and put them in the stack." He got up to change the cone of string on the machine. "See the string on the machine now is thinner than this other string that I have to put on." He separated the strands of string so I could see. The thin string had 6 little strands and the other had 8 strands. The Sunday paper is bigger than the daily paper, and it needs the heavier 8-ply string. "Mr. Johnson told me I should change the string on Saturday night."

"Where does Robert sit?" I asked, because I wanted to sit in his chair. Dad pointed to the chair behind the driver.

Dad let me pretend to do Robert's job by folding the scrap papers and tying a string around them. It was a fairly simple concept. Fold the paper in half, then fold it again in half, put it in the tying machine so the string went around the paper, and turn the crank once clockwise. Dad let me tie up about 20 papers and practice throwing them out in our yard. I was only six years old at the time and the whole process was very thrilling.

Mother let me take a rolled paper to school on Monday to share with my classmates during show-and-tell. The students weren't nearly as interested as my first grade teacher, Miss Parsons. She received the Star at home but didn't realize how the string was tied so neatly around her paper. She asked if I could bring the tying machine to school, but I told her it was attached to the truck and I didn't imagine it could be taken out, but I would ask my dad if he could bring the truck to school.

Tuesday morning, the Star had press trouble and the papers were very late arriving. Robert got home too late to catch the school bus, so Dad took him to school. Normally, if he missed the bus, Robert had to walk to school. Dad thought it was probably partly his fault for making Robert late because he didn't drive the paper truck as fast as Myron did. Billy and I both had to walk to school every day, so we didn't understand why walking was such a big deal. It wasn't until much later we discovered the short 5-block walk to our grade school was nothing compared to the mile and a half trek to William Chrisman High School. When Dad got back home from Robert's school, he told Billy and me he would take us to school in the paper truck. Then my teacher, Miss Parsons, and Billy's teacher, Mrs. Burlison, could both come out and look at the set-up if they wanted to. Miss Parsons brought my class out but Mrs. Burlison didn't. She said she didn't have time. Dad sat in the back of the truck and explained how the whole job was done. Several of the guys in my class said they wanted to work on a paper truck but my dad said they would probably have to wait until they got out of grade school.

Friday morning, Dad said the stars were shining when he left home at 2:00, but by 4:00, some clouds had rolled in and lightning sparked off to the west. He had the boys wrap the wax paper around the rest of the papers and by the time he got home, it was pouring. Although most customers were very understanding, there were a few who complained loudly. If the paper happened to get wet, most customers took it in their house and spread it out to dry. Dad redelivered all of his extra papers. He even had to go back to the stores to get more papers to redeliver to the rest of the unhappy customers who demanded a new, dry paper.

He found out on Friday afternoon when he went to pick up the papers that three of the other carriers didn't wax any of their papers. They were already home before it started to rain. Dad was afraid Myron would be unhappy about all of the complaints on Friday, but Myron just laughed and said the same thing happened to him about once a month. He said, "The weather around this area is impossible to predict. The weatherman can tell you what happened yesterday, and if he looks outside, he can tell you what it's doing now, but if he tries to tell you what's going to happen tomorrow, it's just a guess. My guess is just as good as his. The only thing constant about Missouri weather is change. If you don't like the weather today, stick around til tomorrow and it will be totally different."

Myron was very pleased with how Dad took care of the route and gave him several opportunities to run the route in the coming months. Sometimes, Myron didn't even leave town, he just worked around his house. I believe Myron realized our family needed the money and he just let Dad drive to help our financial situation.   Eventually, all of the other boys working on the paper truck quit. As each one left, Myron asked Robert if he could handle more work. If Robert could do the work by himself, he could make more money. Robert worked every afternoon and morning by himself in order to help the family financially. He slept downstairs and set his alarm for 2:00am. If he happened to oversleep, Myron came up to the house and pounded on the dining room window. It took about three hours to deliver the papers. Then Robert came home and took a short nap before school. As soon as school was over,

Robert walked across the street and met up with Myron to throw the afternoon papers. When they finished, Myron brought Robert home and we always waited supper on him. Mother said Robert was helping the family and the least we could do was wait a few minutes to eat our supper together. On Saturday, after working the morning route, Robert didn't get a break. He mowed a few yards during the day and then went on the route in the afternoon. Even though there was just a morning paper on Sunday, it was twice as tough. The paper was always quite large and it was harder for Robert to roll the papers fast enough to keep the truck moving. By the time he got home, he was worn out. But he still didn't get a break. Missing church on Sunday was not an option and even if it was, Robert would have wanted to go anyway. He had many close friends at church.

Robert finally could take a breather from the paper route on Sunday afternoon. That was the only afternoon with no paper. With the free time, he was happy to attend MYF, which stands for Methodist Youth Fellowship. As in most churches, the youth meetings offered an opportunity for the youth of the church to meet for fellowship and fun. Our house was a frequent destination for several of the MYF members after the meeting. They descended on our house and, while my mother made popcorn or candy, the teens listened to records and danced. Even though we loved to be a part of the party, Billy and I were usually sent upstairs to bed.

Robert continued to work for Myron for about three and a half years. After he finished his Junior year in high school, he bought a car and went to work at Sears. Dad continued to drive for Myron and also drove for other carriers. One of the other carriers was Earl Jones. Earl's route was a little bit larger than Myron's and he employed two boys to work every trip. When Dad worked for him, he only had to drive and the boys threw all of the papers. Dad said it was easier but it took a little longer. At the time, Dad was working full time at two jobs. He worked nights at the steel mill and drove the city bus during the day. With his two full-time jobs and working on the paper route occasionally, and with some financial help from Robert, we were able to get by. Dad had constantly asked Myron and Earl if there was any possibility he might, some day, have his own paper route. They both appreciated Dad's dependability and willingness to help whenever asked. They both told him if they ever decided to get out of the business and sell their routes, they would give him first shot at the purchase.

Dad thought originally his chosen path would be farming, but it wasn't meant to be. Then, after moving back into town, he thought owning a business would be his chosen path. Grandpa Parrish owned his own business which proved very successful. Frequently, when he chatted with my dad about financial stuff, he would ask him the same question. "Bill, would you rather RECEIVE a check for doing a job making $100.00 an hour or WRITE it?" The first time Bill heard that question he thought doing any job making $100.00/hour seemed unreachable and the obvious answer would be 'Receive it' but then he realized 'if I could afford to write a check that big, I would need to have a lot more in the bank'. So his answer was, "Write it!" Grandpa Parrish was happy to see his daughter's husband understood what it took to be successful. "You tried farming but it didn't work out. You'll probably try out several other jobs before you find the right one. If you're lucky, you'll find a job that pays the bills. If you're truly fortunate, you'll find a profession that gives you more after the bills are paid. If you happen to love that particular profession then you should consider yourself to be blessed."

Dad had been lucky. He had found several jobs that paid the bills, but didn't have anything left over without working at multiple jobs. Fortunately, Dad had been able to get quite a bit of overtime at the steel mill. That extra income combined with the fact that the garden allowed us to save quite a bit on groceries, was helping our family get a little ahead for the first time since Mom and Dad got married.

Dad used his skills as a farmer to raise a pretty large garden. The extra lot next to our house was about 75 feet wide and about 150 feet deep. Dad planted twelve rows across of potatoes, eight rows of corn, six rows of green beans, six rows of peas, six rows of tomatoes, four rows of radishes (two white and two red), two rows of onions, two rows of carrots, and two rows of lettuce. We also had a strawberry patch, a raspberry grove, a peach tree, and an apple tree. Dad's brother, S.B., had a farm and about twice a year he slaughtered a cow and a pig and gave the meat to us. Once Mother suggested selling some of the extra food, but Dad totally disagreed. "We'll eat what we need, can what we have room for, and give the rest away. God has always provided for us and when we needed help, He sent it our way. I'm not about to sell what He has given us. We'll just give it to someone who needs it more than we do."

I liked to go with him when he took food from our garden to others. One day when he took some tomatoes and corn on the cob over to Myron's house, I went with him. "That looks delicious!" Myron said, as he met us in the driveway. "How much do I owe you for them?"

"God didn't charge me anything for the rain or the sunshine, so I don't suppose it would be right if I charged you anything for eating them."

Dad really enjoyed giving to others. "Maybe someday you can see fit to let me have a chance at your paper route. That would be more than enough payment for anything I could give you out of my little garden patch."

Dad talked to Myron on several occasions about the potential income from the paper route. He also discussed the cost of buying one. Dad thought if he could just find some way to get his own route, he would be truly fortunate. He managed to be relatively successful in the retail business but didn't really enjoy it. The steel mill paid him handsomely, but it was very hard work, and it required a great deal of overtime. The work was certainly not joyful and he missed spending time with his family. Driving the bus gave him a feeling of independence, which he did enjoy, but it didn't pay much money. Working at two and even three jobs at the same time was, occasionally, the only alternative. He was willing to do whatever necessary to provide for his family. He had not gone to college, but he wanted to make it possible for all of his children to have the chance. For him, the paper route provided a feeling of independence, offered excellent financial rewards, and blessed him with an enjoyable experience.

OBITUARY: ABIGAIL JONES

EARL JONES CALLED DAD LATE ONE EVENING AND ASKED IF HE COULD RUN THE ROUTE FOR A FEW DAYS. Earl's wife had suddenly taken ill and was in the hospital. Even though Dad was scheduled to go into the steel mill that night, he called in sick and ran the route for Earl. The boys were a little surprised to see Dad driving the truck but they both said they preferred having him drive because he was funny. It was on that trip Dad figured out he really did love the paper route. He was more relaxed driving the truck than at any other time. He really enjoyed working with the boys and hoped someday he would get the opportunity to work with his own sons. If he could just get his own paper route, he would feel truly blessed.

When he came home that morning, Mother had breakfast ready and they sat down to the table and talked. It was a quiet time before the rest of the family was up and moving. Dad always said the same blessing before every meal. But that morning, he added a line. "Heavenly Father, bless this food to its intended use, and our lives in Thy service, and if it's Your will, help us to get a paper route. We ask in Christ's name, Amen."

Mother reached across the kitchen table and touched his hand. "Is this really what you want to do?"

Dad relayed the advice he had received from Dorothy's dad. "I've worked at a lot of jobs since we've been married. We've managed to pay the bills, so I guess you could say we're lucky. Since I've been working at the steel mill, we've even had a little bit left over, so I guess your dad would say we're truly fortunate. I just enjoy working on the paper route. It's fun to talk with the boys and make them laugh. I know a lot of responsibility goes along with running our own route, but I think I can handle it. It might even be something we could do together, because I would certainly need some help with the billing and bookkeeping. If it's God's will for us to get a paper route, then I think we should consider ourselves blessed."

"You know I will support you in whatever you decide to do and I would really feel like I was contributing something if I could help. When Billy and Johnny get a little bit older, they could even work on the route and we could keep the money in the family." The more Mother talked about it, the more she began to smile.

"The good Lord is probably not going to just hand us a paper route, but if someone gives us the opportunity, I think we should do everything we can to make it happen." Dad was already trying to think of a way to come up with the money to buy a paper route. "You know either Myron's or Earl's would cost us at least $50,000.00."

"Are you sure it would cost that much?" Mother began to rethink the idea.

"Myron told me the value of a route was basically the yearly cost of the paper to the subscriber, which is about $24.00, times the number of subscribers, times 2. For Myron's route, that would be about $48,000.00 and for Earl's it would be about $75,000.00. How could we ever come up with that?" Dad had done the math.

"If it's meant to be, then we'll find a way." She said it, but I don't think she truly believed it.

Dad already had been working on some possibilities for financing. "No one in my family has any money. Your Aunt Ella already gave us our inheritance and we spent it on this house. I don't think your parents could help us much. Carlton might be able to help us a little, but I don't think he's got that much to spare."

"Maybe we could take out a loan." Mother was thinking out loud.

"Who would loan us that much money? This house is only worth about $10,000 and it's the only thing we have to put up for collateral." Dad was realistic but hopeful. "Our only hope is if Myron or Earl trusts us and carries the note."

Dad was working for Earl every day, so he quit driving the bus and switched to working days at the steel mill. His day started at about 2:00 AM, when he got up to go on the route. When he got home from the route, he would clean up, eat breakfast, and leave to go to the steel mill. He went straight from the steel mill to the gas station to meet up with the boys to deliver the afternoon paper. When he got home from the afternoon delivery, we would eat dinner, and go to bed.

Mother said Earl's wife had some disease called cancer. She was very sick and they didn't know how long she had to live. She said there was no cure for Abigail's illness. Earl spent all of his spare time at the hospital. Sometimes he would come over to our house and give Mother his books and show her how to do the billing. Earl and Abigail had a lot of money but not much family. They had no children of their own but there were some relatives in Oklahoma and Florida.

We had just finished eating dinner and Dad was watching the news on television when the phone rang. As Dad answered the phone he asked me to turn down the television. Mother and Barbara were still doing dishes and the kids were not allowed to talk on the phone. Mother constantly told us the phone was not a toy.

"I feel so sorry for Earl." Dad said as he hung up the phone.

"Is Abigail worse?" Mother came in from the kitchen.

"No. She's about the same, but his voice is so sad. They have a nice home, a nice new car, the paper route, and plenty of money, but all of the money in the world can't help her." Dad paused as Mother put her hand on his shoulder. He looked at her and at Billy and me watching television and then he said, "I guess we sometimes forget just how much we have to be thankful for. Earl said he was going to bring the books over if we could help him with this month's billing."

Dad turned back to watch the news and I turned the volume back up. He was watching the news but his mind was somewhere else. "It's a shame they don't have any children." He wasn't really talking to anyone because Mother had gone back into the kitchen. I didn't like to see my dad so unhappy, but I didn't know what to do. I just climbed up on his lap and he put his arm around me and we watched the news together.

I think Dad had fallen asleep because he jumped when someone knocked at the door. I had heard someone come up on the porch and since he said Earl was coming over, I thought it would be him.

Dad went to answer the door and I went with him. As he opened the door, Earl walked in carrying some books. "Hello, Bill. Where do you want me to put these?" Earl didn't sound so sad to me.

"Just put them on the dining room table." Dad said as he took one of the books.

Mother had already cleared the table and she came in from the kitchen to sit down. I started to sit down at the table with them and Earl said, "Hello there young man. Which one are you, Billy or Johnny?" Most people couldn't tell Billy and me apart.

"I'm Johnny, the youngest." I wanted people to know even though we were about the same size, I was two years younger than Billy.

"It's about time for you to get ready for bed." Mother motioned for me to go upstairs. It wasn't time for bed, but she wanted me to leave, so they could have adult talk. I didn't mind because I knew I could listen through the register. We didn't have a furnace upstairs. Our house was heated by a furnace in the basement, but it only heated the first floor. There were two holes cut through between the floors and each hole had a register in it that could be opened to let heat up from the first floor or closed in the summer to keep the heat from rising. It was cool enough that the registers were open, so I could position myself over one of them and hear plainly what was being said in the dining room. I listened for a little while, but I didn't understand what they were talking about so I found something else to do.

Dad continued to run the paper route seven days a week and work at the steel mill six days a week. Once a week, Earl came over to our house and brought records so Mother could update the books and send out more bills. Some people paid without being billed but she still needed to send out about 1000 bills each month. Each month, Earl gave her $40.00 to cover the cost of the stamps. I hardly ever saw Dad during the time he was running Earl's route. He was home each night for dinner, but I had to compete with Robert,

Barbara, and Billy for his attention. Robert always seemed to have some urgent problem with his car or his job. Barbara just wanted to sit on Dad's lap and comb his hair while she relayed her exciting events from school. Billy and I had our artwork from school, which we thought was terrible, but Dad said it was the best he had ever seen. Mother stayed in the kitchen in order to give us time with Dad. Once she had cleared the table and done the dishes, she started doing book work. After a short while, she came in and reminded Dad he should get some sleep. Our television was in the living room and their bedroom was right next to it. Dad told us we could watch television, but we had to turn the volume down.

There were not many shows to choose from on television, but we sat glued to every one of them. Mother and Dad always liked to watch 'The George Burns and Gracie Allen Show'. Sometimes it was pretty funny. They also liked to watch 'The Ed Sullivan Show' on Sunday night. Dad never missed watching 'The Friday Night Boxing'. Some of the family favorites were 'I Love Lucy', 'Candid Camera', 'Ozzie and Harriet' and 'This is Your Life'. Saturdays were a real treat with 'Howdy Doody', 'The Cisco Kid', and 'The Roy Rogers Show'. Barbara always wanted to watch 'American Bandstand'. Billy and I loved to watch the westerns. There were many cowboy heroes we loved to imitate. Our bed was an old iron frame bed with a large head board and a smaller foot board. We tied a pillow around the iron foot rail and suddenly, through the magic of a child's mind, that iron foot rail became Trigger or Diablo, and later it became Champion or Silver. Cowboys were not the only choice on television, because a new show came on that introduced us to a cowgirl. She could ride and shoot as well as any cowboy and 'Annie Oakley' could always get her little brother Tag out of whatever trouble showed up that week. As a family, we always watched 'Lassie' on Sunday night right before 'The Ed Sullivan Show'. There was another new show that had started to creep into our home. It would remain a favorite for years. Although it started out as 'Disneyland', its name changed several times and introduced us to many new characters, some cartoon and some real life. I think I can still sing all of the words to 'Davy Crockett'. After we were all supposed to be in bed, Mother liked to watch another new show I didn't know much about, called 'The Tonight Show'. Mother also liked watching television during the day. She'd never admit to being a soap opera addict, but I was home from school one day for some holiday and I wanted to watch cartoons but Mother had to watch 'The Secret Storm'.

The phone very rarely rang, but when it did, it was like a fire alarm going off. We only had one phone in the house and it was in the dining room. Frequently several days passed between incoming phone calls and when the phone did ring, it seemed like it was always bad news. When it rang, as Mother hurried to answer it, you could hear her say, "Oh no, what's the matter now." This time she answered it, her fears were justified. "Oh no!... When did it happen?... Were you there?... What do you want us to do?... I'm so sorry... Let us know if we can do anything." She sat down at the dining room table. I didn't know it at the time, but an event had occurred which would affect the rest of my life. A woman I had never met, Abigail Jones, had died. I felt sorry for Earl because I knew he had lost his best friend.

After a couple of weeks, Earl came over to our house. He told Dad and Mother he appreciated everything they had done for him since Abigail went into the hospital. He said he didn't have much family and none of them wanted to mess with the paper route. They just wanted money.

"Bill and Dorothy," Earl paused for a moment to think just what he wanted to say. "I am a man of my word and I promised you if I ever decided to give up the paper route, you would get first shot at it. Talk it over. See what you can do about financing. I know you don't have much cash, but I would rather not carry the note. Make me an offer, but be aware there are other people who will be making offers also. I have a former employee who wants the route, too. His name is Lester Heman and his dad has some money, so I believe he has some financial backing. He gave me $1000.00 to show his sincerity. That's just a down payment and he said he would be making an offer. If you want the route, I would appreciate the same down payment from you. If you don't want the route, I will sell it to him. If you are certain this is what both you and Dorothy want to do, then I will split it between you and Lester. I really do appreciate everything both of you have done to help me over the last several months. I don't know how you do it, Bill. You take excellent care of the route by running it every morning and afternoon and still work at the steel mill during the day. I know you can't have much time left for family activities. If I can give your family time back to you by selling you this route, I would be very happy. I don't want to stay around this area. My home is just too lonesome. I think I'll go to Florida for a while. I have some family there and I'd like to spend a little more time with them. I don't know if you have a bank or a financial advisor, but I put all of my trust in my friend, John Steinhauser. He's the most honest man I've ever met. Do you know him?"

"As a matter of fact, we do." Dad was a little surprised anyone he knew might be suggested. "He and his family go to our church. They're such nice people."

"You'll never find a more honest and trustworthy man. If anyone can help you, he can." Earl got up to leave. "I really want you to get this paper route, if it's what you want for sure. Just talk to John and make me a fair offer."

Mother and Dad just looked at each other after Earl left. Finally, Mother spoke, "I don't know whether to cry or laugh. I'm so sorry for Earl's loss, but if she hadn't died, we may not have ever had a chance to get our own paper route."

"And we stand a better chance at being able to afford half of it than the whole thing. I never thought about splitting it up." Dad was more excited than I had ever seen him. "Who would have ever guessed he knew John Steinhauser? I'm going to talk to him at church on Sunday. God may not just hand us a paper route, but He is sure opening some doors."

The next few days were spent at the dining room table. Dad and Mother were going over all of the possible questions John Steinhauser might have. They calculated the potential income, deducted a percentage for non-pays, estimated charges for supplies, estimated labor expenses, figured in truck expenses, added the Star charges, and even allowed for postage. They had two sets of numbers, a high estimate and a low estimate. They wanted to appear prepared and professional. According to Myron's calculations, if they bought half of Earl's route, it would cost them around $37,000.00. If someone would loan them that much money, they could afford to make payments of about $75.00 per week. They didn't know if Mr. Steinhauser had that much money or if he would just arrange with the bank for them to borrow it. If they did need to go to a bank, what could they possibly use for collateral? The mortgage on the house was paid off, but it was only worth about $6,000.00.

"Do you think Carlton would loan us any money?" Dad was trying to work out a plan. "If we could just borrow $1000.00 from him for the down payment, then we could show both Earl and John we are serious and committed."

Mother thought for a minute and then said, "Isn't there anyone else we can get the money from? I hate to ask family for money. They all do so much for us in other ways. Mother and Dad give us a lot of clothes from the store. Aunt Ella gave us $2000.00 for the mortgage on the house. S.B. gives us meat and brings us coal for the furnace. Didn't you say the steel mill has a credit union? Maybe we could borrow it from them."

"Yeah, they have a credit union, but they'll probably want some kind of collateral." Dad wasn't very optimistic. "I'll talk to them tomorrow."

When Dad talked to the people at the credit union, they told him they could loan him the $1000.00, but he would need to get someone to co-sign the note. Mother called Carlton and told him the whole story. He said he didn't have $1000.00 to loan to them but he would co-sign the note. The next day, with Carlton's help, Dad and Mother took their first step towards buying a paper route and heading down a brand new path. They didn't want to take any chances with that much money, so they went straight to Earl Jones' house and gave it to him. Dad told him he had not talked to John Steinhauser yet, but they wanted him to know they were serious about purchasing the route. Dad told Earl he would be ready to make an offer after he spoke with John. Even though Dad and Mother felt very prepared with all of the necessary information, they were still nervous about approaching Mr. Steinhauser.

"He's pretty much our only hope," Dad told Mother, as we went to church. "If he refuses to help us, we can try the bank, but I think it would be a waste of our time. Earl already said he didn't want to carry the note. I just don't know of any other place where we could get that amount of money."

"Quit worrying Bill!" Mother knew he would continue to worry until the whole process was completed, but she was trying to relax him. "You worry too much. We'll cross that bridge when we get to it, and I guess if that bridge isn't there, then we'll just find another one. You never know, John Steinhauser may be happy to help us."

She didn't realize it at the time, but that was precisely the case. After the morning church service was over, while we were on our way to Sunday School class, John Steinhauser approached Dad with a big grin on his face and said, "Good Morning Bill! How are you this morning?"

Dad smiled, shook his hand, and replied, "I'm still alive, so I guess I can't complain. How are you?"

John rubbed my head and said, "How are you, Johnny?"

It was a compliment to me that he knew my name. Maybe it was because he and I shared the same first name, but it still made me feel important. I just smiled and said, "Okay."

John turned back to Dad and said, "I hear from Earl Jones that you and Dorothy want to get into the newspaper business."

Dad was a little surprised John brought up the subject. "Yeah, we really like it."

But before Dad could even bring up the possibility of financing, John asked, "Why don't you come by our house around 2:00 and we'll talk all about it?"

Dad was relieved the ice had been broken, "Sounds good to me. We'll be there."

"Do you need to check with Dorothy first?" John wanted to be sure they would both be there.

"No, she is always glad to go visiting. I'm sure she'll love chatting with Pearl." Although Mother really did want to be a part of the route operation, this financial talk was 'man talk'. As soon as we got home from church, Mother hurried us through lunch and began to fix a double batch of ginger cookies. While she was busy baking, Dad was putting the final touches on the paper work. Mother set out one batch of cookies for the family and packaged the other batch to take to the Steinhauser's. She said she remembered a church pot-luck dinner when John said how much he liked her ginger cookies. It's funny how women remember when anyone admires their culinary accomplishments. Pearl was probably busy making some delicious snack to serve to Mother and Dad. I didn't understand why my parents acted so nervous about visiting some friends from church. I was just happy to have some ginger cookies.

Mother and Pearl were both totally aware of the situation but they left the negotiations to the men. This was a time of evolution in our country. Women were not yet included in this type of financial discussions. Obviously, Mother had talked with Dad regarding this business and its effects on our family, and I'm certain Pearl had talked to John about getting financially involved with a friend. Those discussions were private, but at least they were happening. In my grandparent's families, women were not consulted about financial decisions. Right or wrong, the men made all of the important decisions. In my grandparent's generation, women weren't considered capable of making that type of assessment. In my parent's generation, women had moved one step closer to equality. Husbands frequently consulted wives. Men actually talked to their wives regarding their opinion of potential decisions. Women saw situations from a different perspective and were a new source of evaluating a problem. Men could evaluate a situation, consider possible changes to that situation, and decide if involvement was advantageous. By involving another person, a man was increasing his likelihood of success. In addition to the factual appraisal he could provide, he was given the additional assistance of a woman's perspective. Mankind had always been aware of the phenomenon known as 'women's intuition', but had not yet found a way to use it to his own advantage. By the middle of the twentieth century, women were, at last, being given the opportunity to become involved in business dealings. From the nineteenth century when women mainly existed to make man's life more comfortable, to the 21st century when men will probably exist mainly for the purpose of making a woman's life more comfortable, this, the twentieth century, was a period of transition. Could we be in the middle of a sexual evolution? Were we in the midst of a switch from submission, to equality, to supremacy? Or would women be satisfied with equality?

Although Dad understood the importance of this meeting with John, and was concerned about the outcome, he openly discussed the potential dealings with Mother. They both felt they were well-prepared for any questions John might ask. Dad's job was to convince John this was a favorable transaction and it was Mother's job to reassure Pearl the outcome would not affect their friendship. They soon realized their concerns were unnecessary. John was not only a very honest man, but he was also very wise. He had done his homework. He had already discussed the financial pros and cons of the newspaper delivery business with Earl Jones. He knew the business could be profitable and it appeared to be a relatively safe financial venture for him. He was satisfied Dad was a hard-working, conscientious man, because he had talked to both Earl and Myron Johnson about Bill's work ethics. He took a trip to Norborne to meet Dorothy's parents. Frank and Mona reassured John that Bill and Dorothy were honest, hard-working people who just needed a break to be successful. John believed in the financial potential of the business and Dorothy's parents believed in the human potential.

When Dad and John sat down to discuss the business, Dad placed his notebook on the table, opened it up and began to lay out papers. John could see Bill was nervous and he smiled and asked, "What's all of this?"

Dad looked at all of the papers with numbers and messages written on them and then he looked at John. "I think this is my chance. I've worked hard my whole life, and I'm working hard right now. I deliver the paper route in the morning, work at the steel mill during the day, and run the paper route again in the afternoon. I believe if I could have my own paper route, our family could be happy. I enjoy running the business and this is the first time I could actually say that about any job. The problem is I need financial help. That's why I'm here. I need your help. I don't have anything to offer as collateral, except my house which is only worth about $6000.00. In order to buy this route, I'll need about $35,000.00. I know that's a lot of money, probably more than I've made in my entire life, but I believe the route is worth it. That's what these papers show. What I can't show on any paper is my integrity. I pay my bills. Before I buy groceries or clothes, I pay my debts."

John looked at all of the papers and then looked at Dad. "I know what the financial possibilities are for the newspaper business. I, also, believe I know what kind of a man you are. There is nothing written on these papers to convince me to loan you any money. However, I believe your solemn promise and your handshake are sufficient to secure the deal."

Dad's eyes began to water as he stood up and offered his hand to John. "I promise I will repay this money to you and I will make sure you are never sorry for making the loan."

John smiled and said, "Just make sure your family doesn't go hungry. If you find your cupboards bare, know you and your family are always welcome at our table."

Pearl and Mother appeared from the kitchen with a tray of ginger cookies and a pitcher of lemonade. Pearl said, "If you men are done with your serious talk, how about enjoying some of Dorothy's famous ginger cookies and my lemonade?"

The loan was made and the deal was sealed with lemonade. This was a time when a man's word was worth more than all of his worldly assets.

BABY-BOOMERS OFF TO SCHOOL

DAD CONTINUED TO WORK AT THE STEEL MILL FOR ABOUT THREE MONTHS AFTER BUYING THE PAPER ROUTE. He wanted to be sure the route could pay all of the bills without needing the money from the mill. As soon as he felt comfortable depending solely on the route for the family's income, he quit the steel mill. Up until that time, I hardly ever saw Dad, except on Sunday. After quitting the mill, it seemed as if he was always home.

When talking to other kids at school, it was fairly common that most of my friends' dads went to work early in the morning and returned home in time for dinner. Most of the mothers were at home all day. Very few women worked outside the home. Even fewer men worked at home. Whenever parents came to school to help the teacher with activities, it was always the mother who showed up. There were obviously women in the work force but it was not common. With the exceptions of elementary school teachers, nurses, and waitresses, there were very few women employed away from home. I remember once, before we got the paper route, my mother offered to go to work at the neighborhood drug store. It was at a time when Dad was between jobs and money was hard to come by. He told her if she went to work, then she should just stay there. He would not allow his wife to go to work. He believed there was no greater honor than to be a full-time mother to their children. Mother just wanted to do her part to help the family financially. She was very happy to be able to work with Dad on the paper route. Even though he did all of the actual deliveries, Mother spent just as much time doing billing and collecting.

In order to save money, Dad did not mail monthly bills to the customers. Instead, each month he and Mother went door to door collecting for the service. Each morning of the last week of the month, he used a rubber stamp and placed a red notice on the front page of about 125 papers that said 'Collector Will Call Today'. Then, at about 9:00am, Dad and Mother walked from house to house collecting the fee. The monthly charge for the paper was $1.95. Since the customers received the notice with their morning paper, they were usually prepared. If the customer needed to leave their house on the morning of collections, they left their money in an envelope pinned to the front door. Some left it in their mailbox and some left it with their next door neighbor. Dad was very business-like. He knocked on the door. If the person was home, he collected the money, punched their card for the appropriate month, and left. If the person was not home, he left an envelope with his name and address on it and the customer could either mail it in or drop it in a drop box. Dad had three drop boxes. One was located at the Safeway store, one was at the Watts Drug Store, and one was at the Standard Oil gas station. Each drop box was a small mail box with a padlock on it. Customers could drop their payment in the slot in the top and then Dad could open the box to take the payments out. Dad liked to collect, but Mother liked to talk. Dad could collect three or four customers while Mother chatted with one. As Mother and Dad became acquainted with the customers, they both liked to chat. In the beginning, it took them about two hours to collect for each day. After a few months, the time had expanded to four hours.

We lived in a very trusting society at that time. No one locked their doors. Windows were left open, day and night. There was no air conditioning, so people sat outside in the evening to cool off. Fans were the only relief from the heat of the mid-day summer sunshine. Customers only paid by cash because checks weren't widely accepted yet. Many customers left their doors unlocked and told my parents to step inside and the money would be on the table by the front door.

One morning, during a regular collection day, Dad knocked on a customer's door, but no one answered. This happened to be one of the customers who always had the money ready, but had previously told Dad that if no one answered the door, to just step inside and pick up the money from the table and punch the receipt. When Dad opened the door, he saw the money right on the table as usual. As he put the money in his pouch, he happened to look up and see the man sitting in his chair. Startled at first, Dad then laughed and said, "You scared me!" When the man didn't respond, Dad thought he must be asleep. He spoke louder and said, "I punched your receipt and it's on the table." The man still didn't move. Dad stepped closer and asked him if he was okay. When the man still didn't respond, Dad reached down to shake him. The man slumped over in his chair. He was dead. Dad went to the phone and called the police. The police arrived soon and had the body taken away. The man lived alone and no one knew who to contact. The man left enough money on the table to pay for the whole month. Before leaving the house, Dad put the appropriate amount of money back in the envelope and wrote on the receipt 'Paid in Full'. It may have only been a dollar, but it was the honest thing to do and Dad would not have considered doing anything else.

After my parents finished their collections, Dad didn't want Mother to have to go home and fix a meal, so they always treated themselves to lunch at a restaurant. They had several favorite places to eat. I think Mother's favorite was either Clem's or Mug's Up. Both of those restaurants served the loose-meat hamburger she preferred. They also liked going to Slover's, Pete's Café, and the Big Burger Restaurant. Any place was a treat, because we hardly ever ate out. Collection days were the monthly exception to eating at home. It took six days to complete the collections for the whole route. If the weather was agreeable, they could complete the route in one week. If rain or snow was predicted, they didn't do collections on that day. After a few months, Mother and Dad knew just about everyone on the route. When it was necessary for customers to leave town, they called our house to stop delivery and left instructions to start the service again when their car or truck was in the driveway. It was a very personal relationship.

The home delivery system was very popular at this time. It was also used by the milkman, the Manor bread man, the Fuller brush man, the Watkins man, and the Avon lady. I never saw the milkman because he delivered the milk to our house early in the morning, about the same time as Dad delivered the paper. Mother always left the empty milk bottles on the back porch with a note in the top of one of the bottles telling him what she needed. This was the only way to get truly fresh dairy products. She usually ordered two quarts of regular milk and occasionally she ordered a quart of chocolate milk. The glass bottles of regular milk had about a cup of cream risen to the top. She carefully poured off the cream and kept it in another container.

I did see the Manor bread man. His name was Orville Jones and when he walked to our house, he blew on a two-note whistle to let Mother know he was approaching the house. I always loved hearing that whistle. In addition to bread, which was kind of boring, he always had a huge assortment of goodies and snack cakes. Home delivery was the only way to get fresh bakery items.

The Watkins man did not visit us as frequently as the milk man and bread man, but he had the neatest stuff. Mother bought all of her spices from the Watkins man and she also bought concentrated juice. One quart of his juice made about five gallons of drink for us. She also bought certain medications from him. He sold a special liniment for sore muscles Dad always used and a medication for cuts called Petro-Carbo Salve. Mother just called it carbolic salve and she placed it on every cut and scratch. Occasionally, if the cut looked infected, Mother reached for the iodine, but I protested vehemently. The pain from the iodine was worse than getting the cut in the first place. There was no pain when the salve was used and it had mysterious healing powers. Just smear the salve on a clean, open wound and cover it with a band-aid. Wait a day or two and remove the band-aid to discover the injury had been totally healed. This salve became a lifelong staple in all of the Morrison medicine cabinets. I realize the major purpose of the salve was to heal open wounds, but I trust it so much, I think if I was having a heart attack, I would reach for the salve.

The Fuller brush man only visited about once a month and I didn't find his wares as exciting as the others. He mainly sold brooms, mops, dust pans, and other cleaning supplies. I didn't care about anything the Avon lady sold either, but I did like seeing her come to our house, because she always smelled good and had little packets of free samples to give us. Everyone liked getting free stuff even if it was just soap, shampoo, or lotion. My mother mainly bought perfume, lipstick, nail polish, cologne, after shave, and shampoo from her.

It was a time when products were brought to the consumer instead of the consumer going out to search for the products. There were no shopping malls. There were no supermarkets. There certainly was no place for one-stop shopping. I suppose the closest thing to a super store was Wild Woody's Bargain Barn. It was located on the southern edge of Independence on Noland Road between 39th Street and 40 Highway. Our family made the trek to Wild Woody's about once a month. I think it must have been a barn in earlier years, because the floors were dirt and it smelled like Uncle B's barn. It was stocked full of all kinds of merchandise. Things were very cheap, and if you knew what you were looking for, you could find some real bargains.

For the most part, we have become a society dependent on air conditioning. We live in air conditioned houses, drive to work in air conditioned cars, work and shop in air conditioned buildings, and worship in air conditioned churches. During these early years of my life, we had never heard of air conditioning. On those hot summer days, our only relief from the heat was a fan, some shade, and Mother's Kool-Aid Ice Cubes. One of the first buildings to have air conditioning in Independence was the Katz Drug Store on the Square. Since we only had one car and Dad used to drive it to work, if it became necessary to go to the drug store, Mother walked the five-mile round trip to the Square with Billy and me tagging along. I was just a little kid, so the heat didn't bother me too much, but it always felt hotter when we came out of Katz than when we went in. The Granada and Englewood Movie Theaters didn't wait long to jump on the a/c wagon. Since the doors had to be closed and there weren't any windows, the fans could only do so much. The churches were about the last to conform to the new cooling opportunities, because the buildings were big and difficult to cool, and they were only used for a few hours each week. Many homes began to switch over to window unit air conditioners, but it would be several years before the central a/c unit was a standard in just about all homes.

Just as on the farm, the paper route was a full-time business. Seven days a week, 365 days a year, even on Christmas Day, the newspaper had to be delivered. Dad never complained about the demands of the route, but his main problem was keeping good help. Many boys started working, but it was difficult to get up at 2:00 every morning and then work again after school with no break on the weekend, so most of them quit after a month or so. Dad thought he might be expecting too much for one boy to handle the responsibilities by himself, so he hired a second one. One worked Monday, Wednesday, and Friday and the other one worked Tuesday, Thursday, and Saturday. They both worked on Sunday. Dad was anxious for Billy and me to start working full time. We both helped out during the week and we alternated working on Sundays, but we were too small to handle it by ourselves.

The first day I actually began working on a regular basis was June 1, 1954. School was out for the summer, and while other families planned vacations and summer relaxation, our family was tied to home and dedicated to making the route as successful as possible. During the summer, it was acceptable for Billy and me to work both mornings and afternoons. The afternoons were easy and fun. The mornings, however, were a little more difficult. There's nothing easy about being awakened in the middle of the night to go out and work on a paper route. The first few mornings were fun, because it was exciting to be up when everyone else was asleep. It didn't take long before the new wore off and I was sleepy. Occasionally, if we happened to see a milk man, Dad stopped him and bought a quart of chocolate milk. There weren't any stores open, so if we wanted anything to eat, we had to bring it from home. In the afternoon, we could stop and get a candy bar and a drink from Pierce's Drug Store. My favorite candy bar was the green-wrapped Brach's Mint Bar. Dad had to go in to the store to leave them papers to sell, so he didn't have to make an unscheduled stop. When it was extremely hot, Dad liked to stop by a new hamburger joint called The Candy Stripe and get a cup of ice. They had a new machine that froze the water and then a large wheel with a sharp knife went around and shaved off a layer of ice. The ice wasn't hard like ice cubes, so it was very easy to chew. When the temperature topped ninety degrees, there was nothing as refreshing as a cup of shaved ice from The Candy Stripe.

ELVIS INDUCTED IN ARMY

BY 1957, I WAS WORKING ON THE PAPER ROUTE EVERY AFTERNOON WITH ANOTHER BOY. I walked from Alton Grade School to the Standard Oil Gas Station at the corner of 23rd Street and Crysler Avenue, where I waited for Dad to pick me up. I was only 10 years old and in fifth grade. By today's standards, these actions would probably be considered mean or cruel, but to me, it was fun. I enjoyed feeling mature and independent. All of my friends from school went home and watched television or played after school. I went to work and I thought it was exciting.

Several events happened earlier in the year that made me see life a little differently. Robert married Earline in April. How strange to see my brother married and living in a house with a woman! When I look back, I guess it just made me feel a little older. Robert moved out of our house when he started college and he never moved back in. He worked his way through college by preaching at small rural churches. When he married Earline, Billy and I were the candle lighters for their wedding. Robert and Earline didn't kiss and hug a lot in public, like many young people in love, but they appeared very natural together. Like Dad and Mother, they just seemed to belong together.

In July, Grandpa Parrish died. That was my first close encounter with death. I heard about other people dying, but I never actually attended a funeral. I remember the day he died. Dad and Mother took me to Boy Scout Camp to visit Billy. Grandpa Parrish was in the hospital in Kansas City. He was certain people were trying to hurt him. As long as he took his medication, everything went okay. Mother tried to visit her dad every day at supper time to make sure he took his medicine. Since we had been away for the day, Mother could not be with him at supper time.

Apparently, Grandpa didn't take the medicine and tried to escape from the hospital. He thought his room was on the first floor, but he was really on the fifth floor. When we arrived to visit with him, his room was empty. When Mother asked where he had gone, the nurse broke the news that he had fallen out his window to his death. Mother found the medicine in his room and she blamed herself for not being there in time to make him take it. Dad felt responsible because we were at Scout Camp too long and he wanted to stop and eat before we went to the hospital. Grandmother Parrish felt responsible because she wasn't with him. Everyone blamed the nurses and the hospital staff for not doing their jobs. I discovered when someone dies, everyone left behind, in his or her own way, feels responsible. I handled most of the funeral service okay, but I couldn't keep from crying when they put him in the ground and started shoveling dirt in on top of him. I guess that's when I realized I would never see him again.

About two weeks later, I found myself in a position to deal with death again. My mother's grandfather had died. Grandpa Fidler was a lot of fun to listen to. When we visited Norborne, he lived in the house directly across the street from Grandmother Parrish. I loved to listen to him tell stories about the past. He used to say, "Past is all I got. At my age, there can't be much future." When he was 95 years old, he built a small house for a friend. One day, he was up on the roof, patching a leak, and he fell to the ground. A neighbor saw him fall and went to get help. The city mortician was only a block away and when he arrived, he couldn't get a pulse and didn't hear Grandpa breathing, so he assumed the old man was dead. He took my great-grandfather back to the mortuary. While the mortician was writing down the time and conditions of death, Grandpa Fidler woke up. He looked around, recognized the mortician, and said, "What in the hell you doin'? I ain't dead yet. You'll get your hands on me soon enough. Next time just wait til you're damn sure I'm dead." He went back to the house and finished patching the roof.

Grandpa Fidler told me when he was about my age, he was 'fightin' in the war'. When I asked him if he shot anybody, he said he was 'too young to tote a gun', so he just ran along behind the lines carrying water and information. He was talking about the Civil War. At the time, I didn't realize the importance of communicating with a person who had actually been involved in the Civil War. To me, it was just another one of Grandpa Fidler's stories. In his lifetime, he had witnessed, first hand, many major changes in the world. When he was a child, his world was only as large as he could travel on foot or on horseback in a day. Before he died, he witnessed global communication by phone and television, global travel by jet planes, and outer space exploration. My only regret in knowing Grandpa Fidler is that I didn't know him better. He held the key to the door of our country's past in his head and I loved sitting at his feet and observing as he opened up that door and displayed his history to all who would listen.

One day, while we sat on his front porch, he asked me why I didn't want to go and play with the other kids. I imagine he would have preferred to have me leave him alone, so he could take a nap, but I told him I could play any time. I wouldn't always have him to talk to. He was already over 100 years old, so certainly his time was very limited. When I asked him why he thought he got to live so long, he said, "Living a long time isn't a reward, it's a punishment. God brings the good folks, like my Anna, home to be with Him sooner. I guess I must have been pretty ornery for Him to leave me here for so long. I'm ready to go home when God decides it's time." I didn't cry at Grandpa Fidler's funeral. I think most people just thought I didn't know him very well. I think the reason I didn't cry was because I did know him well. I knew he was happy to be going home to be with his wife, Anna, again.

It was a long time before I thoroughly understood that type of love and devotion. Girls were not particularly interesting to me until I entered 6th grade. That's when I first started noticing there was something about certain ones that made my stomach kind of queasy. It was not sick-queasy. It was that kind of queasy feeling I would get in my stomach when I came up to bat for the first time in a baseball game. It was like being a little bit scared and a little bit excited at the same time. I had reached a whole new perspective on the role of females in my life.

There was a young lady in my class I really liked. We tried to always be on the same team during competitions and spent time together during recess. When she held my hand for the first time, I felt like I had just won the World Series. I wanted to spend time with her away from school, but we lived far apart. We attended different churches, so we didn't see each other on the weekends. One afternoon on the route, I mentioned to my dad I had a special friend at school and I would like to take her out on a date. He said he thought I was too young, so I dropped it for a while. She gave me a Valentine card that said she loved me and I gave her one that said I loved her, too. Before I knew it, it was May and school was almost out for the summer. How could I possibly go for three months without seeing her? I had memorized her phone number, but I had not yet called her. After hearing Dad's original response, I tried a different tactic. Barbara was dating a boy by the name of Gary. Since they could go out on dates, I told her about Christy. My sister thought the whole idea was very cute and, even though I don't think Gary was too excited about the idea, he agreed. Barbara told me to call Christy and the four of us could go miniature golfing together at Coolcrest.

I wasn't quite prepared for all of the dynamics that go along with dating. I liked Christy and I enjoyed spending time with her, but when we were on the dating stage, neither of us knew what to do. We sat close together in the back seat as we drove to the golf course. The radio was blaring a song by some new guy named Elvis something. I wasn't a big fan, but Barbara liked him. I think Gary thought he was just as accomplished at singing as Elvis, because he sang along, even though he didn't even know the words. I wasn't a real big fan of Elvis' music, but I admired him as a person. We talked about him at school and our teacher said he was inducted into the Army. He was rich enough that he could have bought his way out of the military, but he chose to serve. In my opinion, that made him okay.

When we got to Coolcrest, I paid for Christy's admission because I had a job and could afford the price. Besides, I was the one who asked her out on the date and I felt it was my responsibility to pay. She committed the unforgivable faux pas of bringing her purse with her on the golf course. Obviously, she couldn't hold her purse and putt the golf ball, so she asked me to hold it for her. I think that was the first time I ever actually held a woman's purse, except my mother's. I was devastated. My sister must have noticed my devastation, because she offered to hold it while Christy putted. After finishing the obligatory 18 holes, Christy asked me if I was thirsty. Without considering the possible ramifications, I said yes. She was already digging in her purse to get enough money to buy both of us drinks. That embarrassed me, because I felt it was the man's responsibility to pay. I'm certain she just wanted to show me she liked me and was willing to buy something for me, but I felt emasculated. My first date was not a rousing success, but, to this day, I still like Christy and enjoy visiting with her at our high school reunions.

As the summer passed, I only talked to Christy one other time. I called her to see if we had any classes together. The only class we shared was band, but we wouldn't be sitting close together because she played the clarinet and I played the trumpet. I thought I would still see her a lot, but had yet to experience the difference Junior High School made. In sixth grade, we sat in the same classroom all day. When we got to Junior High, we changed rooms every hour. First hour band was the only time I got to see her, and then it was only the back of her head. I did have some classes with friends from Alton Grade School, and I also was in class with friends from church. During the year, my circle of friends grew larger.

My first year in Junior High was our last year we lived in the old house. Billy was a freshman at William Chrisman Division II (the original William Chrisman), and Barbara was a senior at the new William Chrisman Division I High School. I walked to school for the first seven years, but then I rode the bus to Palmer Junior High School. I didn't ride it home because I had to work on the paper route. After school, I walked about six blocks to meet up with my dad at Harry White's gas station at the corner of Truman Road and River. I walked right past Harry Truman's home every day, but I never saw him out mowing his grass. I did encounter him one afternoon on my way from school to work. I approached the corner of Truman Road and North Delaware, and noticed Mr. Citizen walking north on Delaware. We were on a collision course. I stopped to let him walk by and he stopped and stuck out his hand. "Hello there, young man. My name's Harry Truman. What's yours?"

I was a little dumbfounded, but managed to speak, "My name's Johnny Morrison. It's a pleasure to meet you, sir."

"People called my father 'sir'. Just call me Harry"

"Yes, sir. I mean Harry."

Some people drove by and yelled 'Hi, Harry!' and Harry waved his cane. "See, everybody just calls me Harry." He turned to cross Truman Road and then he said, "Did you just get out of school?"

"Yes," I said, "I'm on my way to work."

"That's a pretty good school. I went there when I was your age and look what happened to me. Work's important, too, but never give up on education." He crossed the street and was followed closely by a black car. I assumed they were secret service agents. Anyone who lived in Independence at the time knew, and was accustomed to seeing, Harry Truman walk the streets around his home, greeting people as he walked. I'm not sure I was as impressed as I should have been, but I was only 12 years old.

Right next door to Harry White's gas station was Morford's Diner, which was a place where we could buy sandwiches and carbonated drinks. I was always starving after a hard day at school, so the diner became my after-school snack place. Morford was the first person to introduce me to a cherry limeade. Through sixth grade, my world was pretty small. My home was the center of a five-block world. School was five blocks west. Our little neighborhood grocery store was five blocks southeast. Most of my friends lived with in that range, and I rarely ventured beyond that five-block perimeter. When I entered seventh grade, my world had grown immensely. I had met the President of the United States and enjoyed my first cherry limeade.

Seventh grade was the only year I played the trumpet in the band. I eventually had to drop band because, thanks to the paper route, I couldn't stay after school for marching practice. That was just one of the many activities I had to pass up because of the route. Many changes affected my life during seventh grade. I would like to say the most exciting thing to happen to me was meeting the ex-President of the United States, but that wouldn't be honest. The most exciting event to change my life was the opportunity to begin attending MYF. I didn't realize it then, but during the next six years, I would formulate friendships that would last a lifetime.

PRESIDENT IS SLAIN IN DALLAS

DAD AND MOTHER CONTINUED RUNNING THE PAPER ROUTE AND I GUESS IT WAS FINANCIALLY SUCCESSFUL BECAUSE, IN ABOUT FIVE YEARS, THEY WERE ABLE TO BUILD A NEW HOUSE. They paid off the note at the steel mill and were ahead on their payments to Mr. Steinhauser. Dad and Mother had become good friends with an elderly couple who lived on the route, named Paul and Anna Meyers. They owned an empty lot next to their home. Paul had retired from the railroad and their home was right across the street from the railroad tracks. They agreed to sell their vacant lot to Dad and Mother. Dad contracted with a family of house builders. They were a religious family and they were known to be very honest. The men never cut their hair or shaved their beards. The women always wore head coverings and long dresses. Dad worked along with them and did all he could to help with the cost. The new house was quite a change from our old one. We had three bedrooms, two bathrooms, kitchen, living room, dining room, large family room, and two-car attached garage all on one level. We also had a full basement Dad finished as a recreation room.

By the time we moved into the new house, I was starting eighth grade and working on the paper route every day. Robert moved away to college and decided to become a Methodist minister. He worked his way through college by taking positions as student minister at small churches. The churches furnished a place for him to live so he never lived at home again. Thanks to Grandmother Parrish and Aunt Carolyn, Barbara was enrolled at the Warrensburg State Teachers College, and Billy was a sophomore in high school. Until I graduated from William Chrisman in 1965, I worked on the paper route every day. Because of the work, I was unable to participate in any extra-curricular activities at school. I would have loved to play baseball or football, but they were not options. I couldn't even join any clubs at school because their meetings were always after school during my work time.

I had to plan everything around the paper route. The inconvenience of the route in the afternoon was nothing compared to the nuisance of getting up at 2:00 every morning. As a teenager, I wanted to stay up late, but I usually had to head for bed around 10:00, when the news came on television. I used my own money I had earned on the paper route to buy a clock radio. I loved to listen to the Kansas City A's baseball games on the radio. We couldn't afford to actually go to the stadium very often, but I rarely missed hearing a game on the radio. My clock had a feature that allowed me to set a sleep time of up to an hour, so if I fell asleep, the radio would automatically go off after sixty minutes.

Three of the A's, Norm Siebern, Whitey Herzog, and Bill Tuttle, all lived on Dad's route and subscribed to the Star. I continuously asked Dad if he would talk to those players and ask them for free tickets, but he said that wouldn't be very professional. There were many nights I laid awake to see if the A's could pull out a victory, but their victories were few and far between. I learned to live with the frustration, but constantly hoped for a winning season. If the game happened to be close or if the A's were winning, I frequently stayed awake listening. When my sleep timer turned the radio off, I turned it back on for another hour. If the A's happened to be playing on the west coast, the game didn't end until around midnight. There wasn't much time for sleep and then my Dad had a difficult time waking me up for the route.

After working on the route for a couple of hours during the night, I normally had time for a short nap before going to school. I existed on an average of 5-6 hours of sleep per night while school was in session. I did manage to get a little more sleep on weekends and during the summer.

The route did, however, offer some positive elements. My dad always bundled up all of the left-over papers and saved them for recycling. As a money-making project, our youth group at church decided to ask church members for all of their old papers. Every week, the youth group gathered to stack and tie up papers. Then, about once a month, we used my dad's truck to carry the papers to the recycling company. The paper route, in a round-about way, was bringing the youth together for a common project.

Some of the guys at church actually worked on the route for my dad. The girls never worked on the route, but it was a fun activity just to go along and watch. The girls who went the most frequently were Carolyn and Jane. They rode along in the back of the truck and sat on bundles of papers. On their first trip, when we neared the end of the route, and all of the bundles were gone, the girls either had to sit on the floor of the truck or find some other possible perch. Jane spied the hydraulic jack by the back door. She wanted to know if it was safe to sit on. I told her it was a 2-ton jack so I thought it would hold her. Even though she was 15 years old, she was very small. I never ventured to ask, but I imagine she weighed less than 100 pounds.

Hydraulic jacks have a valve that must be turned in order to raise the vehicle, or in this case the 15 year-old girl. Before she noticed the valve, she tried raising the jack, but it just kept going back down. Convinced it was a defective piece of equipment, she tried sitting on the saddle of the jack while it was only three inches off the floor of the truck. The saddle was a little dirty, so she put a piece of scrap paper on it and then tried to sit down. My dad was somewhat oblivious to the antics in the back of the truck, so he continued to turn corners as if we were all buckled in. The first time Dad turned a corner after Jane found her perch, she went rolling. Once we were certain she was not hurt, we all started laughing. I was more concerned about her than I was my job and I missed throwing a couple of houses. Dad stopped the truck abruptly and scolded me for not doing my job.

After he realized Jane's dilemma, he got out of the truck and came around to the back door and showed her how to raise the jack. He raised it to the maximum point and, since it was on wheels, he rolled it up to the seats where Bill and I were sitting. The floor of the van had grooves running from the back to the front. As soon as Dad started going forward, Jane started rolling backward. The wheels of the jack were in the grooves in the floor and she rolled to the back door. I'm not certain who enjoyed the ride more; Jane, who experienced it first hand, or the rest of us who saw the ride and observed the look on her face as she helplessly rolled to the back of the truck. After placing the jack perpendicular to the grooves, she could still sit on the saddle and face forward, holding onto the backs of my chair and Bill's chair. Once it became stable, it was not nearly as much fun, so she decided to share my chair.

I threw the papers on the right side and Bill threw them on the left. Jane sat on the left half of my chair and handed papers to me so I wouldn't have to bend over and pick them up. It didn't take long for her to decide it would be much more fun throwing the papers herself. I warned Dad he had a rookie throwing the papers. Even though she had been watching me throw papers for quite a while, and observing that the preferred method was to throw them like a Frisbee, she still tried to throw them like a baseball. Her first throw hit the edge of the window, fell into the street, and rolled into the ditch. Dad was being very good-natured about the whole ordeal and he just laughed and told her she would have to be in a convertible to throw like that. After showing her the preferred technique, she managed to get the papers over the ditch and into the yard. After trying herself, she was somewhat astonished Bill and I could throw the papers clear up to the porches with, what seemed like, little effort. We all had a great time, and the paper route became the topic of many discussions at our church MYF meetings. Although several other members said they would like to go, I always made some excuse why they couldn't. I knew the experiences we had could not be duplicated and perhaps the mystique of the exciting paper route was far better than it could actually be in reality for someone else. Besides, Jane was the only one I really wanted to spend a great deal of time with.

The pews in our church sanctuary had racks on the back of them to hold hymnals, registration pads, bibles, and offering envelopes. The offering envelopes had short one-paragraph stories about Christian discipleship written on them. One Sunday as the minister was making his third of four points, I noticed Jane had pulled out one of the envelopes and was reading the story. I looked at her face, and her eyes appeared glassy. A tear filled each eye but not enough to fall out. I asked her if I could read it and she handed it to me. It was a witness from a woman who had gone to Africa to help with the sick people. She was a nurse who had wanted to help and use her skills to make a difference in the world. It really didn't move me much and I gave it back to Jane. She put it in her purse and said, "I think someday I'd like to be a nurse and make a difference in the world." She went on to become a nurse, teach nursing, achieve her nursing doctorate, and lead the nursing staff at a large Chicago hospital. When I observed the reaction she had to such an innocuous written message, I witnessed the power of the written word. I wanted to some-day become a writer and be able to move people the way she was moved.

I continued to deal with the written word every day on the paper route. Newspapers are made up of a compilation of millions of writers telling millions of stories to millions of people about millions of events. Through the written word, those newspaper readers were given the opportunity to visualize countless experiences that they, otherwise, would not have known. I worked daily on the route all through high school. The benefits of working were obvious. I had a regular job with a regular source of income. My parents were able to keep the money in the family by having Bill and me working every day. I didn't make a lot of money, but managed to save nearly $3000.00 by the time I graduated. I saved most of what I earned.

I did take a trip to the west coast in 1962. Bill planned to go with me, but at the last moment, he decided he couldn't afford it. I was only 15 years old and had never been away from home for any extended period of time, never traveled a long distance by myself, and certainly never on an airplane. When I boarded the plane in Kansas City, I tried to appear mature and worldly. I wanted to act nonchalant, but I'm certain the crew had been made aware this was my first flight. My itinerary called for a two-hour layover in Denver before changing planes and heading to Seattle. When I arrived in Denver, I located the gate number where I was to board my next plane and then set out to explore this new world. I discovered a restaurant and just had to get something to eat. After spending about a week's income on a hamburger, fries, and a Coke, I resumed my explorations.

While I was roaming about the Denver Airport, my name was called over the loud speaker. "WILL JOHN MORRISON PLEASE REPORT TO THE UNITED AIRLINES TICKET COUNTER?" Even though I was sure there must be another John Morrison, I went to the ticket counter and said I thought I had been paged. The ticket agent told me to come around the counter and go through doors marked "EMPLOYEES ONLY". Right through the doors, I was greeted by a very attractive, young stewardess. She verified I was the same John Morrison heading to Seattle on United Airlines. When she was satisfied she had the correct person, she told me to stay with her. When a young, attractive air line stewardess tells a 15 year-old boy to stay with her, she had better be prepared to bear his children. I could tell she was smitten by my charm. She put her arm around my shoulder and took me through another door into a large room where everyone, except me, was wearing a uniform. She approached two men, called one of them Captain, and introduced me as a special customer. I still felt they must be making a mistake, but I was going to enjoy it as long as I could. The stewardess told me to go with the Captain and she would see me on the plane.

The Captain took me into another room and asked me to sit down while he looked over some important papers. After about fifteen minutes, he came back and told me it was time to board the plane. We went through a couple of rooms and down a long ramp to a plane. When we got on the plane, it was empty. He took me up to the cockpit and told me to sit in a chair while he made certain the plane was ready to fly. Three other officers entered the cockpit and asked if I was a new pilot. The Captain just told them I was a special customer. One of the officers introduced himself as the navigator and explained the purpose of the dials and switches. I didn't understand most of what he was saying, but I appreciated the attention. All of the officers assured me the plane was very safe and I was lucky to be traveling with such an ex- perienced crew. After about twenty minutes, the Captain said the rest of the passengers had been seated on the plane and told me to go find a seat in the cabin. He said I could sit in any empty seat, but he would suggest sitting in the back with the stewardesses.

As I exited the cockpit, several passengers sitting in the front of the plane looked up and probably wondered if the plane was being piloted by children. I slowly walked down the aisle toward the back of the plane and noticed there were several empty seats. When I booked my ticket in Kansas City, I asked for a window seat. I checked my ticket and located the seat assigned to me. It was next to the window and there was an older woman sitting in the aisle seat. She asked me if that was my seat and I told her it was. I glanced to the rear of the cabin and observed the stewardess who had been so friendly with me. She saw me and motioned for me to come to the back of the cabin. Given the alterna- tives, I quickly chose the obvious. There were three other stewardesses busily involved with pre-flight chores. Mandy put her arm around my shoulders and whispered, "You can sit in your assigned seat if you want, or you can sit back here with us." The seat she pointed to didn't have a window but, at that time, I really didn't care about panoramic views. The view of the stewardesses was much more enjoyable.

The navigator had referred to our flight as a 'local', but he said many passengers referred to it as a 'puddle-jumper'. After leaving Denver, we landed in Salt Lake City, Utah, Boise, Idaho, and Walla Walla, Washington before reaching our ultimate destination of Seattle, Washington. Mandy asked me to stay on the plane because she wanted to walk out with me. Of course to a teenage boy that was the same as a marriage proposal. As we left the plane, she asked me if someone was scheduled to meet me at the airport. As much as I wanted to say 'no', I told her my older sister was going to meet me. When we left the gangway, I saw Barbara and Larry looking for me. Barbara ran up to me and hugged me and said, "We were wondering if you were on this flight. They told us everyone except the crew was off of the plane."

Mandy spoke on my behalf. "I asked John to wait for me so I could make certain he found someone." Barbara was living in Bremerton, Washington and her husband, Larry, was stationed at the Naval Base there. Larry was scheduled to be released from the Navy in July, 1962. The World's Fair had been in Seattle and there were many interesting things to see. Barbara told me if I came out to see them, we would travel down the coast to visit family and maybe even go into Mexico. After Larry's release, we traveled north into Canada and visited Vancouver. We drove south down the coastal highway to San Francisco, and inland to Sacramento to visit some of Larry's relatives. We left our trailer in Sacramento and went further south to Los Angeles and even into Mexico. Upon our return to Sacramento, we hitched up the trailer and headed east towards home. The trip was a very enjoyable experience and I managed to see eight other states and two foreign countries. Another of the benefits of the paper route was I could take an extended vacation and not worry about losing my job.

There were definitely times I wished I could get fired. The paper route totally infringed on any kind of additional activities. For about 2-3 hours after school, I was on the route and then it was dinner time. On school nights, I really needed to be in bed by 11:00 in order to get my 5-6 hours of sleep. During my sophomore and junior year in high school, I dated Jane. I dated other girls before and after, but I would have to say she was my first true love. We experienced all of the anticipated events that normally accompany teenage dating. We spoke to each other either in person or on the phone every day for almost two years. I offered to carry her books at school, but she informed me she was perfectly capable of carrying her own books, but she did appreciate the sentiment. Our relationship felt so natural. When we held hands, it felt as if they belonged together. When we hugged, our bodies melted together. Her kisses were addictive. One was never enough and ten only deepened my need for more. It was as if something inside of me recognized something inside of her and those two souls yearned to be one. We spent a great deal of time together. We saw each other at school every day. We went out to some activity almost every Friday and Saturday night. She was in the Pep Club so her attendance at all school sporting events was compulsory. I attended all of the events I could but, since she was in Pep Club, we couldn't sit together. Every Sunday, we attended Sunday School, Church, and then, in the evening, MYF together.

After youth group on Sunday evening, we always managed to find some activity to extend the evening. Occasionally, we would travel to someone's house to hang out til it was time to go home or we might even visit the new hamburger stand, McDonalds. On other occasions, we discovered other, less wholesome, activities.

One of our favorite projects was teepeeing (toilet papering) someone's house. I'm not certain if my age group was the one to invent this procedure, but my parents had never heard of it. In case this cultural event has evaded your locality, this is the process. In order to avoid bringing attention to anyone individually, each of our group took turns going into different stores and purchasing 4-roll packages of toilet paper. When we had accumulated a sufficient number of rolls, we then proceeded to our chosen victim's house. Sometimes the chosen recipient was a friend and sometimes it was not. We met at a location close to our destination and then carpooled to our target. We could usually all fit into one vehicle, thereby bringing less attention to ourselves. We parked a short distance away from the house and the driver stayed in the vehicle looking out for any neighbors who might hear the disturbance. The boys were usually responsible for throwing the rolls up into the trees. The ultimate purpose was to have strands of toilet paper hanging like draperies from the trees. The taller the tree, the longer the strand of toilet paper left waving in the breeze. The girls generally decorated the bushes and small trees. If there was sufficient time and toilet paper, we adorned the lucky recipient's car and house with the beautiful garlands of white and pastel colored paper. As soon as the deed was accomplished, the driver slowly neared the house and all of the participants jumped in and we sped away. If done properly, the house appeared to be hidden behind a screen of gently flowing paper curtains. The bushes and small trees appeared to be wrapped as gifts anxious to be opened. The yard looked as if it had been covered with a fresh, soft, white blanket of snow.

The clean-up, however, was quite difficult. Due to the perforations in the toilet paper, when the homeowner attempted to pull the paper out of the tree, it would tear up higher than one could reach. If it happened to rain or even have heavy dew, the paper fell apart on contact. It was inevitable that some small pieces of paper would be blown into neighboring yards. In most cases, remnants of the event could linger in the trees for months.

If we happened to get caught in the act, it was very simple to reverse the process and appear to be cleaning up the mess instead of making it. Our repudiation would be that we just happened to be passing by and observed the dreadful deed executed on the premises of our friend. We wanted to clean it up before anyone saw it. We wanted to spare our friend the embarrassment of discovering such a reprehensible event.

We were caught once when the girl's father opened the front door. "Hey, Mr. Thomas!" I yelled very loudly, so all of the other participants would hear me and know to reverse the process.

Gary, one of my best friends at church and my blood brother in Boy Scouts, approached the front door with an armful of toilet paper and asked Mr. Thomas, "Do you happen to have a barrel or bag we can put this stuff in?"

About that same time, Jane appeared from around the corner with an equally large armful and said. "That's okay. We'll just take it with us and throw it in the dumpster at church." As she started walking to the car, she added, "We didn't want Carolyn to see this mess."

Mr. Thomas was confused. He thought he had caught criminals in the act of committing a crime, but apparently he had interrupted some 'good

Samaritans' in the midst of a good deed. "That's real nice of you to clean this mess up. I didn't even know it had been done. There's a trash barrel by the garage. Just put that stuff in there and then come in the house. We've got some cider and soda pop and Anne just made some cookies. I sure do appreciate your help. It would have taken me a long time to get that out of the trees."

Carolyn came out to help us clean up the mess. She knew we had been caught in the act but she was not about to tell her parents. She was aware that for us, being teepeed was not an act of malice but one of acceptance and love. We were each teepeed at least once during our term in high school.

While we were on the paper route, my dad and I saw many teepeed houses. The first time we saw it, Dad stopped the truck and tried to figure out just what that stuff was hanging from the trees. When I told him it was toilet paper, he said "Why in the Sam Hill (one of my dad's favorite expressions, but I have no idea who Sam Hill is) would anyone hang toilet paper in their trees?" I explained the whole concept to him, but he just saw it as vandalism.

When it happened to our house, he wanted to call the police and try to find the guilty culprits. I dissuaded him and told him I would clean up the mess. It wasn't long until all of the parents communicated with each other and discovered nearly all of the members of our youth group had been victims of this terrible act of defacement. Realizing their children were probably guilty parties, the youth-parent-staff committee decided it might be advantageous for the group to hear from some law-enforcement individual. A representative from the police department was invited to come to our church and lead a discussion on teenage vandalism. The policeman appeared in full uniform with his sidearm and tried to scare us straight. Our first impulse that night was to teepee the policeman's house, but cooler heads prevailed and we decided we should cease the activity for a while. All of the parents were going to be especially vigilant.

In 1963, I passed the long-awaited driver's test and got my driver's license. With that one accomplishment, I was able to shrink the world. With my license and car keys, I could eat dinner at home, pick up Jane and have dessert at Velvet Freeze, attend a movie on the Plaza, visit friends in Westport, go parking on Cliff Drive, and be home and in bed before midnight. Life was perfect.

On a cool Friday afternoon in November, I was sitting in Economics class. We didn't do much in that class. I think the teacher agreed to teach that subject just because the school district needed an economics class. He was a young guy who wanted to be cool and popular. There were rumors spreading through the halls between classes of an assassination attempt on President Kennedy, but we didn't know whether to believe them. When we entered the room, we asked Mr. Campbell if the rumors were true. He said if they were true, Mr. Shelton, the school principal, would make an announcement over the intercom. After about ten minutes, the announcement was made. President Kennedy had been assassinated in Dallas, Texas. Most of the girls cried. Mr. Campbell just sat at his desk looking out the window. I was sad, but I was more angry than hurt. This man was OUR president. He was a representative of the YOUNG people of the United States. He had taken a position that had previously been held by old politicians and claimed it for the youth of America. He was young. He had a pretty wife and young children. He made the office of President seem personal to us. He made the position vibrant. Now, someone had taken all of that away. Why?

I only had to wait until shortly after school to obtain more information. The Star had all of the pertinent facts. I anxiously opened the first bundle of papers and read most of the front page before I started rolling. Dad told me I would have plenty of time to read the entire paper when I got home, but I should get to work, because there were many customers who wanted to read about the events of the day. I took a paper in the house when we got home from the route. I wanted to know all of the details. I thought if I read enough data, I might understand why this happened. For that weekend, I stayed glued to the television.

When it came time to go to church on Sunday morning, I asked my parents if I could stay home and watch the events. I'm certain they realized the importance of the proceedings, so they allowed me to miss church, which was a rare exception in our house. As I watched television, the newscasters said the assassin would be transferred from one jail to another. I had seen pictures of Oswald, but I wanted to see him walk and talk. Again, I thought if I could just get enough knowledge, I might be able to understand the purpose. As he was led to a police car, someone came out of the crowd, stuck a gun in his abdomen, and shot Oswald. I'm certain it had never happened before, and I doubted if it would ever happen again, but a man was just shot on live television. What has happened to our world? Why would this man kill our president? Now we would never know. He was dead, too. We could only speculate. When President Kennedy died, the feeling of hope died with him. Innocence died. Camelot disintegrated. I needed something to depend on. I needed something that would always be there. I knew the paper route would always be there, but I searched for something more.

Jane and I dated for nearly two years. She was astonished to find out her father and I shared the same birthday. She told people the two most important men in her life shared the same birthday. Even though we talked for hours at a time, I am not certain we both totally understood the other's feelings. I felt she was more than a girl friend to me. I thought I was more than a boy friend to her. I told her on many occasions I loved her and she responded the same. When I was with her, I felt complete. Being together was so natural. I always dreaded the eventual parting. When we were apart, I thought about her constantly and counted the minutes until we would be together again. I longed for some special technique to allow me to communicate my love for her in a new and different way. The words came out so easily that they were becoming automatic. I wanted to tell her about my adoration in a special way she had never heard before. We both were enrolled in French class at school, and I thought it would be romantic to explain the depths of my eternal devotion in French. She was a better student than me and I felt she would certainly understand whatever I might say. We had taken over two years of French by that time so I used the vocabulary I knew and I practiced several times before I actually spoke to her.

We had been out for the evening, sat in my car talking and making out for a while, and then when I walked her to her front door, I said, "Je t'aime."

She quickly responded, "Je t'aime, aussi."

We kissed and I added, "Je t'adore et je t'adorai, toujours. Je veut que nous serons ensemble pour tous les temps."

I thought she understood what I had said, but I'm not certain if she did because she answered, "Merci." She kissed me again and said "Bonsoir." Then she went in the house. I didn't find out until many years later she didn't understand a word I said after 'je t'adore'. I guess my plan to be romantic needed a little more work.

We broke up shortly after that night. I thought it was because she didn't want to become any more serious. I believe that in reality, I may not have been serious enough or, at least, not clear enough. She loved to have fun and dated many other men before finally marrying another man when she was nearly 30 years old. The man she married was named John and shared my, and her father's, birthday. I'd like to think there is some cosmic explanation to all of that, but I would, in reality, just have to chalk it up to a quirk of fate.

IT'S BETTER TO HAVE LOVED AND LOST

I CONTINUED TO WORK ON THE PAPER ROUTE. It was a constant that was welcome in my life at the time. I knew whatever else may change in my life, the paper route would always be there. Jane and I remained friends during our senior year in high school. We couldn't possibly be anything less and were destined to be nothing more.

I managed to earn enough money to pay for at least one year of college. I was offered scholarships to all of the major colleges in Missouri, but I didn't use them. My parents thought in order to use scholarships, one had to show financial need. I believed them and didn't pursue any of the offers. If I had only known, most of my college would have been paid for. I really felt college was my only chance to escape from the paper route. With a college degree, I would have the opportunity to make a living in another profession. I wasn't certain what field I should enter; I just felt I needed to get away from the paper route. I thought I might want to become a lawyer, but my heart just wasn't in it. My mother wanted me to become a minister, but I never felt the call. My grandmother thought I would make a great teacher, but I had always heard 'those who can, do; those who can't, teach'. At the time, I had no interest in teaching. I hoped after a couple of years at general education, something might interest me. After graduating from high school, I decided to attend Southwest Missouri State in Springfield, Missouri. I knew several of my friends from high school were attending SMS, and I couldn't afford to go where Jane went, so I decided to try it out.

Everything went smoothly for most of the first month, and then I started dating Yvonne. She was in my religion class. It was a very small class and was scheduled to meet in a small room on the second floor of a two-story house just off-campus. The professor had been out of town and he had given the class assignments to be completed in a workbook. Our first class meeting was not until the third week of the fall term. As I approached the house, I couldn't help but notice the most attractive girl I had ever seen standing on the front porch. She was talking to a guy whom I assumed must have been her boyfriend. I thought at the time he was the luckiest guy in the world. She looked like she had just come from the tennis courts. She was wearing a white shirt and very short white skirt. As I walked up the steps to the front porch, the guy walked down the steps toward the street. He turned and yelled, "I'll see you in Civ on Wednesday."

The girl yelled, "Okay." But then very quietly she said, "Not if I see you first." The guy was not her boyfriend. She knew I heard her comment and we both smiled. I held the door open for her and we walked in together. Just inside the door was a staircase with a note on the banister directing students to the second floor. She was a couple of inches shorter than me and had very pretty long blond hair. She was tanned and had an athletic body. As we walked up the stairs, I noticed her legs were quite muscular. She must have been a cheerleader in high school. It would have been impossible for her to walk across campus without attracting the attention of every guy in sight.

Although the course was a study of major world religions, the professor was more concerned with how those religions affected our fundamental beliefs. We were encouraged to keep our religious preferences to ourselves, but on the first day, as we were introducing ourselves, most of us shared our name, hometown, home church, and reason for taking the course. I was drawn to Yvonne by her beauty, but hooked by her sense of humor. As we went around the room, each person stated the basic info and stopped. When it was Yvonne's turn, she said she was from Nebraska, her father owned a

Volkswagen dealership, and she had been raised a Baptist, but could probably be persuaded to become a Methodist by the right guy. I'm sure she didn't know I was a Methodist, but it is fairly well-known among Protestants, that Baptists and Methodists are fundamentally the same, except Baptists are much more strict about what they believe is proper behavior.

My Baptist friends basically believed all smoking, dancing, drinking alcohol, and gambling was sinful and to participate to any degree was wrong. The Methodists generally believed although those things may not be preferred behavior, they were only sinful when practiced to an excess. Methodist doctrine does not dictate what one can or cannot do. It focuses more on the positive side of living. Simply, the Baptists were more closely tied to the Old Testament doctrines and focused on the negative; thou shalt not smoke, thou shalt not dance, thou shalt not drink alcohol, thou shalt not gamble, and the rest of the Fifty Commandments, while the Methodists were more closely tied to the New Testament doctrines and focused more on the positive; you should love God, accept Jesus as your personal Savior, love one another, and treat others as you would like to be treated.

I was sitting next to Yvonne and after she spoke, I offered her my right hand, smiled, and said, 'Hello, Yvonne. My name is John. I'm from Independence, Missouri. I am a Methodist and I took this course so I could persuade you to become a Methodist.' After class, I stayed for a couple of minutes to ask the professor if he knew my brother, Robert, because he said he had attended the same Seminary Robert attended, Drury Seminary in Springfield. He didn't know Robert, so the discussion was short. When I went out the front door of the building, Yvonne was waiting on the front porch. She asked me if I had to hurry to another class and, even though I did, I told her I didn't. I wasn't about to allow a small thing like a class stand in the way of any potential relationship with her. I asked her if she had a class to get to and she said she was done for the day. We decided to head over to the Student Union to grab a snack. We talked as if we had known each other for ten years. Instead of hearing new information about a new friend, it felt as though I was becoming reacquainted with an old friend I hadn't seen for a long time. When she spoke, I really listened. Her favorite food was McDonald's french fries, but to look at her body, you would think she had never eaten anything fattening. Her greatest fear was spiders. When she described her family, I felt I could see them. When she described her home, I'm certain I could have driven down the street and picked it out. I told her about my family and friends, and found myself saying very personal things. I told her information I had never told anyone else. I even heard myself telling her the series of events leading up to and including my profession of eternal love to Jane in French.

After talking for nearly an hour, she hesitated for a minute and seemed to be carefully considering what to say next. She looked very serious and then she said, "Persuade me to become a Methodist."

I looked into her beautiful green eyes, remembered our initial introduction, and said, "Do you think I am the right guy?"

She didn't hesitate to answer, "If you were not the right guy, you couldn't convince me to eat McDonald's french fries, but if you are the right guy, you could convince me I would be perfectly safe to let a spider crawl on my arm."

I reached across the table and touched the back of her hand. She rolled her hand over and squeezed mine. Neither of us said anything, but I know we both felt the strong bond that had already been made. I wanted to kiss her, but we had only met a couple of hours before. I thought if I tried to kiss her, she might think I was only interested in sex. I should have known better. After a few seconds, she said, "I'm sure you could convince me to kiss you." We both leaned forward and for the first time in my life, I felt the need to keep my eyes open during a kiss. I just couldn't stop looking at her beautiful face. As our lips touched, I couldn't keep my eyes open any longer. They just melted shut. It wasn't a long or deep kiss, but I could feel my toes actually curl up. Our lips parted and she was the first to speak, "I need some fresh air. I feel really light-headed."

As we got up to leave, she put her hand down and touched the table to keep from falling. I asked, "Are you okay?"

She moved her hand from the table to my arm and said, "My legs feel a little weak, but I'm more than okay. For the first time in my life, I feel perfect."

We went outside and sat on a bench. The sunshine had lost some of its strength from the summer and its warmth felt pleasing. There was a slight breeze but certainly not cool. I looked at the cloudless sky and said, "Isn't this the most beautiful day you've ever seen?"

She glanced at the sky, looked at me, and said, "This is, without a doubt, the most beautiful day I have ever experienced."

I put my arm around her and she rested her head on my shoulder. We sat there, frozen in time, not needing to speak, but fully understanding each other's feelings. After a short while, I didn't want to end the moment, but I felt the need to be fully understood. This was the most stunning person I had ever known. Her physical beauty was obvious and her inner beauty radiated through every pore. How could I be so lucky? I couldn't risk losing her. I had to make her aware of my feelings. What were my feelings? Could I really love her? I thought about when my dad first expressed his love for my mother. 'Like' wasn't strong enough to describe my feelings for her. When I woke up that morning, I had never met Yvonne, and yet before the sun went down, I had fallen in love. I couldn't risk letting this day end without telling her how I felt. For the first time since we shook hands in religion class, I felt uncertain about what to say.

She looked so comfortable that I hated to disturb her, but I felt I must say something. I cleared my throat, but before I could speak, she said, "You'd better not be going to say something to me in French."

That was just the levity I needed to relax and relay my true feelings. "I know we just met a couple of hours ago and I know I like you a great deal."

"Oh, John, I like you, too. I was just sitting here dreading the moment when we have to say 'Good Night' and each head off to our separate dorms."

I hadn't considered that moment yet. It would definitely be difficult. Weren't those the same words my mother had said to my dad? I felt compelled to get the words out. "I hadn't thought about that moment yet, I'm still having a hard time understanding this moment. 'Like' just doesn't seem quite strong enough. I really do feel as if I love you."

She lifted her head from my shoulder and looked into my eyes. It felt like hours before she spoke. "I don't know if there is any such thing as love at first touch, but when you shook my hand in religion class, I felt shivers all over my body. My grandma says when you feel that, it's the Holy Spirit blessing the moment. From that first touch to this second in time, I feel I have learned what love really is. Grandma also said 'when it comes to love, throw out the rules'. How long you've known each other, or how you met, or differences in age, race, and creed don't mean anything when you're in love….. and I know I love you, too."

As our lips touched, sealing the moment, we became one. I couldn't tell where I left off and she started. As we hugged, she spoke, "We'd better spend some time in public with a lot of other people around or we're going to be explaining a pregnancy by Christmas."

It was inevitable our relationship would ultimately be consummated, but we didn't want to do anything that could tarnish it. We decided to go for a walk. I think we must have walked for miles, but I couldn't really tell you where we went. We shared memories, experiences, and dreams for the future. We went to dinner together and then went to the television lounge. Batman was on TV that night and we both enjoyed the experience. On college campuses all over the country, students just like us crowded into small rooms to live the Batman experience. We all understood the story line was preposterous, but we enjoyed screaming out 'POW!!!! OOOPH!!!! SPLATT!!!!', or whatever words were shown on the screen. It was necessary to arrive in the room at least an hour before the show in order to get a seat. In the television room, there were two couches, four over-stuffed chairs, two tables, and the television. There were usually at least 20-30 other people sandwiched in around the walls. We managed to arrive in time to get one of the coveted chairs. I told Yvonne to sit in the chair and I would sit on the arm. She said, "I have a much better idea. Why don't you sit in the chair and I will sit on your lap, unless you think I'm too heavy."

I wanted to suggest that arrangement in the first place, but I didn't want to seem presumptuous. While we waited for Batman to begin, we continued to chat. One of the other students, who was trying to hold the couch for his late friends, said, "I hope you guys don't plan to talk during Batman."

Yvonne whispered in my ear, "He's just jealous he doesn't have a girl sitting on his lap." I just smiled and thought to myself how every guy in the room would be jealous of me.

I whispered to her, "I couldn't be happier than I am right now."

She whispered again, "Are you really happy I am sitting on your lap, or is there a cucumber in your pocket?" We both laughed and the guy on the couch gave us another dirty look. Soon, the room filled to capacity and the moment of anticipation arrived. We screamed and laughed our way through another exciting episode and all agreed to tune in next week to 'Same Bat Time, Same Bat Channel'. We left the Student Union and headed in the general direction of the girls' dorm.

Yvonne stopped about twenty feet from a door and said, "That's my door, but don't make me go in yet. I feel like today has been a dream and if I go in and leave you here, I'll wake up and you'll be gone."

I shared her feelings, but knew we had to do some homework and get some sleep. I reached in my pocket and pulled out a cross I carried with me all of the time. It was given to me by the MYF when I left for college. It was a small cross and it had the words 'I Am Loved' inscribed across it. "Just take my cross and if you begin to feel this has been a dream, just read the words and know they are true."

She took the cross, closed her eyes, and squeezed it. She opened her eyes looked at me and said, "The Holy Spirit just blessed this moment." She frantically started rummaging through her purse, looking for something.

"Are you looking for your room key?" I thought that seemed logical.

"That's it!" she said, as she pulled a key out of her purse. "It's not my room key. It's the key to my home in Nebraska. As far as you're concerned, it's the key to my heart. Take it and hold on to it and if you think I'm not real, just look at it and know you hold the key to my future."

We kissed again as if I were being deployed overseas for a year. We parted and she turned to walk inside. I remembered reading Romeo and Juliet and thinking how stupid Romeo sounded. Now, if I knew the words, I'd gladly sing them to her, but I just said, "I love you."

She ran back to me and said, "I just need for you to hold me for 23 seconds. If I don't put a time limit on it, I'll be here all night." I looked at my watch, but didn't bother to count the seconds, because I didn't want her to leave either. She backed away and said, "Did your watch stop?"

I just glanced at it and said, "When I'm with you, time flies. I'm afraid when I am not with you, time will stand still. I know we will see each other tomorrow morning, but right now, that seems like years away."

She turned to go inside and I stood there waiting until she disappeared down the hallway. I waited a few minutes longer and then turned to head towards the men's dorm.

When I got back to my room, my roommate was gone. I was glad for the silence. There was no way he would be able to understand my day. I took out my books and tried to get started on my homework. I couldn't read a sentence without thinking of Yvonne. I took her key out of my pocket, squeezed it in my hand, and the Holy Spirit visited me. I spoke out loud, "As long as you're here, Holy Spirit, will you please help me to get my homework done?" I laid the key down on my desk and managed to get all of the necessary work done. When I went to bed, I laid the key on my night stand right next to the bed. I thought I would never get to sleep, but did manage to drift off around two.

I woke up to the sound of my roommate getting ready to leave. I had told Yvonne I would meet her at the Union for breakfast at about 8:00 because we both had classes at 10:00. When I looked at the clock, it was nearly 7:30. Richard had an early class at 8:00 and would probably just run by the Union and get a banana for breakfast. I hurried into the shower but it didn't take long, because the hot water was already gone. I dressed quickly, grabbed Yvonne's key and the necessary books, and ran out the door. I wanted to be waiting outside her dorm door as if I had been there all night. I couldn't wait for the elevator, so I ran down the five flights of stairs. I ran out the door and nearly leveled a girl standing right outside. It was Yvonne.

"I couldn't wait any longer," she said. "I wanted to see you as soon as possible." It was true. She did exist and she was more beautiful than I had remembered. She extended her right hand very formally and I gently took it in mine. "I want that to be our own private way of saying 'I love you!'. I know most lovers kiss when they first see each other, but we were brought together by a handshake and it's very special to me. When we shake hands and gently squeeze, it's as if love is transferred from one to the other." We embraced as if we hadn't seen each other in years.

That was the way we spent our lives for the next couple of months. We were together as much as possible. We hated to be separated, but learned to live with it. There were a few times when one or the other of us had to go home for the weekend. When one of us left, the other one would usually go home, too. The weekends lasted about two years when we were separated. We were both dreading the long Thanksgiving weekend and the, even lon-ger, Christmas break. Our plan was to tell our parents and our families about our relationship over Thanksgiving, and then meet each other's family over Christmas break.

As the Thanksgiving holiday approached, Yvonne acted nervous. When she was apprehensive, the best way to settle her down was to talk about our future. She loved thinking about how wonderful it would be when we could be together all of the time. We had discussed marriage, but deemed it a mere technicality. Nothing was going to change our feelings for each other. Just because we got married wouldn't make us love each other more, and just because we weren't married yet didn't make us love each other less. Marriage would give us another means of expressing our feelings. We were both very anxious to be joined together. However, we also knew we couldn't allow anything to hinder our relationship.

The week before Thanksgiving, her nervousness turned into depression. I tried to lighten the mood a little bit by suggesting, "My roommate has a box of spiders he is trying to train to run down his arm and jump to the floor. Would you like for me to go get them and let them practice on you?"

She smiled and realized I was only trying to make her feel better. "If they were your spiders and you REALLY wanted me to do it, you know I would do anything for you." She paused for a minute and appeared to be in deep thought. "Let's run to McDs and get some fries. Sometimes I can talk better while I'm driving."

I knew there was probably some logic in there somewhere, but I didn't see it. "Okay, you know I'm always ready for McDonalds fries."

I didn't have a car in Springfield, so we had to take hers. She was going to take me to Independence on Tuesday before Thanksgiving and then I would drive my car back to Springfield on Sunday so I could take some stuff home over Christmas. As we walked to her car, she said, "Do you really HAVE to go home for Thanksgiving?"

I wasn't exactly sure where this was going, but, to tell the truth, no trip home was mandatory. "You know I don't HAVE to go home, but I am looking forward to telling my family about you. I can't wait until you can meet them over the Christmas break."

She was still trying to figure out a way we could be together. "Do you realize the longest we have been apart was 71 hours and that was when I had to go home for my cousin's wedding? She couldn't figure out why I was crying like a baby. I told her they were tears of joy and I was so happy for her. You and I both know why I was crying. That should have been us getting married. I want a Spring wedding but I don't know if I can wait that long. Do you think we might be able to just spend the holiday here in Springfield together?"

We pulled into McDonalds and I went inside to buy the fries. I took the opportunity to think for a minute. In fact, the clerk said it would take a couple of minutes because she had to put down a fresh batch. Should I remind Yvonne of our plans or should I go along with the new ones? We had discussed marriage a great deal and our decision was to break it to our families gradually. We were going to tell our respective families over Thanksgiving we had met a special person. Then we were going to buy an engagement ring between Thanksgiving and Christmas. We would announce our engagement over Christmas and make plans for a Spring wedding, as soon as school was out. I knew she was depressed about being apart, but I knew it wouldn't be much longer until we could be together permanently. I was concerned if we moved too fast, our families might think we were irresponsible. Maybe before we made any changes, I needed to uncover her motives.

As we enjoyed the fries, we were both very quiet. She had been the last one to mention the time apart, so I needed to respond. "Seventy-one hours was tough, and five days over Thanksgiving will be even worse, but soon, we will be able to be together permanently. You know I will do whatever you want, but don't you think we can wait just a little longer?"

I offered her the last french fry. She took it, ate half, and gave me the other half. Finally, she spoke, "I've been thinking about this a lot and I want to see how you feel about it."

"Okay," I said, "but, you know I have a great deal of difficulty telling you, no, about anything."

She smiled and said, "Please, don't interrupt me. I've been rehearsing this and I want to get it right." I nodded my head and took her hand. She continued, "Before I met you, I had my life all planned out. I was going to get my degree in Veterinary Medicine and then go back home and open a Veterinary Clinic in Nebraska. One of my clients would be a handsome, intelligent, professional man with a great sense of humor. After dating about a year, we would get engaged, and then in about another year, we would have a large, fabulous wedding and go to Europe for our honeymoon. After returning to Nebraska, we would go on to raise four children and live happily ever after."

She hesitated and looked at me. I'm sure she could tell I wanted to speak and I had a sad look on my face, as if I had hurt her. She continued, "Don't look so sad. You are, without a doubt, the most wonderful thing that has ever happened to me. When I met you, my life was turned upside down. All of my priorities changed. Nothing was important any more except making you happy. I didn't want to do anything that didn't include you. I discovered my happiness was not dependent on a degree, a lavish wedding and four kids. I could never be any happier or more satisfied than I am right now, being with you. I know we can still have a beautiful wedding, a honeymoon, and as many kids as you want, but I don't want to miss out on the chance of completing our love. What if something happened to you or to me and we never had the opportunity to consummate our love?"

Again I wanted to speak, but she placed her fingers on my mouth. "Anything can happen at any time. Either one of us could get killed crossing the street. Before we separate for Thanksgiving, I want to be with you. I want for us to become one and when I return to Nebraska I want to be carrying part of you inside me. I have done the calculations and I know there is no chance of pregnancy at this time. I have called the motel on the north edge of town and made a reservation for Monday night. I have thought about this a lot and I have prayed about it and I believe it is the right thing to do. I know we wanted to wait until we were married to have sex, but I believe in God's eyes, we are already married. We have both committed our lives to each other and we have expressed our undying love for each other. The wedding ceremony is just a celebration of that love. I'm not suggesting a long term sexual relationship before marriage; I just feel the need to be with you. I have desired being with you from the first day, but now it feels more urgent. The desire is obviously still there, but the need is overpowering. I don't really understand why, I just feel before we are apart for Thanksgiving, we must be together. I will have a difficult time being away from you, but the memory of the experience will carry me through. I don't want you to answer now. I want you to think about it and pray about it. If you decide to say yes, it needs to be because you believe it is the right thing to do. Don't just do this for me; do it because you know it is the right thing to do. Never second guess it and never apologize if it feels wrong later. It has to be right for both of us or it shouldn't happen. Okay, you can talk now."

I sat there silently for a few seconds, trying to come up with the right choice of words. I needed to be very careful, because I didn't want to say anything that might be taken the wrong way. I, very tenderly, took her right hand in mine. "I will honor your request, and not answer right now. However, my first inclination is to do as you want."

She quickly interjected, "Don't make this decision based on my feelings. You need to make the decision based solely on your own feelings. This has to be right for you or tell me no. I will love you completely, no matter what you decide. You can't give me a wrong answer. If your answer is yes, then I will know you love me. If your answer is no, I will still know you love me."

She had given me a lot to think about. The ride back to the college was pretty quiet. As we drove past the men's dorm, I asked her to pull over and let me out.

"You're not mad at me, are you?" She asked, as she stopped the car.

I smiled and said, "I don't think it is possible for me to be mad at you. How could I ever be angry with you for asking me to make love to you? No, I'm definitely not mad, but you have given me a lot to think about. You have already taken this step; now it's my turn. I need to be alone and think. Tomorrow is Sunday. Why don't you pick me up here tomorrow morning at about 9:00 and we'll go get some breakfast before church?"

She leaned over and gave me a goodnight kiss and said, "Just remember, you can't give me a wrong answer. I will love you, no matter what!"

As I started toward the dorm, I looked up and saw my room light was on. That meant Richard was there and I wouldn't be able to think with him in the room. He would probably want to chat or play cards or something. I decided to go for a walk. Before long, I found myself sitting on 'our' bench outside the Student Union. I was going over scripture in my head and trying to remember all of the reasons why pre-marital sex was wrong. I felt sex was wrong if it was done for individual pleasure. A lot of young people were having sex just because it felt good. Our purpose was not carnal pleasure, but spiritual fulfillment. When Yvonne and I have sex, it will not be just because it feels good, it will be because it completes our loving relationship. I reached in my pocket and pulled out Yvonne's key. As I held it tight in my hand, I asked the Holy Spirit to sanctify my decision. I should have remembered the Holy Spirit doesn't respond to demands. It moves at its own will.

Generally, Yvonne and I attended church every Sunday. We did not always go to the same church. In fact, we alternated between the Baptist and the Methodist church. She liked the Baptists, but I could tell she was beginning to lean more to the Methodists' beliefs. She said she would be perfectly happy attending a Methodist church after we got married. On this particular Sunday, it was the Baptist turn, but I asked Yvonne is we could go to the Methodist Church. She had already dealt with the issues and arrived at a decision. I was still wrestling with my conscience and I wanted to talk to the Methodist minister.

After breakfast, we went to the Methodist Church and it was a very nice service. Nothing was actually said that would move me one way or the other. It was the Sunday before Thanksgiving, so the obvious sermon was about being thankful. After the service, as we shook the minister's hand, he jokingly said, "Hey, when are you two going to give me the honor of performing your wedding?"

We had already told him we were planning to get married, but probably not until next Spring. Yvonne answered him, "You're welcome to come to the wedding, but John wants his brother to perform the service."

"I'm certain that would be a big honor for your brother and a very meaningful experience for both of you."

I hated to take up his time on a Sunday afternoon when he probably had other plans, but I really wanted to talk privately with him. "Do you think you could give us a few minutes of your time, now?"

He didn't hesitate, "Certainly. Just go in and sit on the bench right outside my office. I'll be there in just a few minutes."

After a short time, he came by and motioned for us to follow him. We went into his office and he closed the door. As he was taking off his robe, he said, "This is two weeks in a row you've been here. Hey, John, are we winning out over the Baptists?"

He knew we had been attending both churches. I looked at Yvonne and smiled, "I think she's leaning our way, but I'd still marry her if she wanted go to the Baptist church."

He didn't sit in the chair behind his desk. He just sat on the corner of his desk and said, "What can I tell you that will make your life better?"

Yvonne said, "Just tell John it's okay."

He looked a little bit more serious and said, "I'm afraid you may need to expound somewhat."

I took Yvonne's hand and explained to him about our whirlwind courtship. I also told him about our future plans concerning our families and the holidays. He said everything sounded great to him and we seemed to be a very mature responsible couple. Then Yvonne explained how she felt about the need to consummate our relationship. He looked very pensive and he went around his desk and sat in the chair. Yvonne explained she had made plans for Monday night, but those plans were contingent on my agreement. She told him she would still love me, no matter what I decided. Then I told him I had been struggling with my conscience all night. I had replayed the scriptures and the advice I had received over my whole life. I wasn't asking him for his approval, only his guidance.

He picked up his Bible and said, "Before I give any advice, I want to ask both of you a few questions. Yvonne, I heard what John had to say, but can you tell me in your own words if you really want to marry him."

"Without a doubt. I'd marry him today if he wanted to."

"Okay, that's pretty clear. How about you John, do you think Yvonne is the right woman for you to marry?"

I looked at Yvonne and said, "The day we get married will be the happiest day of my life."

He started thumbing through the Bible like he was looking for a particular passage, and then he said, "Marriage is not all happiness and bliss. It sounds to me like you two have never even had a slight disagreement. What's going to happen when things are not so rosy? What if you can't pay for college and are forced to drop out?"

I said, "I don't know what path God has intended for me. I just know I want to walk down that path with Yvonne."

Yvonne said, "I would like to become a Veterinarian, but if I only care for my own dog or cat, I would be happy as long as it is in a home with John."

The minister spoke again, "I have some older couples in this church. There is one couple in particular who has dealt with a great deal of medical problems. He has had a stroke and is not able to take care of himself. She feeds him and takes care of all of his needs. I realize you are both young and healthy today, but do you think you guys could do that?"

Yvonne and I looked at each other. This was a subject we had already discussed. She told me to go ahead and speak. "We have already talked this over and there is no doubt it would be a difficult situation. We agree taking care of each other would not be a problem, but knowing the most important person in the world is suffering, would be painful."

He said, "The divorce rate in this country is astounding. What makes you two think you can survive against those odds?"

Yvonne spoke first, "I know there are a lot of divorces today. My aunt and uncle just got divorced last year. There are probably not many families that have remained untouched by divorce, but I believe if two people really care about each other, as John and I do, then any potential problem can be solved."

The minister turned to me to see if I had anything to add. "I know there is no guarantee with a marriage certificate, but there are no guarantees with a birth certificate either. As parents, you do the best you can and make sure every day your child knows he or she is loved. If married partners show the same commitment to their spouse, I think there would be fewer divorces. I thank God every day for bringing Yvonne into my life and I ask his help in making sure that every day, she knows I love her."

He just shook his head in agreement and asked, "Have you guys bought any rings yet?"

Yvonne told him about our plans to buy the rings between Thanksgiving and Christmas. "Until then," she added, "John gave me this cross to remind me I am loved and I had it made into a necklace. I gave him the key to my home to make him know he holds the key to my future."

The minister again shook his head in agreement and said, "Since you have already exchanged tokens of your pledge to love each other, and have come here today professing your love for one another before me, I now pronounce you husband and wife. John, you may kiss your bride."

We both looked at him like he was crazy and Yvonne said, "That's not the way we do it in the Baptist church."

"Let me clarify," he said, as he stood up, "all of the questions I just asked you are the same questions you will be asked in your wedding ceremony. The only difference then will be you will be given a piece of paper signed by the minister and two witnesses. That paper will be filed with the State of Missouri or Nebraska, and then it will be legal. Here, today, before me, and with God as your witness, you made the same commitment. I'm not going to tell you I believe you should have sex, but I am going to tell you I know many legally married couples who are not as devoted to each other as you two are."

He walked around the desk and Yvonne gave him a hug and said, "Thank you, that's just the way I feel."

I shook his hand and told him, "Thank you for meeting with us. You have been a big help."

After class on Monday, Yvonne and I went to the motel to check in. We checked out the room and then went back to campus to eat dinner. We each had classes on Tuesday, so we planned to leave the motel early in the morning, get breakfast on campus, attend the necessary classes, and then leave for home around noon. Since I didn't have a car, she was going to drop me off in Independence, briefly meet my parents, and then head for Nebraska.

We arrived at the motel at about 10:00 Monday night and we left the motel at about 8:30 Tuesday morning. The night could not have been more perfect. Yvonne could not have been more beautiful. At the appropriate instant, we felt the Holy Spirit confirmed our decision. The night was not about pleasure or excitement. It was about love, unity, and consummation. When we physically became one, our commitment was complete.

We attended the necessary classes, packed up the car, and headed home for the Thanksgiving break. Yvonne was much more relaxed than she had been for the last week or so. She hadn't stopped smiling since we got up that morning. When I asked her about the smile, she said, "My history professor asked me if I won the lottery and I told him I did."

I told her, "My main purpose in life is to make you happy and to be certain you know you are loved every single day for the rest of your life."

She responded, "I am so happy we decided to be together last night. I feel so relaxed and …." She was searching for the right word. I know because I had been trying to figure it out, too. "….complete. That's it. Up until last night, I felt as if something was missing in my life. Even though I know you love me, and that will never change, becoming one was God's gift to us. I hope we live to be a hundred and have tons of kids and grandkids as witness to our devotion, but if something tragic were to happen to you and God were to take you away from me, I would always know for one brief, shining moment, I knew perfection."

There wasn't anything I could add so I just said, "Amen!"

The trip to Independence was way too short and soon we would face another 'good-by'. She was surprised to see Independence was so large. I guess she was expecting one main intersection with a blinking stop light. As we headed north on Noland Road, I told her about the way it used to be. It had become much more commercial. We arrived at my house at about 2:30 and I knew Dad would be on the paper route, but I hoped Mother would be home. She was nowhere to be found. I showed Yvonne all through the house and even out in the garage where I found an extra paper tying machine. I showed her how the papers were rolled and tied. She said she would love to go on the route someday. She wanted to meet my mother, but she was a little bit worried about the weather. She wanted to get home before dark. I told her she would have plenty of time to meet the whole family around Christmas. Parting was never easy, but we had developed a routine. We always allowed some time for kissing, then she would say, "23 seconds!" and we exchanged parting comments and then always the last act before parting was a good-by kiss and then we touched hands. I know that sounds really corny but we both knew if we didn't give ourselves a time limit, 23 seconds, we would never part. Expressing our devotion through word and deed and the hand touch was just special because that's how we met. We walked out to her car, stood there for a few minutes, and then she said, "23 seconds!" She got in the car and as I touched her hand with mine, she said, "It's a little easier now because I am taking part of you with me."

I told her I would meet her on 'our' bench at 6:00 Sunday evening. She said she would be there waiting for me. I watched her drive down the hill and stop before turning on 23rd Street. She must have seen me in her rear view mirror, because she tapped her brake about ten times and then she left. I smiled and waved. As I walked back to the house, I calculated in my head....123 hours. I would need to keep very busy to make the time pass.

As I sat down to turn on the television, I heard the garage door go up. Mother was home. I went out to greet her and I scared her. She didn't know anyone was home. She had the trunk full of groceries for Thanksgiving dinner. She asked how long I had been home and who brought me. I told her I had only been home about 20 minutes and a new friend brought me home. She asked if he was from Independence. I said, "Well, first of all, he's a she, and she's not from Independence, she's from Nebraska. You just missed her. She wanted to meet you, but she wanted to get home before dark. She waited about 20 minutes, but decided she needed to hit the road."

Mother tried not to pry, but she wanted more info. "She wanted to meet me? This sounds serious."

"Yes, it is serious. She's very special. She is planning to spend some time here over the Christmas break and meet the whole clan. I, also, plan to go to her home and meet her family."

"Tell me about her. What's her name? What is she studying to be? How big is her family? What does her dad do? What church does she belong to?"

I answered all of her questions as I helped her put the groceries away. I found myself telling her all about our relationship....well, almost all. She began to fix dinner and I knew Dad would be home soon. I asked how the route was going and she said things were going okay now because Dad had found a trustworthy worker. As long as he had at least one dependable helper, his job was a lot easier. I was watching the news when Dad got home. He asked me to come out and help him clean out the truck. I took the opportunity to tell him about Yvonne. As we were standing out in the garage talking, I pulled Yvonne's key out of my pocket to show it to him. As I squeezed it, I felt chills. I assumed she must be thinking of me, so I kissed the key and put it back in my pocket.

That evening at the dinner table, Yvonne was the main topic of discussion. I wanted my parents to realize she was THE ONE, but I asked them to refrain from making a big deal out of it on Thanksgiving Day. We would refer to her as my new girl friend and I would gladly take all of their teasing. Then at Christmas time, they could all meet her and see just how wonderful she really was.

I managed to survive all of the teasing and the joking comments. Bill wanted to know what she looked like. Robert wanted to know what church I had been attending and who the senior minister was. Barbara wanted to know if she had any siblings. Bill said she sounded too perfect and she was probably a figment of my imagination. No one had actually seen her or met her, so I had no proof. I told them I would try to convince her to come to Independence during Christmas break, so they could see she was real. I had hoped Yvonne would call me on Thanksgiving Day, but she didn't. I was certain she was very busy with family activities and I hoped the weekend would pass quickly for her. Talking to me on the phone may have made the time apart more difficult. I would have called her, but I left her parents' phone number in my dorm room. I could hardly stand the wait.

Finally, Sunday arrived and we went to church. There were a few friends there from MYF and I told them about Yvonne. Every time I spoke about her, it made me miss her more. Mother fixed Sunday dinner and soon after, I began to get ready to leave.

As soon as I arrived in Springfield, I went to the girls' dorm and buzzed Yvonne's room. No one answered, so I figured she must not be back yet. I carried my stuff up to my room and decided to try to get some homework done before she got back. We only had a couple of weeks of classes and then finals week right before we went home for Christmas break. I saw the piece of paper with Yvonne's parents' phone number on it, folded it, and put it in my billfold. I didn't want to be without it again. I kept looking out the window, hoping to see her car. She always drove right past the front of my dorm and honked that unmistakable VW horn. I glanced at the clock and it was 5:42. She certainly had more will-power than I did. I know we were planning to meet at 6:00, but she was cutting it close. I hoped she didn't have car trouble. She shouldn't because her car was brand new. Her dad, the Volkswagen dealership owner, gave her a demo to drive. I walked outside to meet with her and sat on 'our' bench for a while. It got a little chilly, so I went inside and sat in a chair so I could see the bench. As it neared 6:30, I went to the girls' dorm and buzzed her room again. Her roommate answered and said she hadn't talked to Yvonne since last Tuesday. She just assumed we were together.

I couldn't wait any longer. I went to the Student Union to use a pay phone to call her parents. I felt like a teenager calling a girl's house for the first time. I was very nervous and I'm sure my voice was probably shaking when someone answered the phone. "Hello, my name is John and I am a friend of Yvonne's. I'm calling from Springfield."

It was a woman's voice, "Oh, hi, it's so nice of you to call. I'm Yvonne's aunt. Her parents don't feel like talking on the phone right now. Can I give them a message for you?"

I was a little puzzled why they couldn't talk on the phone, but my only concern was that Yvonne was on her way and would be here soon. "Can you just tell me when she left there and when she should be here?"

There was silence on the phone and I could barely hear some talking. I guess she must have tried to cover the phone with her hand. Then a man's voice, "Who is this?" He sounded a little cranky; like he thought I was a prank caller. "And what do you want?"

I certainly didn't want to get on the wrong side of her family, so I spoke very clearly, "My name is John Morrison. Yvonne and I have been dating since the beginning of this semester. She probably told you about me this weekend. We were supposed to meet at 6:00 in front of the Student Union and she's always been early. I was just getting worried."

"Hello, John. This is Yvonne's dad. She did tell us about you on the phone and in her letters. We've been looking forward to meeting you. There's no easy way to say this: Yvonne never made it home for Thanksgiving. She was about twenty minutes from here when she had an accident. She didn't survive…."

He was still talking but I couldn't understand what he was saying. I said, "Are you telling me Yvonne died?"

"Yes, she died on impact, so there was no suffering…."

I think he was still talking but I couldn't listen. I just said, "I'm sorry, but I can't talk now." And then I hung up. I walked out of the Union and it was beginning to rain. I sat down on 'our' bench. The tears were washed away by the rain. I didn't want to go inside. I told myself the raindrops were Yvonne's tears and I wanted to soak up all I could. I'm not sure exactly where I went or what I did that night. I know I was in my car for a while, but I don't think I went anywhere. It was about 2:00 in the morning when a security guard tapped me on the shoulder and asked me if I was okay. I told him, "I'll never be okay again." He told me I couldn't stay on the bench all night and took me back to my room. I know I went to some classes that week, but I have no idea which ones. I tried to take two of my finals but it was pointless.

The last Saturday before I went home, Yvonne's parents came down to move all of her belongings back to Nebraska. They called my room and asked me to come downstairs. I met them and they were very nice. They said Yvonne had written and told them a great deal about me and they just wanted to meet me. They said the accident occurred at about 5:30 on Tuesday evening. I thought back. Could that have been when I was showing Dad her key and I got a chill? It didn't matter anymore. They asked me if there was anything of hers I wanted to keep. I asked them if they found the cross that said 'I am loved'. Her mother covered her mouth with her left hand and reached out to touch my arm with her right hand and whispered, "She told us you gave it to her.....and she was wearing it when she......had the accident. It meant so much to her. I hope you don't mind, but we buried her with it around her neck. We wanted to call you to let you know about the accident, but we didn't have your number. We even tried to call down here to the college to get your number, but the offices were closed for Thanksgiving. Since all of the family was in town for the holiday, we decided to have the funeral on Saturday. I'm so sorry we couldn't get in touch with you."

She put her arms around me and I couldn't hold it any longer. I sobbed like a baby. She tried to comfort me, but there was nothing she could do. After a few minutes, I took the key out of my pocket and offered it to Yvonne's dad, "Here, this is Yvonne's key to your house. She gave it to me, but I guess it's really yours."

He put the key in my palm and squeezed my hand around it. "If my baby wanted you to have this key, then you keep it and if you're ever in our town, feel free to use it."

They got in their car to leave and Yvonne's mother put her hand out the window, just the same way Yvonne did. I took her hand just as I had taken Yvonne's hand many times and she said, "Yvonne called me on that Tuesday morning while you were in class. She called to tell me when to expect her home. I could hear the smile on her face. When I asked her why she was so happy, she said, 'John makes me happy. He makes me feel like the luckiest woman in the world. If I live to be a hundred, I'll never be any happier than I am right now.' That's the last time I ever spoke to my daughter and I just want to tell you thank you for allowing her to experience true love before she died."

I never spoke to them again. As they drove off, I felt like I lost Yvonne all over again. I tried to put my life back together and take my last final, but it was in my religion class. I looked at the test and I knew the answers but I just couldn't get anything on paper. There were way too many memories in that classroom.

I went by the Methodist church to see if the minister was there. I knew I couldn't sit through a service but I wanted to talk to him. I found him painting a classroom wall. He apologized for being so dirty, but I reminded him my brother was a minister and I had certainly seen him much dirtier. He asked where Yvonne was and I broke down again. I managed to tell him the whole story and he tried to comfort me. I told him I appreciated his concern, but nothing seemed to help. I asked him if he had any contacts at the college and he said he knew a few people there. I told him my predicament with my finals and I knew I would probably fail most of my classes. I really did want to continue in college but I would probably be academically ineligible for the next semester. He offered to give them a call and see what they could do. I gave him my phone number in Independence and he said he would call as soon as he knew anything.

Richard was already gone, so my room was quiet. I needed to think. I would be going home and Yvonne would not be going with me. I felt as if I couldn't endure another retelling of the events. Perhaps the easiest thing to do would be to just tell everyone we broke up. They had never met her and so they could just consider her as another ex-girlfriend. If the minister wasn't able to clear the path for me, I wouldn't be going back down there to college anyway. I loaded everything in my car, because I didn't know if I would be coming back.

When I got home, Mother and Dad were there to greet me. Mother asked where Yvonne was and I told her we had broken up and Yvonne had dropped out of school and moved back to Nebraska. I would never see her again. I had loved her a great deal and the break-up was not easy for me so I would prefer the subject would not be brought up again and it was not. The day after I got home, the minister from Springfield called and told me he had gone over to the college and explained my situation to the Dean. My grades would have to stand as recorded and I would be on academic probation, but I could come back for the next semester. I should have taken a semester off because I just couldn't concentrate. I slept late, missed classes, and only did about half of my homework. I always felt sick. I either had a headache or stomach ache all of the time. I never went back to McDonalds and I avoided 'our' bench outside the Student Union. By the end of the spring semester, I had failed about half of my classes and I was out of money. I moved back home, broke and unhappy.

I needed a job to pay for college and I needed college to escape from the paper route. As hard as I tried to escape the bonds of the paper route, it was again, pulling me back. Back in Independence, I felt I needed something to keep me busy and take my mind off of my problems. There's nothing better than a 7-day a week job to keep a person busy. Again, I turned to the one thing I knew I could always count on.

TROOP BUILD-UP IN VIETNAM

LESTER HEMAN, THE PERSON WHO BOUGHT THE OTHER HALF OF THE PAPER ROUTE FROM EARL JONES, NEEDED SOMEONE TO RUN HIS ROUTE FOR HIM SO HE COULD PURSUE OTHER INTERESTS IN REAL ESTATE AND SALES. He offered to pay me double what my dad had paid, give me one trip a week off, one weekend a month off, and two weeks a year off with pay. I just couldn't refuse it. I figured if I worked on the route for Lester for 2 or 3 years, I would be able to graduate from college and then step right into my new profession. I knew I had worked on the paper route all through high school, so I felt I would be able to do the same thing in college. Getting up to go to class was more difficult than I thought it would be. Most professors didn't even care whether anyone attended or not. I found it was way too easy to skip class and way too difficult to try to learn the important material without attending class. Viet Nam was becoming a violent whirlpool for young American men. Anyone who did not have a deferment could expect to be drafted into the Army and most Army draftees ended up in Viet Nam. I preferred not to go to a place accepting strong, healthy, young men and returning broken, handicapped, disfigured, angry old men. I needed to maintain my deferment in order to avoid passing through the doorway to Hell.

If the paper route was not enough of a disruption to derail my education, and the pressure of being sent to Viet Nam was not enough of a motivation to excel in my studies, I soon found another distraction. After my experience with Yvonne, I wasn't interested in a serious relationship. I just wanted to go out with a lot of different girls. I confined the merriment to the weekends, until, on one of those dates, I happened to meet the young woman who would eventually become my wife. Actually, I was on a double-date with my friend Mike. Mike was a close friend from church and school. He was a year younger than I and he had just graduated from Chrisman. We both dated several girls from the Northeast area of Kansas City.

On this particular evening out, his date was Edy Jo, and my date was Phyllis. Both girls had attended a private girls' high school in Kansas City and recently graduated. We went to the drive-in and happened to park next to another longtime friend from high school, Kirk, whose date was Pat. Kirk was enamored with Phyllis and I was equally interested in Pat. Between movies, the six of us stood outside our cars and chatted. While Mike and Kirk were looking under Kirk's hood at some engine problem, Phyllis and Edy Jo ran off to the bathroom and I was left to visit with Pat. I discovered she had graduated from Van Horn High School in the spring and had gone to California to spend some time with a boyfriend during the summer. They decided to break up and she had returned to live and work in Kansas City. I enjoyed spending time with Phyllis, but I also wanted to get to know Pat better, so I gave Phyllis' phone number to Kirk and he gave Pat's phone number to me.

Within a couple of weeks, Kirk and I had officially traded partners. After dating for about six months, Kirk and Phyllis were married. In another six months Pat and I were married. I would like to say it was true love, but in retrospect, I know I had not yet escaped the bonds of my devotion to Yvonne. Pat was just an unfortunate victim in my quest for happiness. I quit college in the Spring semester before we were married in the summer. The draft board had already taken away my student deferment and reclassified me as 1A (which was their version of fresh meat for Viet Nam). I did not want to take a chance of being sent to Viet Nam, so I decided to enlist in the Navy. I assumed that in the Navy, I would always sleep between clean sheets and work in a controlled environment.

After four very short months of marriage, I entered active duty in December, just one week before Christmas. The frustration of being separated from my new wife, compounded by the drudgery of boot camp, caused me to have an extremely long 13-week experience. During boot camp, on career day, recruits were given the opportunity to choose their field of endeavor for the next 2-4 years. I originally wanted to go into electrician's school. However, I was told if I went to that school, I would be obligated to sign up for an extension on my active duty time because it was a very long school. I definitely did not want to spend a day more than absolutely necessary as a boy in blue. When the careers officer looked at my test scores, he discovered I had scored quite high on the FLAT portion of the exam. FLAT stood for Foreign Language Aptitude Test. If I wanted to go into that field, the Navy would send me to a school to learn a foreign language and I would be stationed in whatever part of the world spoke that particular language. Realizing there was probably a large contingent of Viet Namese linguists, I asked the officer what was available. The first possibility he mentioned was Serbo-Croation. When I asked about the school and the later deployment, he said the recruit chosen for that particular school would be sent to a land base in Europe and stay there for the remainder of his enlistment time. I, quickly said, "Where do I sign?"

While reading through the papers, he said, "I need to inform you there is only one recruit chosen each year."

I noticeably shrunk down in the chair. I had to ask, "What happens to me if I request Serbo-Croation and don't get it?"

"If you choose Serbo and are not selected, you will be sent out into the fleet and probably assigned to a ship until next year." By the sound of his voice, I felt he thought spending a year on a ship would be a great vacation.

I really did not want to spend a year on a ship. I wanted to go to a school and then finish my tour of duty practicing the trade I learned. I needed to know what my chances were of being selected to Serbo-Croation school. "What are the criteria for selection?"

I'm not sure if he didn't know or just didn't want to take any more time, but his answer was, "I have no idea how the decision is made. I do know if you choose to take Viet Namese, you will be selected. I can't make any guarantees about Serbo. My job is to write down your choice."

"What are my other choices?" I asked.

He was beginning to sound a little frustrated. "If you want to pursue a foreign language, your choices are Serbo-Croation or Viet Namese. If you want to go to the electronics school, you will need to sign a two-year extension on your active duty requirement. If you don't want to choose any of those, then you will probably be sent out to the fleet. What do you want?"

I really wanted to go to the Serbo-Croation school but I did not want to take the risk of being passed over or being by-passed by some other more qualified individual. If I spent a year in the fleet, then I would be obligated to sign an extension in order to go to the language school. Contrary to all of my hopes and plans, I accepted the billet in the Viet Namese foreign language school.

About six months later, I met a guy at the language school who was enrolled in the Serbo-Croation class. He was the only student in the class. He said he started boot camp at the end of January. When he spoke to the career officer on career day, he was told there was still an opening in the Serbo-Croation school. When he asked what qualifications were necessary for that billet, he was told it was 'first come, first served'. In other words, the first person to request the Serbo School in each calendar year would get it. He requested it on February 6. I met with the career officer on January 2. When I realized I could have been the one accepted in Serbo-Croation school, I was not very happy. If given the opportunity, I would certainly like to give that career officer a few limited choices as to where he could go. This was only the beginning of my unrewarding dealings with the Navy – and it didn't get much better. My Navy career could be the source for another whole book, but not this one.

By the time I returned home from my obligatory time in the service, I was anxiously looking forward to renewing my effort to get a college degree. I graduated at the top of my class in the Viet Namese language school, so 24 hours of foreign language credit was added to my transcript. I enrolled in college and recommitted myself to that purpose. I felt I was finally going to be able to escape the clutches of the paper route.

I received a call from Barbara Heman (Lester's wife). "John, do you think you could do me a favor?"

Suddenly, I felt the paper route pulling me back in, but she sounded desperate. She and Lester helped me when I needed it, so I couldn't turn away.

Maybe she just wanted me to run the route for a few days. "What did you have in mind, Barbara?"

"Lester just recently passed away." She hesitated.

"I'm so sorry, Barbara. What happened?"

"It was his smoking. He contracted lung cancer. They tried all kinds of medication, but all it did was make him lose weight and hair. When he died, he weighed less than 100 pounds."

I couldn't turn my back on her. "I'll do whatever I can to help. What do you need?"

I could hear the tears in her voice. "The boys who work on the route know I need them, because I don't know which customers to throw the papers to. The boys who work on the truck are the only ones who know which houses receive papers. They got together and decided I should pay them $100.00 a trip. I don't have any choice. I need them."

I have a pretty good memory and I knew which houses subscribed before I went into the service. I knew there would be changes, but I thought, by watching the boys closely, I could learn about 90% in one day. "I'll be over to your house in 10 minutes."

I went by Barbara's house and found out who the boys were and where they lived. I took the truck home with me and told her I would take care of the situation. I told her to make each boys check out for the regular amount for the trips they had worked.

When I arrived at the first boy's house, he asked where Barbara was, and I told him she was sick. When I picked up the second boy, I told him the same thing. I also told them I didn't know much about the paper business so they would need to give me driving instructions. I focused mainly on the boy on the right side on the morning trip and I focused on the boy on the left side on the afternoon trip. When we finished the afternoon trip, I told them both I would not need them to work any more. I gave each of them his check and told them if there was any problems with the amount of the check to have their parents call Barbara. One of the boys actually did have his father call Barbara, because he thought she had shorted his son the agreed wages. When Barbara explained the situation to the father, he tore up the check and said he was sorry and embarrassed for the way his son had acted.

I had put myself right back into the one position I was trying to avoid. I thought I could train some new help for Barbara and make a throw book for her, which would show all of the subscribers, as insurance. I hoped I would be able to get away from the route in a few months. Pat and I had bought a home and we were hoping to start a family. The income from the route was necessary for us to pay the bills. The route had taken so much of my time that my college career had been limited to just one class at night. My brother, Bill, was leasing a route in Raytown.

It was more profitable to lease a route than to manage one, so I called a friend, Raymond, who owned 4 paper routes and asked him if he knew of any routes for lease. He said he would have a route available in about two months, if I could wait that long. I told him I would probably need that much time just to train my replacement. When I sat down to talk with Raymond about the route, I learned I would be making more money than I had ever made before. The money would be great, but the route still demanded a huge sacrifice; seven days a week, twice a day, except on Sunday, I would be at the mercy of the elements. Whether in rain, sleet, or snow, regardless of temperature, over one hundred degrees or twenty degrees below zero, I was obligated to deliver all of the papers to all of my subscribers. I had a wife and hopes of starting a family, and felt my responsibility to my family was greater than my desire to escape from the clutches of the paper route.

BODY FOUND IN POOL

I FOUGHT THE ELEMENTS FOR ANOTHER SEVEN YEARS. I suffered through the heat of the summer and battled the ice and snow of frigid winters. There were many memorable trips on the route. In addition to pulling the dead woman from the flooded ditch earlier in the day, on previous trips, I discovered another dead body in the motel on 40 Highway. One of my helpers found a dead body in the swimming pool in the apartments. I stopped a robbery at the convenience store on 47th Street with a Butterfinger. I convinced a girl to give life another chance when she was prepared to jump off of the Stadium Drive Bridge over I-70. If the paramedics had been five minutes slower, I would have helped a woman give birth. I pulled a baby out of a wrecked car just before it burst into flames. I observed a college girls' softball team skinny-dipping in the indoor hotel swimming pool. I attended a team celebration in Hal McRae's hotel room when the Royals clinched the Division Championship. It was again time for me to go back out on the route and battle nature. No telling what excitement the next trip might bring.

As I pulled up to Rick's house, he was sitting on the front porch waiting for me. Although he normally was to cool to run, he ran out and jumped in the truck. "Have you decided what story you're going to tell us?"

I really had forgotten about my promise. On the way to Charles' house, I mulled over which story I might tell them.

Apparently, Rick and Charles had talked about the impending tale, because as soon as Charles got in the truck, he turned to Rick and said, "Did he tell you yet?"

"No, dork, he's still thinking about it." Rick tried to appear uninterested.

I decided to let them choose which story they wanted to hear. "Do you want to hear about finding a dead body, stopping a robbery, celebrating with the Royals, helping a woman having a baby, skinny-dipping with a girls' college softball team, or saving someone from a wrecked car?"

Rick quickly answered, "I already know about the dead body. Remember, I was there, too. You didn't find another dead body, did you?"

"As a matter of fact, I found two other dead bodies. Well, in reality, I found one, but one of my helpers found the other one." I would prefer telling the story about the woman having a baby or saving a baby from a wrecked car, but these were teenage boys who were more interested in gruesome tales.

"Do you mean one of your helpers, just like me, found a dead body?" Charles was not sure if he wanted to hear about something that could, conceivably, happen to him.

Rick could see the fear on Charles' face and took the opportunity to scare him even more. "It was probably in the apartments." He knew Charles was already afraid in the apartments.

"Actually, it was in the apartments." As I looked in the mirror, I noticed Rick had a rather serious look on his face. He wanted to scare Charles, but he wasn't real crazy about hearing we had discovered a dead body in the same apartments where he would be delivering papers.

"Was it on a morning trip or an afternoon?" Charles was hoping I would say afternoon, so he could try to scare Rick, who would be running them that afternoon.

I had two different sets of apartments on my route. The short set was located by 40 Hiway and the long set was south of I-70. Usually, one boy would run the short set and the other boy would run the long set. Since Charles had run the long set in the morning, then he would get to run the short set in the afternoon. The short apartments only took about 30 papers and I left with the other boy to throw about 50 papers which took about 10 minutes.

"It was on a morning trip." I said.

"Ha!" Rick interrupted me because he knew what Charles was thinking.

"Like I said, it was a morning trip, but it was in the short apartments." As I spoke, I looked in the rear view mirror and saw a slight smirk appear on Rick's face.

"Guess which apartments you get to run?" Rick began to poke at Charles.

As we pulled into the gas station to load up our papers, Rick jumped out to talk to one of the guys on Charlie's truck. I was sure he was going to relay the events of the morning trip. Charles sat very quietly behind me. I was going to get out and talk to Charlie when Charles spoke up. "Do you think you could wait 'til after I run the apartments to tell the story? Rick will just make a big deal out of it and try to scare me if you tell it before I get out."

"Okay, I'll run that section first and then you and I can get the Sports Complex and the trailer courts while Rick runs the apartments." There was really nothing unusual about running the route in that order. Sometimes, it was advantageous to run it that way to avoid traffic. Since the papers were late arriving, I would have probably started with the apartments first anyway. Rick came back over to the van and wanted to know why the papers were running so late.

We never knew why the papers were early or late until the truck driver arrived with our load. Sometimes he knew why they ran late and sometimes he didn't. It didn't really matter what time we received our papers because the customer always assumed late was our fault. People always expected their newspaper to arrive at the same time every day. I felt they must assume that we collect the stories, type them up, and print them in the back of our van. I know it sounds ridiculous, but most customers blame the carrier when the paper is late. Once in a while, a carrier may have a flat tire or engine problem, but vehicle delays are rare. The Star requires all carriers complete their delivery rounds by a certain time. The times are all easily attainable if the papers are delivered to the carriers on time. The carriers and their helpers all sit at the local bundle drop and wait for as long as it takes. Occasionally, the papers actually arrive early, but not often.

Rick was frustrated because he had plans for activities after the route and we were going to be late getting home. "Why can't the Star always get the papers here at the same time?"

I didn't know if he really wanted an answer or if it was just a rhetorical question, but the response could kill some time. "It's a fairly long and sometime arduous task. The people in charge decide how much of the paper will be advertising and how much will be personal interest news. Then the advertising department sells ads to appear in the paper. That department fills up their assigned amount of space. The big shots assign reporters to gather stories and prepare them for print. Once the stories are prepared, editors check them for accuracy and grammar. Advertisers and reporters are given deadlines and it is their responsibility to have everything ready for print by a set time. Once all of the information is gathered, the typesetters arrange the words and pictures to fit on the correct page size.

As soon as the press plates are prepared, the presses actually begin to print the paper. One of the first papers off of the press is pulled out and checked for mistakes. If there are problems, the presses are stopped, the mistakes corrected, and the presses are started up again. After the papers are printed, they are sent down a long conveyor belt and are joined with other sections of the finished product. The final creation is then folded and stacked. The stacks are sent through a compactor which presses the stack down and puts a strap around the loose papers to form a bundle. The bundles are then sent down another conveyor belt to the loading dock. At the dock, the truck drivers take the bundles off of the conveyor and stack them in the delivery truck to be brought out to the carriers.

If any part of the process is delayed, we get our papers later. Sometimes, the editorial staff will say they need a later press time in order to get the latest news concerning an important topic. The important topic could be anything from the flood to the Royals final score in a West coast game. The newspaper bigwigs don't like it when television releases more current information than can be found in the paper, so they try to wait as long as possible to get the latest news. The editorial staff may be the culprit today because they want to get every bit of information concerning the flood. The presses could have broken down. Occasionally, they experience a jam or a newsprint tear. When the newsprint tears, the press needs to be rethreaded. That all takes time. Sometimes, a new bit of information becomes available and, if the editorial staff believes it is important enough, the presses are stopped and the plates are changed in order to produce a new and improved up-to-the-minute product. It is possible everything could run as smooth as possible downtown and then the truck carrying our papers could break down on the way here."

Rick appeared to be a little bored by most of my explanation but he hadn't considered the Star truck breaking down. "What do we do if that happens?"

"There's not much we can do. We just have to sit here and wait while the driver uses his two-way radio and calls the Star to tell them he is stranded. Then they get another truck and another driver and send him out to transfer the load."

"Has that ever happened?" I think Charles was hoping for something that had never happened before.

Unfortunately, I think about every possible option has occurred at least once. "Yeah, I know of several times it's happened. Once, the driver was using a CB radio and we heard him call the Star for help. He gave his location and we drove down on the interstate and met him. We took turns backing up to the back of the Star truck and loading our papers. We were all done and on our way before the replacement driver showed up to help."

Rick was trying to figure out a way to eliminate this potential problem. "Why can't all of the truck drivers use CB radios?"

He didn't realize it, but we had already discussed that option with the circulation department in our monthly meeting. "We discussed that possibility with them, but the CB radios have a very limited range and, besides, not all carriers have CB radios either. Maybe one of these days, someone will invent a phone that doesn't need a wire connected to it. If we all had pocket phones, then we could be in constant contact with the Star, the truck driver, and each other."

"Wow! That would be cool." Charles had temporarily forgotten about the late papers. He was thinking of other possible inventions. "Maybe someday, we can carry televisions in our pockets, too. It would be cool if we could ride around in the truck and watch television."

Just then, the Star truck pulled in and we all jumped out to get our papers. We liked to joke around with the truck driver and accuse him of doing something to cause the papers to be late. "Hey, Chuck, did you find a new place to stop and get a cup of coffee?"

He didn't see anything funny. The Star caused his day to run long, also. "I wish I was doing something fun, instead of just sitting down at the dock watching the morons run in circles."

Charlie was all business. "Did anybody give you any reason why they're so late? I know our customers are going to be asking and I'd like to be able to tell them something."

Chuck was just standing back, letting everybody grab bundles. He wasn't making any attempt to count. He knew we were all pretty accurate. "I left the Star with the right number of bundles, so if anyone is short, talk to your buddies." He turned towards Charlie. "Nobody tells me anything. I heard the presses stop three times while I was loading my bundles, but I don't know if they broke down or just stopped to update the news."

Everyone grabbed their bundles and left the station in a big hurry. My first stop was the Sheraton. I dropped off the correct number of papers at the front desk and then went to the Gift Shop. Geraldine, the manager, was in a snit. "Where have you been? I've had a dozen people in here wanting to buy the afternoon paper."

I don't think she wanted an answer. She was like most other customers. She just wanted to let me know she was unhappy, but I gave her an answer anyway. "The presses shut down several times. I don't know if it was for updates or if they were just having press trouble. I can't bring the papers to you until the Star brings them to me."

We headed straight for the first set of apartments. I let Charles out and explained to Rick why I was running the route this way. We then picked up Charles and continued to the other apartments. After I let Rick out, Charles and I journeyed down 43rd Street towards the Cut-Off. I stopped in at Holiday Inn and put papers in the machine in the lobby. There was no one at the front desk, so I didn't have to answer any questions there. We cut through the Sports Complex and headed to the trailer courts. When we got back to the apartments, Rick wasn't quite done, so we delivered the papers to the townhouses. Charles said he wanted to get out to try to scare Rick but I didn't want to waste any time on foolishness. We were already running late.

As soon as we picked him up, Rick said, "You didn't start the story without me did you?"

I had temporarily forgotten about the story. "No, I haven't started it yet."

As we started heading south on Pittman, I began the story. I knew I would
have enough time to relate all of the events while we delivered the South part
of the route.

"It was a cold, winter morning. There wasn't any snow on the ground and
the roads were clean and dry. There were two guys working for me that you
wouldn't know. One was Darryl and he was kind of a nerdy guy. He wore
glasses and he was pretty skinny. He had a difficult time carrying all of the
papers in the long apartments."

"That sounds like you, Charles." Rick couldn't resist a dig at Charles, but
he was right, they were a lot alike.

"I ran the route a little differently back then. I let one boy, who happened
to be Darryl, out at the long apartments, and then I went North on Pittman to
40 Highway and proceeded East to the short apartments. There I let the other
helper, Tim, out. He was a rather large boy. Due mainly to his size, he moved
very slowly. It always took him about twice as long to run the apartments as
any other boy. After letting him out of the truck, I continued by myself, throwing papers on both sides of the street. I threw the same area then as I do now.
It took me about ten to fifteen minutes to make all of the throws and get back
to the apartments to pick him up.

As I was heading East on 40 Highway, I saw someone running towards me.
As I got closer, I could see it was Tim. I was surprised, because I had never
seen him move so fast. I slowed down to pick him up, but he ran right past
me. I started backing up, but he didn't slow down. I turned the truck around
and started following him.

As I drove up next to him, I said, 'Come on Tim, get in the truck.', but he
just kept on running.

He said, 'I ain't gettin' in that truck! You can't make me! There's no way
I'm goin' back to those apartments!'

I finally figured out where he was headed. He lived around the corner in
the first house. I passed him up and pulled into his driveway, got out of the
truck and opened the back door for him to get in. He had depleted his oxygen
supply and started walking. As he approached the truck, I said, 'Okay, Tim
what's the deal?'

He stopped and sat down on the back bumper of the truck. He was still breathing rapidly as he attempted to talk. 'There's some dead guy at the apartments and I ain't goin' back there.'

I assumed he was wrong. He had probably seen some laundry or fire wood that just looked like a person. When I suggested that to him, he said, 'I don't care if you believe me or not. I know it's a dead guy and I don't want to see it again.'

Still not believing him, my thoughts turned to the paper deliveries, so I asked him, 'Did you finish delivering all of the papers?'

Newspapers were obviously not very high on his list of concerns because he said, 'I figured all you cared 'bout was the papers. No, I didn't finish delivering all of 'em. When I saw the dead body, I dropped the bag and started runnin'.'

I knew I had to go back to the apartments, whether Tim went or not. 'Where did you see the dead body?' Even though I didn't really believe there was a dead body, I figured the only way I could get information was to go along with him.

'I'll tell you where it is, but I ain't goin'.' I reassured him he would not need to ever go back to those apartments again, if he didn't want to, but I also told him he couldn't work on the route without running the apartments. He thought for a minute, because he really did like the money, and then he said, 'Could I still work on the route if I run the long apartments every day?'

I told him I felt certain Darryl would be happy to run the short apartments every day. It reminded me that Darryl was still in the apartments and I would need to hurry to pick him up. 'Okay, Tim, I need to know where the dead body is located.' As I was talking to Tim, I shut the back door and walked around the truck to get in the driver's seat. I think Tim wanted to go on the route, but he definitely didn't want to go back to the apartments.

He asked, 'Are you just gonna leave me here?'

I told him, 'I'm going back up to the apartments to finish delivering the papers. If there is a dead body, I'll call the police. I'll probably have to stay and talk to them.'

As I put the gear shift in reverse, Tim said, 'I delivered the first six doors and the body is in the pool. I saw it when I walked past on my way to the next building. I just dropped the bag with the papers in it right there. If you want me to go the rest of the way on the route, you can come get me after you leave the apartments.'

As I left Tim's house, I was wishing for one of those pocket telephones. I glanced down at my watch in order to register the exact time. I subtracted about 15 minutes from it and wrote it down on a piece of paper. I figured that was when Tim actually saw what he believed to be the dead body. If I was going to be discovering a dead body, I would rather do it in the presence of a police officer.

When I turned out onto 40 Highway, I reached for my CB radio to ask someone with a land line to call 911. Then I spotted a police car in the parking lot behind Cool Crest. I pulled into the parking lot and up to the police car. He had his dome light on and it looked like he was writing his reports. Don had told me they do that whenever they get a chance. I didn't know how to relay my story without sounding somewhat suspicious. I said, 'Hi, I'm the newspaper carrier for this area and I just let one of my helpers out to deliver the papers to those apartments about 15 minutes ago.'

He just looked at me and said, 'Okay, so how can I help you?'

I said 'My helper said he saw a dead body in the swimming pool. It may just be some old clothes, but do you think you could go check it out?'

His face became much more serious as he reached for his radio. He said something in the radio and we both hurried to the apartments. He followed me and I parked at the door nearest to the pool. We both got out and cut through one of the buildings. The swimming pool was in the middle of the apartment complex surrounded by the apartment buildings so it couldn't be seen from the street or the parking lot. When we came out of the apartment building into the courtyard area, I saw the canvas bag with the papers in it Tim had been carrying.

The cop was walking in front of me and he reached the pool area first. There was a ten-foot fence around the pool. The manager had told me the insurance company made them put up the fence in order to prevent little kids from just wandering into the pool area and falling into the water. As I reached down to pick up the canvas bag, I saw the body in the pool. It was winter and the pool had been partially drained and the diving board had been removed. The entry gate into the pool area was chained and locked. The cop shined his flashlight into the pool and there was definitely a body. From our position, we couldn't tell if it was male or female. The body appeared to be in men's clothes but it was laying face-down in the murky water.

The cop turned to me and said, 'Do you know where the manager lives?' I said I knew the manager and I would go wake her up. I took the bag with the papers in it and went to the manager's building. I rang her doorbell and waited for a response.

After a couple of minutes, she opened the door. 'Hey, John, what's the matter? Did someone skip out without paying their bill?' Whenever someone skipped out without paying, I would check with her to see if she had a forwarding address.

I said, 'Not that I know of, but I believe there's a dead body in your swimming pool. I can't be sure he's dead, but at least he's passed out. I found a policeman over at Cool Crest and he's out by the pool now. He needs the key to the gate.' She reached for a key on a hook behind her door and handed it to me.

She said, 'Here's the key. I'm going to get dressed.'

"Was she naked?" Rick interjected. He knew the manager was an attractive young woman. Trust Rick to be more interested in seeing a naked woman than the possibility of a dead body.

"No, she wasn't naked. That's a different story."

"I want to hear THAT story!" Charles hurled the words out before Rick had a chance to say them.

There definitely was a story about a naked woman, but I didn't want to share it with them. "No, you guys are too young to hear that kind of story. Besides, I haven't even finished this one yet."

As I headed back out to the pool area, I noticed there were a few residents looking out their windows. I mentioned it to the cop and nodded towards the curious onlookers. "Looks like we've got an audience."

He didn't pay much attention to them. I handed him the key and stood close by in order to enter the pool area with him. He wasn't going to allow it though. "You're going to have to stay outside of the pool area, because it's a potential crime scene." He unlocked the padlock and entered the pool area. I waited at the gate as he reached the body. He turned the body over and discovered it was a deceased male. "It's too late. He's dead. I'm going to need your name and the name of the kid who discovered the body."

Just then, Tanya, the apartment manager, walked up to my side. "Is he dead?" She asked, as she looked into the pool.

I told her he was dead and the cop asked who she was. I introduced her to the cop and he asked her if she recognized the man. She said, "He's not a tenant but I have seen him around. I think he has friends who live here." As she was talking, three more officers came running up to the pool area.

The initial policeman turned to the other three and said, "This guy (pointing to me), is the newspaper carrier who delivers papers to these apartments. His helper discovered the body about 20-30 minutes ago. She (pointing to Tanya), is the apartment manager. Get their names, addresses, and phone numbers and tape off this area. I don't want anybody in the pool area til the investigators get here."

One of the officers ran back towards his car to get the tape and the other one reached in his pocket and pulled out a pad of paper and pen. I told him I was in the middle of delivering my papers and I really needed to leave, if that was okay. After getting approval from the initial officer, I gave him all of the necessary information, including Tim's name and address, and I left. As I picked up the bag to continue delivering papers to the rest of the apartments, he was talking to Tanya. When I finished delivering all of the apartments, I walked back past the pool area, which was roped off with yellow crime scene tape. Tanya told me they didn't have a positive identification yet, but he had not been living in the apartments. I told her I would stop back by after I finished the route to find out the details. When I drove down 40 Highway, I noticed there was a police car in front of Tim's house. I thought I might pick him up to help finish the route, but I didn't want to wait until the police were done talking to him.

Darryl was done with the long apartments and was sitting on the sidewalk waiting for me. He was not very happy when he found out he had to roll the rest of the papers by himself, so I told him I would give him double pay for the trip, if he could roll fast enough to keep us in rolled papers during the south part. The additional monetary incentive was sufficient for him to handle the job easily. He was interested in the exciting events in the other apartments, but he did not envy Tim for having discovered the body in the pool. He said he would probably not have even seen the body because he never walked close enough to the pool to see down inside. He was pretty fast in the apartments and he usually ran from one door to the next without looking around.

Tim walked very slowly and looked at everything along the way. One time I found out from Tanya that Tim had been seen stopping outside a window and looking in at a woman getting dressed. When I confronted Tim with the accusation, he denied looking in anyone's apartment. I told him I would be spying on him and if I, or anyone else, happened to observe him looking in an apartment window, he would no longer have a job. As it turned out, he never worked another trip after discovering the body. He said his parents wouldn't allow him to work because it was too dangerous. I actually think if he really wanted to work on the route, they would have let him.

After I finished the route and took Darryl home, I stopped back by the apartments. There were still two unmarked police cars in the parking lot on the west side of the buildings. I drove on down to a spot close to Tanya's apartment. There were always extra spaces there for prospective residents to park. Before going to her apartment, I looked out the patio door to see the pool area. There was still yellow tape all around the area and four detectives inside the pool area down by the diving board end. I didn't see Tanya with them, so I assumed she was back in her apartment. I tapped lightly on her door because I didn't want to awaken her if she had been able to get back to sleep.

She opened the door as I was tapping. She said, 'I saw you pull up, so I figured you would stop by.' I told her I had just looked out to the pool area and saw the investigation still under way. She said there were also two other cops, a man and a woman, going door to door to interview all of the residents to find out why the guy was here and try to figure out what happened to him. They said they could smell alcohol around him and it looked as if he hit his head on the diving board support pipes.

She was in the kitchen making coffee and muffins, and asked me if I would like some breakfast. She said she had asked the police to notify her with their findings because if there were any illegal activities going on, she would make the culprits move out. She said she already contacted the owners of the apartment complex so they would hear about the situation from her instead of on the news. The television was on but the sound was turned down low. She asked me to watch the TV, while she finished cooking. As I was watching the news, I realized I should probably call home, so I asked Tanya if I could use her phone. She said it was okay as long as I didn't live in Alaska. I called home and told Pat what happened and I would probably not be home before she left for work.

As we watched the news and drank our coffee, we could see out Tanya's patio door as the investigators wrapped up their examination of the area. One of them left the area and headed towards his car and the other one was carrying a clipboard and he headed towards Tanya's apartment. Shortly, we heard a solid knock at the door along with a stern voice saying, 'This is the police.'

Tanya was near the door by the time he knocked and opened it as he was speaking. She invited him in and asked him if he wanted a cup of coffee.

He looked at me and said, 'Is this your husband?'

I stood up and walked toward him offering my right hand and said, 'No, I'm not her husband. I'm the newspaper carrier for this area. My employee is the one who discovered the body and I just stopped by to see what happened.' He looked as if he didn't believe me, but I guess the nature of his business is to be suspicious.

He looked down at his clipboard and told us the name of the deceased. He then went on to say the guy had been to a party at one of the apartments in the complex. He had a lot to drink and told people at the party he wanted to go for a midnight swim. No one at the party actually observed him leaving, but apparently he went to the pool area and found it locked. He was determined to go swimming so he must have climbed the fence. The investigators found a piece of his clothing on the top of the chain link fence. His clothes obviously got caught on the top of the fence, and he must have staggered and hit his head on the diving board support pipe and fell into the pool. The investigators found skin fragments and some blood on the pipe. There would be an autopsy to be sure, but it appeared the blow to the head killed him. It looked like a fluke accident. The police locked the chain on the gate and gave the key to Tanya. He reminded both of us they had our phone numbers, and if anyone had any further questions, they'd give us a call.

"Did they ever call you?" Rick asked.

"No, I never heard from them again but some reporter called Tim and interviewed him on television. Tanya said she didn't hear from the police, but the guy's family filed a law suit against the people who owned the apartment complex. The suit never made it to trial but it was settled out of court. I think the insurance company gave the family some money but didn't accept responsibility for the accident."

Charles was still thinking about another potential story. "Will you tell us the story about the naked lady tomorrow?"

I really did not want to tell them that story. I never should have even mentioned it. "I don't know Charles. I'll think about it and see if I can tell the story and still keep it G-rated."

Rick also wanted to hear the story. "My parents let me see R-rated movies all the time."

They weren't going to let me drop it. "I'll think about it. I might tell you part of the story." We finished the south part and headed north on Pittman to take them home.

STAR CANCELS ALL CARRIERS CONTRACTS

BEING A NEWSPAPER CARRIER IS SIMILAR TO BEING A FARMER. Every day, twice a day, the papers must be delivered. Life goes on. People are married and divorced. Babies are born. Loved ones pass away. All life-changing events take place and still the paper must be delivered. The temperature may climb above 100 degrees or drop below zero and in spite of everything, the papers must be delivered. There is no snow deep enough and no flood high enough to deter the carrier from his obligation. If the delivery vehicle breaks down, it must be repaired or replaced. If all of the employees quit, the carrier is left to complete the rounds by himself. If the carrier is fortunate, he may have some family members to count on, in case of emergency. If a carrier should shirk his duty, his contract could be cancelled immediately.

My parents had encountered a great deal of difficulty keeping dependable employees. Almost every day, Dad came by the house and picked up my mother to help him with deliveries. She helped roll the papers and my dad threw whichever side was needed. My mother said the only benefit was each morning she worked, Dad took her out for breakfast. They were both very worried about the employee situation. Dad knew he couldn't handle the rolling and throwing by himself, but he hated for my mother to be pressed into service. He expressed the frustrations with some of the other carriers, and one of the carriers said he knew someone that might like to lease the route. Dad and Mother had always been totally involved with the operation of the business, but they didn't know anything about leasing it to someone else. Since Bill and I had both leased paper routes, we explained to them how the process worked. Larry, the guy who wanted to lease their route, contacted my parents to discuss potential arrangements with them. He agreed to a one-year lease, and took over the actual delivery of the papers. My parents greatly enjoyed their free time, but had to learn to exist on a reduced income.

However, newspaper delivery in this area was destined to undergo a big change. The Star had been owned by William Rockhill Nelson since its initial publication in 1880. Even though the family tried to maintain ownership after Nelson's death in 1915, it was only about ten years until the employees purchased the company with the help of Nelson's son-in-law, Irwin Kirkwood. Ownership continued to rest in the employees' hands until 1977. After turning down many offers to buy the company, they finally relinquished and sold it to a large corporation, Capital Cities. Since the direction of the Star was being decided by another company, all of the workers and associates were concerned for their positions. Management was afraid they would be replaced by someone from the parent company and everyone was wondering if the Star intended to continue in the same method of operation.

In late September of '77, I received a letter in the mail from the Star. That, in itself, was not a strange occurrence. I received countless communications from them regarding various elements of delivery. This particular letter would probably live in infamy with all of the contract carriers in this area. To paraphrase the contents, the Star decided to cancel all contracts with all carriers. They wanted the carriers to continue with their responsibilities and each carrier was invited in to sign a new contract. The only major difference between the two contracts was the carrier relinquished all rights of ownership of their respective routes. Each carrier was required to sign a statement granting sole ownership of their route to the Star. Routes could no longer be bought or sold. The customers were the property of the Star and the carrier would be compensated for delivering the newspapers in a designated service area. In essence, the carriers would receive similar compensation for their efforts, but they would not have any vested financial interest in the route.

Fortunately for me, I did not own the route I was delivering. I just leased it from Raymond. However, my parents owned two of about three hundred routes in the Kansas City area and Raymond owned four. If my parents had sold their routes before the letter, the market value would have been about $100,000.00. Prior to receiving the letter, they discussed the possibility of Larry purchasing the route, but he couldn't afford it. He wanted to lease it for a couple of years and then, perhaps, he might try to arrange financing to buy it. Raymond's routes were larger and they were probably worth close to a half million dollars. This was, obviously, devastating news for all route owners.

Since the carriers were not employees, they could not belong to a union. However, they could, and did, form an association. Out of the 300 carriers in the area, about 25 of them regularly attended the association meetings. The main purpose of the association was to give the carriers one voice in dealing with the Star. The carriers association really didn't have much power but it did give the carriers a place to meet, compare ideas, vent frustrations, share solutions, and recommend improvements. Raymond regularly attended the meetings but my parents only went occasionally. As soon as the letter was received, an emergency meeting of the carrier's association was scheduled. Nearly all of the 300 carriers and their spouses attended the meeting. The consensus was to contact an attorney to educate the carriers on their possible alternatives. One week later, the carrier's association met with an attorney and he said he would attempt to get a temporary restraining order against the Star. If he was successful, then the Star would be obligated to continue operations as they had been until the final decision was made in court. The main concern of the carriers was their financial investment in the business. If the Star had offered a reasonably fair financial compensation to the carriers for purchase of their routes, most would have accepted it.

The attorney was successful in obtaining the temporary restraining order. This accomplishment took a great deal of pressure off the carriers. Thanks to the association, the carriers were in a position to expect some kind of compensation from the Star. The attorney agreed to handle the case on a cost-settlement basis. That meant the carriers were not required to pay him for his services. The association would pay him for any incurred expenses and he would receive a percentage of any final settlement from the Star. If the courts ruled against the carriers, the attorney would get nothing. The case would probably linger on in court for years.

The association calculated the costs incurred by the attorney and divided those up between all of the carriers. My parents paid their fair share, but any additional expense obviously reduced their profit margin. The regular monthly meetings of the association became a popular place to be. The regular attendance had gone from about 25 to an average of over 300. At least 50% of all routes were represented at each meeting. If any carrier was unable to attend, he would send someone in his place to get an update on pertinent information. I frequently attended the meetings with my parents and, if they were unable to attend, I represented them. Each month, the association put out a promo listing all of the information to be discussed at the meeting. No matter how exciting the meeting sounded, there was very little new information. Carriers were operating in limbo. If the carrier owned and operated his route, then business continued as usual. If the carrier was unable to operate his route, and leased it out to another person, then that person could, conceivably, obtain a delivery contract directly from the Star. By doing that, the carrier would be left with nothing.

I would have been happy to stay with Raymond, because I liked and respected him. I was making more money on that route than I ever made before. The major source of income was the retail paper sales. The home delivery portion of my income basically paid the monthly bills. The income from the hotels and stores was mainly profit. Since my parents leased their routes to Larry, they were not personally involved with the delivery any longer. They, along with most carriers in the area, were very uncertain as to what might happen to them if they were not actually involved in the delivery of the newspaper. They were afraid they might lose all rights to any potential financial settlement the Star might offer. Since the one-year lease with Larry was nearing its term, my parents asked me if I would consider leaving Raymond and taking over their routes. Financially, it was not a good idea, but I wanted to help my parents.

No one else in the family was in any position to help them out. Robert, or Bob, as we had starting calling him, had been a Methodist preacher for nearly 20 years. He was not living in the Independence area. Barbara was working at

John Knox Village as a nurses' aide, so she was not able to help, and Billy, or Bill, as we had started calling him, had his own paper route in Independence. I was going to lose about three hundred dollars a week, but my parents really wanted me to take the route. Mother said they could both sleep comfortably knowing I was taking care of the business. My living expenses were relatively small so I knew I could afford to make the change.

The transfer from one route to the other was simple. I already had a truck with all of the necessary equipment. I had bags and other supplies that could be used on any paper route. My employees on Raymond's route already knew the correct customers who were subscribers, so I left them on that route. There were already three boys working on Dad's route, so they stayed to work for me. One day, I was delivering papers by the Sports Complex, and the next day, I was delivering papers by my parents' house. Since I was already familiar with my dad's route, the transition was very easy. The hours were basically the same, and the daily dedication was unchangeable. I still had to do all of the monthly billing. The retail accounts were very small. I had two vending machines that sold daily and Sunday papers, and two 7-11 convenience stores that sold papers on consignment. On Raymond's route I had two large apartment complexes, but on Dad's, there was just one small complex that had around a dozen subscribers. The total delivery time was about the same on both routes, but Dad's route was a little closer to home.

One day melted into another and the law suit appeared to be everlasting. The carriers won one round, but the Star appealed and won the second round. The case was headed for the Supreme Court. It could be years before a final verdict would be reached. I continued to employ a seemingly endless string of helpers. The Star had started sending out the Sunday papers in two parts, so I needed one person to do nothing but assemble the papers for sale in the stores. Since the helpers assembled the papers and then put them in a bag to be thrown, I needed to use another person to sit in front and throw the right side while I threw the left side. On Sunday, I was using at least four people to help me with the deliveries. It had turned into a much more complex arrangement than it was in the old days.

TOP TEN LIST

MY PERSONAL LIFE WAS ALSO DESTINED TO END UP IN COURT. Pat and I had been having marital problems for quite some time and we were headed in opposite directions. She was a very nice person and, in the beginning, she was very devoted. She traveled with me to Monterrey, California while I was in the Navy and she also moved to Texas with me when I was transferred to San Angelo. She stayed in Kansas City and worked while I was overseas. When I came home from the Navy, we bought a house and settled down with the hopes of starting a family.

My experience with Yvonne confirmed the possibility that true love is achievable, but my marriage to Pat was not fulfilling. I truly thought I was going to be married to her for the rest of my life. I think if we had been able to have children, we probably could have stayed together. We had both been to the doctor to be checked for any medical issues, but there were no obvious reasons for the inability to conceive. The doctor only told us to decrease the frequency, employ optimum timing, and modify positions. We tried every suggestion, but even after ten years, there were no pregnancies. We were very conscientious about making daily efforts, but children were not in our future. After several years of frustration, Pat began to modify her priorities. Having a child did not seem so important any longer. Perhaps because of her apparent inability to conceive, she had decided she did not want children. Her decision to exclude children from our relationship did not coincide with mine. It was still very important to me. She had accepted her role of being childless, and she wanted to move back to California. She was happiest when we lived there and she wanted to go back. She didn't like the frustration that accompanied sibling relationships. She was an only child and she wasn't comfortable with my brothers and sisters and the dynamics that accompanied larger families. Bob had three children, Barbara had four, and Bill had two and I believe that she was feeling pressure from everyone, not just me. She wanted me to give up the paper route, sell our home, and move to California with no prospects for employment.

We probably could have worked our way through most of the problems, but we didn't really try, and the children issue was a deal breaker for me. There were a few other personal problems that affected my willingness to exert the effort. She had made contact with an old boyfriend from high school and I didn't have the energy or desire to compete. It hurt me deeply to discover that my wife had gone elsewhere to find companionship. In the end, it was a very amicable divorce. She didn't want the house or any alimony as long as I could come up with a substantial cash settlement. I managed to come up with the money, so once we met with the judge, our need for communication ceased. We went to court on her thirtieth birthday. When I gave her the check and her freedom, I told her 'Happy Birthday'. We did maintain contact for several months after the divorce. Within a year, she was married and pregnant. Once my mother heard the news that Pat had remarried and was pregnant, she rationalized that 'God had never seen fit to bless our marriage with children'.

With my second round of bachelorhood, I was anxious to take advantage of my new-found freedom, but at the same time, I realized I was thirty-one years old. I was resolute in my desire to have children, so there wasn't time for an extended period of carousing. I enjoyed the occasional one-night stand, but after having been married for ten years, I was more interested in potential long-term relationships.

Throughout my life, there have been many times I have felt totally lost. I dealt with the loss of my grandfather, great-grandfather, and uncle in less than a year, but the paper route was there to give me stability. It certainly wouldn't die on me. My first love decided to trade me in for a newer model, but the paper route never turned its back on me. I turned my back on the paper route and tried to escape to college, but the paper route was there when I returned and needed it. My first true love died before we could build a life, but the paper route offered me the opportunity to make a living. I answered the call of my country to serve in the military, and then I answered the call of another carrier to come back to the paper route. Even with my divorce, and the Star threatening to divorce all of the carriers, my parents again called me back to the paper route. I was back where I started, right on the same route I had grown up on. The one constant thread that had wound continuously through my life had been the paper route. It had always been there, either demanding my constant attention, or hovering in the background, waiting like an old friend for my return. I was not forced, but enticed into a lifelong relationship with newsprint. I suppose, at any juncture, I could have gone a different direction, but the paper route path was broad and well-traveled. The job was so easy and paid so well. I always thought it would be very difficult to find a job that required so little time, but offered so much income. I found myself thirty-one years old, divorced, with no college degree, living alone, and the only dependable facet of my life was the paper route.

Divorce is not easy, even under the best circumstances. I wish that there was a class I could take to learn how to maintain a fulfilling marriage. It would be nice if there was a learner's manual for people to study before getting married. I had to take a test in order to obtain my driver's license, but no test is necessary to get married. When I married Pat, I thought I would be with her for the rest of my life. I was very fortunate to have a supportive family. I told my family that I was going to marry Pat, and they accepted her as if she had been born into the family. That should be what all families do, but I know of many friends who have not been so lucky. Their spouse was not completely accepted by all members of the family and the relationships were tenuous. By the same token, families should also accept decisions to divorce. When it becomes necessary to erase a marriage, all family members should be supportive. Just as I chose to bring Pat into our family, I also chose to remove her from our family. I believe the decision to divorce Pat was more difficult than the one to marry her, but I knew I could count on my family to support my decision. Once our divorce was final, my family never contacted her again. Perhaps some members of my family may have called her or exchanged cards, but there was never a question of where their loyalty rested and I knew if I was lucky enough to marry again, they would unanimously accept whomever I chose.

It became crucial for me to embrace the route as an ally instead of an enemy. There were many positives to the newspaper delivery business. The actual delivery only took about 2-3 hours. I didn't have a malicious boss constantly looking over my shoulder, waiting for me to give him an excuse to fire me. The bookkeeping was elementary. The income was more than I needed to pay the bills, and I did enjoy riding around in the truck for a couple of hours talking to young people. I guess my grandfather would consider me lucky, and maybe even blessed. There have been many young people who worked for me. Some just put in their time and grabbed the paycheck. Others became friends. As I continued the search for a new wife, the paper route again offered stability to my life.

It may seem a little ridiculous, but I decided to resort to logical methods in my approach to the complex task of finding the love of my life. I certainly hadn't been very lucky up to this point. I thought love should be an outcome of chance, not of planning. Christy, Jane, Yvonne, and Pat all were chance meetings. I didn't search them out or hunt them down. I decided I would have a much better chance at finding the right girl if I knew what I was looking for, so I started writing down things to look for in a potential companion.

First, and foremost, she needed to be a woman who loved children. Many people get married and decide when the time is right to have children. They take the normal steps and within a few months, they are painting a nursery. I'm not sure if they appreciate how truly fortunate they are. After spending nearly ten years trying to conceive, I valued the blessing. It wouldn't take very long to find out if a woman was looking forward to the opportunity to hear the pitter patter of tiny feet.

The second item on my list was a good sense of humor. I guess, in a way, if any woman was looking forward to giving birth, she would need to have a good sense of humor. What woman can seriously say she is looking forward to the wonderful opportunity to put on about 20-30 pounds, feel like a beached whale, deal with terrible mood swings, just to have the auspicious prospect of suffering through the worst physical pain known to mankind? I try to see the light side of everything and I needed to have a companion with that same outlook on life.

Item number three was a little more solemn. I was raised in a Christian environment and take my religion very seriously. I suppose it is possible for people with drastically different theological viewpoints to be happily married, but I didn't want to deal with that much drama. Even if we were able to respect each other's positions, the thought of trying to raise a child in a religiously diverse household, was more than I felt I could handle. My first choice for the religious conviction of a spouse would be Methodist, but I knew I could probably accept just about any Protestant faith.

I almost hate to mention the next item on my list. Some people will probably think I was narrow-minded or maybe even a little prejudiced, but I was looking for a girl with above average intelligence. Some of the women in my past have been lacking in intellectual aptitude. I didn't mean she had to be a nuclear physicist or even a philosopher, but it would be nice if she knew what they did. I discovered an intelligent person is much more likely to get involved in a stimulating discussion.

I'd better move on before I get in any more trouble. The next item was a little less confrontational. I would hope to find a girl with ambition. I didn't really care where her ambitions lead her; I just didn't want someone who was easily satisfied. Whether she aspired to be a great nurse, and make a difference in the world, or if she wanted to be the best Veterinarian in Nebraska, or the best mom in town, I just wanted to be with someone who always looked for some way to be better at her chosen vocation. My parents taught me I should always do my best in everything I attempt.

Age was not a primary concern, but since I was anxious to have children, it would be better if a potential spouse was my age or younger. Pregnancy can be difficult, or even dangerous, if the woman is in her thirties. Therefore, if there were a large number of potential candidates for the coveted position of becoming my wife, and I narrowed the field down to two finalists, one 20-year-old and one 40-year-old, age could sway my decision.

The next item on my list was a little difficult to describe. I simply expressed it as Mother-like. I didn't mean I wanted my spouse to look like my mother, but I would like for her to have the same wife skills. Before someone screams 'chauvinist', let me explain. I certainly believe in the liberated woman. I believe every woman should have the right and the opportunity to work and advance in any field of her choosing. In today's world, it has become much more difficult for a family to flourish on just one income. However, someone needs to cook, clean, sew, do laundry, and make the nest a comfortable place to call home. In some families, the wife was the homemaker and in some families, the husband was the homemaker. There were more and more families with shared responsibilities. My mother never worked outside the home, but was on call 24 hours a day as our domestic engineer. I would hope I could find someone who not only accepted the position of homemaker, but desired it.

For most of my life, I have had a pet. I have always enjoyed the unquestioning love of a dog and the occasional affection of a cat. I realize many people do not share my adoration of dogs and cats, but I hoped I might locate someone who could appreciate their value in the home. Since humans have domesticated dogs and cats, it has become the responsibility of the pet-owner to provide the pets with food, shelter, and medical care. I would prefer house-pets but, by living inside the home, the animal would inevitably shed hair on the carpet and furniture which would cause additional trouble for the home-maker. In order to fill this item on my list, she would not only need to love animals, but be willing to share in the effort of maintaining them.

Coming in at number nine on the list was a rather obvious item. There must be some type of mutual attraction. I was not looking for a girl shaped like a Barbie doll, or one who was drop-dead gorgeous. Physical desirability should be automatic. Just like any wrapped gift, the true beauty of each person is under the wrapping. However, in order to have the opportunity to unwrap the gift, one must first be drawn to it. I was drawn to people who were polite, friendly, and cheerful. I made an effort to become better acquainted with someone who also saw those traits in me. I didn't look like a Chippendale dancer and I wouldn't expect my wife to look like a Playboy bunny, but I would like to think we were both equally attracted to the other.

The last item on my list accompanies that attraction. Each person brings a diverse collage of traits to the relationship. Separately, they might be a mess, but when both people share their qualities with each other, the result should be a beautiful image. The glue that holds all of the pieces of the collage together is the physical expression of love. If both partners are openly communicating with each other, then this should be an extremely enjoyable experience for both of them and the never-ending supply of glue should be used frequently and liberally. My hope and prayer is my future soul mate will appreciate and desire that expression. If a married couple maintains a platonic relationship, disagreements last longer and there's no means of absolution. People are destined to have discrepancies, but the beauty of sex is it offers a method of acceptance and forgiveness rolled into a mutually enjoyable experience. In short, I guess I would say the more of this glue used in a relationship, the stronger the bond created.

When I started putting together this list, I thought it sounded simple. All of the characteristics were important to me and I hoped to find someone who possessed all of them. After looking over the list, I decided I might be expecting too much. It would be quite unlikely for me to find anyone with ALL of the qualities. It became necessary to prioritize the list in the order of importance, just in case I didn't locate the perfect mate. The items are listed in order of importance with the exception of the last item. The only reason it is listed last is because it's the only item that can be truly known after marriage. The physical expression of love should be discussed and understood by both partners before marriage, but my hope was the obligation to be joined should only be surpassed by the desire. Love is a remarkable phenomenon. I suppose everyone has, or at least should have, their individual definition of love. To me, love is placing another person's happiness, fulfillment, and wellbeing ahead of my own. It would be my responsibility to my partner to be certain that every day, she knows she is loved. The truly extraordinary quality of love is when it exists it is reciprocal.

Once I was equipped with my Trusty Top Ten list, I began my search for the perfect spouse. All I needed was to find an attractive, young, ambitious, intelligent, Methodist girl with a great sense of humor, who loved children and pets, and was a great cook, who was also anxious to do whatever it took to make me feel happy and loved. As preposterous as it may sound, I thought it was a great idea. It would have probably been easier to discover a cure for cancer.

I knew this whole process sounded ridiculous, but I really felt I needed something concrete to help me know what I was looking for. If I didn't know who I was looking for, how would I know if I found her? Okay, I'll admit, there are exceptions to the rule. Sometimes, it's just kismet. I didn't have any list when I met Yvonne, but that relationship was just not meant to be. I loved Jane, but regrettably, the feelings were not reciprocal. I thought I loved Pat, but when I looked at the list of characteristics I valued, she didn't have four of the ten items. I probably wouldn't have married her if I had made and used my newly discovered list.

If you want to find fish, then you should probably look in water. Since religious beliefs were high on my list, I decided I should probably start looking in a church. When I compared my list to the girls I had been dating, I realized I had been concentrating on the wrong priorities. It appeared I was only interested in number nine, physical appearance, and number ten, sex. Karen was definitely attractive and she certainly enjoyed playing with glue, but she was an orphan and she had very strong beliefs about not having children. She was ambitious, but her future plans did not include a husband and certainly not children. She would probably become a rich, top executive with a trophy boy-toy companion. She was not deeply disturbed when I told her I felt our relationship was not going anywhere.

Mary could not walk across the lobby of the hotel without turning the head of just about every guy in sight. She was the front desk clerk at one of the hotels on my paper route. I definitely was not thinking about number three when I asked her to go out on a date. However, she did not attend any church and she was about as dumb as a sack of rocks. I found it almost impossible to carry on a discussion with her. When we went out, her mind may have been on physiology and anatomy but I know she couldn't spell or define either one of them. When I told her I was looking for a more consequential relationship, she said, "You mean like Truth, or Consequences?"

I couldn't help but notice Tina. She was a customer on my route and she lived in an apartment with two other girls. Every afternoon when I delivered her paper, she was sitting on her front porch. I first noticed her long blonde hair and pretty figure. Okay, I'm a guy. On closer scrutiny, I observed she had very pretty blue eyes. I realize eye color is not on my list of requirements, but I have pretty blue eyes and I am partial to anyone who shares that trait. Tina ran a day-care facility out of her apartment. At first, I thought all three children were her own, but she was very quick to tell me only one was hers and the other two were children of people who lived in the apartment complex. She said she loved children and hoped to have more someday. In the meantime, she decided she would do what she loved most, take care of little children. She had graduated from college with a degree in Early Childhood Development. She was very intelligent and had a great sense of humor. She had eight brothers and sisters and had a great deal of experience in the kitchen. She loved to cook and her apartment was immaculate. Her husband was killed in a car accident, so I felt an affinity with her situation. After his death, she moved in to the apartment with her two friends in order to reduce expenses. Although it appeared she fit right into my list, there was one point I couldn't overlook. She was a Catholic. I respected her beliefs, but I did not share them. I was sure many people could raise their children in a home with a Protestant father and a Catholic mother, but it wasn't what I wanted for my children. When I explained my situation to her, she was very understanding. She agreed that raising children was very difficult under the best circumstances. We parted, but remained friends.

LOVE/LOVE

THE PAPER ROUTE GAVE ME THE FREEDOM TO PARTICIPATE IN MANY OTHER AREAS OF INTEREST. While Pat and I were married, we did not have a huge amount of activities away from home. The main object of our time commitment was our church. We enjoyed being active members in our adult Sunday school class, which actually met on Friday nights. With Bill and I delivering the large Sunday paper from about 3:00 until 7:00 on Sunday morning, 8:30 church was difficult. Four couples, the Bearleys, the Mulveys, my brother and his wife, and Pat and I were the founding members of the young adult class at church. The class continued to grow in numbers and dedication to our church program. Through that involvement, we were asked to join other committees and groups. One of the obligations Pat and I were asked to accept was the position of youth group coordinators. Since we were under thirty, we were acceptable to the MYF members as okay. With that connection, we developed many life-long friendships.

During our tenure as coordinators, we became trusted confidants for many of the young people. Several of the boys were able to open up with me about their concerns. Most of the girls felt a close relationship with Pat. We received many late-night phone calls. I was called to the police station on two occasions when group members had been taken in. These weren't serious violations, one was for curfew violation and the other one was caught teepeeing a house, but the teens involved were required to contact an adult to pick them up. They didn't want to call their parents, so they called me. I did later meet with the teens, their parents, and our youth minister to discuss the situation. The youth members never wanted their parents to be told, but we had to use our own best discretion.

Pat and I tried to catch as many of the group members' extra-curricular activities as possible. We had MYF members in five different schools, so we weren't able to attend all of them. Since all of the schools played football on Friday night, we could only catch one game each week. When two of the schools played each other, we made a concerted effort to attend that game. We also attended baseball, soccer, volleyball, and tennis. We tried to remain neutral when we attended sporting events, but always cheered for individual accomplishments.

After Pat and I divorced, we decided it was in the best interest of the youth group to give up our position as youth coordinators. I missed the regular involvement with the youth group and still attended many activities alone. Once we separated, Pat never attended any church activities.

With my new-found bachelorhood, I buried myself in the dating scene. Most of the girls I dated were great dates, but not great potential partners. With list in hand, I endeavored to find a way to locate the perfect mate. I was apparently looking in the wrong places. I decided to visit some different churches in the area to see if I might find a candidate. After visiting six other churches, I decided there were not very many available girls in Independence. Finally, on a hot July Sunday, I went to another Methodist church in town. Right inside the door, there was a very attractive girl, who was probably in her twenties. She was a greeter and she was handing out bulletins. Striving for levity, I asked her if I needed a reservation. She laughed and said even though reservations were preferred, there was an empty seat on the third row from the back. She went on to say her reserved seat was on the aisle, but I could sit next to her. As I took a seat, I thought over my list. She's an attractive, young, Methodist, with a sense of humor. That was a good start.

On this particular Sunday, this church was celebrating communion. Methodists normally only celebrate communion about 5-10 times a year. After the service, I introduced myself to the young lady. I told her I was a member of another local church, but I was just checking out the other churches to see what programs were available for young singles. I extended my hand and asked her name. She took my hand and at the same time, said, "Hi, I'm Yvonne." Chills went down my back and I must have cringed, because she said, "Is that the wrong name?"

I apologized and said I had previously dated a girl named Yvonne and she held a special place in my heart. My expectations immediately soared. I told her the communion had not been very filling and wondered if she would like to go with me to get some lunch. She said she would love to grab something to eat and it would give her an opportunity to tell me about her church's young singles' activities. The church was near Noland Road so I asked her where she would like to go. She said she loved Mr. Steak but would only go if we agreed to go Dutch. Financial position was not on the list, but it was nice to know she was insistent on paying her own way.

We each drove our own car and met at the restaurant. When we entered, I was surprised to see the hostess was Sheryl, a member of my church, who was also a member of the MYF group. She graduated from high school in the Spring and was also working at an insurance company in downtown Kansas City. I introduced Sheryl to Yvonne and was a little embarrassed I didn't know Yvonne's last name. I explained we had just met at church and Sheryl jokingly scolded me for going to another church. Once seated in our booth, Yvonne explained all of the activities for singles at her church. Unconsciously, I found myself glancing at Sheryl. I was very inconspicuous, but it appeared each time I looked at Sheryl, she was looking at me. I figured she was just checking out my date.

During the course of our dinner, I found out Yvonne had completed her Bachelor's Degree in Science and was enrolled in post-graduate studies at Johns Hopkins. She was planning to be a neurologist and settle on the east coast. She didn't know if marriage would be in her future, but it would be about ten years before she considered it. I thought I was very discreet with my observation of Sheryl, but Yvonne said she knew something about chemistry and she definitely felt it between Sheryl and me. As Yvonne and I walked out of the restaurant, Sheryl was seating another family. Once outside, Yvonne said, "I hope to see you at church again, but right now I think you should go back in and make a date with that hostess."

I dismissed the idea, because of our age difference and went to my car. I sat there for a few minutes thinking about what Yvonne had said. Then my thoughts were directed towards my list. How did Sheryl fit in? She was an attractive, young, intelligent, Methodist girl, with a great sense of humor, and I had witnessed her love for children in the church nursery. I wondered what she thought about sex. I shook my head to try to straighten out my thinking. I had to remember she was twelve years younger than me. I thought about the irony that another Yvonne had entered my life, not as a potential mate, but perhaps to introduce me to one. Out of all of the churches in the area, I chose the one she attended. Out of all of the restaurants in the area, Yvonne chose the one where Sheryl was working.

Just then, I looked up to see Sheryl walking towards my car. I rolled my window down and asked, "Are you on a break?"

"No," she said, "I was only scheduled to work during the lunch rush. I worked from ten til two. Did you make Yvonne walk home?"

I was a little surprised she remembered the name. "No, we drove separate cars from church and she had someplace she needed to go." I wanted to change the subject from Yvonne and talk about her. "It sure was nice to see you again. I didn't know you still worked at Mr. Steak."

"I probably won't be working here much longer. I can only work on weekends and I just work when they are in desperate need of help. After being inside for so long, it really feels hot out here."

"I'm sorry," I said, "Get in here where it's cool."

She didn't hesitate to get in the car and put her face up to the air conditioning vent. As she sat back, she said, "Now I think I know why Julie backed out of playing tennis this evening." Julie was her tennis doubles partner in high school and ranked as Chrisman's number one player. She continued, "I haven't had a chance to play since we graduated."

I always enjoyed playing tennis with her and I had no other conflicts, so I said, "I don't have any plans for this evening, so I can play with you."

"That would be great," she said, "but I was hoping to play tennis."

I was probably a little slow in the dating department and certainly not 'the Fonz', but I thought she was flirting with me. Didn't she realize I was 12 years older than her? I tried to pass over the comment and said, "I'm not as good as Julie, but I'm available for this evening."

She was quick to answer, "Julie is tough but I would much prefer playing against someone I know I can beat."

I don't think confidence was on my list, but it was certainly one of her attributes. We decided to meet at the tennis courts in Mill Creek Park at 5:00. Being an accomplished athlete was not on my list either, but we did have a lot of fun. She was very competitive and only played to win. I appreciated her ambition, but when we played, I was more interested in just doing something together. Even though I really enjoyed playing tennis, I was certainly no Jimmy Connors. I had never produced any kind of an effective serve, and I blame the paper route. After throwing about a million papers, my right shoulder didn't function properly. My forehand was above average, and my backhand was okay, but I had a very difficult time hitting overheads. The doctor said I had rotator cuff damage, and at that time, I wasn't sure exactly what that was. I did have fairly good hand-eye coordination, so I could usually make contact with the ball. It just didn't always go where I intended for it to go.

After playing tennis for a couple of hours, Sheryl asked me if I would like to come back to her apartment for something to eat. She had moved out of her parents' house and into a small apartment close to Hill Park which happened to be on my paper route. I remembered she said she loved Dr. Pepper and Hershey's Special Dark, so I stopped by the grocery store and picked up a six-pack and a big candy bar.

When I arrived at her apartment, she met me at the door wearing a robe. I told her I picked up drinks and dessert. She told me our dinner was on the stove, so if I didn't want it to burn, I should watch it while she took a quick shower. I was a little surprised at how comfortable she seemed. Call me old fashioned, but I felt a little funny standing in her kitchen, while she showered on the other side of the wall. It was a very small, one-bedroom apartment. The front door opened into the living room, which was about eight feet deep and about fifteen feet across. There was a door on the left wall which opened into a very tiny bathroom. In the left rear of the apartment was the kitchen. It had a refrigerator, stove, and sink with a few cabinets. There was room for me to turn around but that was about all. In the right rear of the apartment, was the bedroom.

As Sheryl disappeared into the bathroom, I ventured into the kitchen to see what we were having for dinner. It looked like my mother's hash. It was basically brown gravy with chunks of meat and potatoes. There was also a pan of peas cooking. I stirred them both and took a quick look around the apartment. The living room was neat and clean. There was a magazine on the couch with a picture of Chris Evert on the cover. There was also a stack of about six or seven paperbacks on the corner table. I wondered what kind of books she was reading, so I picked them up and they were all murder-mysteries. When I peeked into the bedroom, I noticed the clothes she had been wearing at the tennis court were in a basket by the foot of the bed. The bed was made and there was nothing out of place. I thought about my list. She had made a clean comfortable nest and I would soon be testing her culinary skills.

I scolded myself again for thinking of this young girl as a potential mate for me. I had to remind myself that she was twelve years younger than me and even though she was currently an eighteen-year-old high school graduate, I had known her since she was fourteen. Just then, the shower water shut off and I hurried back to the kitchen to check on dinner. I would have a difficult time explaining how dinner burned while I was supposed to be standing there watching it. The peas and the hash were both boiling, so I quickly stirred them to make sure they weren't sticking to the bottom of the pan. Everything was okay, so I turned down the heat. I expected for her to come out of the bathroom fully dressed, but she came out wearing the robe and her hair wrapped in a towel. She hurried into the bedroom asking me if I knew which end of the spoon to hold. I explained I was a perfectly capable cook, so she told me to put some biscuits in the oven.

I turned on the oven and while it was heating, I found the biscuits and proper pan. When the timer went off, she appeared out of the bedroom. She said, "I guess that bell means dinner's ready."

I had found the necessary plates and silverware, so the table was set, but I hadn't put dinner on the table yet. I said, "If I knew you were waiting for the bell to ding to come out here, I would have set it to go off ten minutes ago."

She said, "Oh, did you miss me or did you just want me to do the work?"

I had to be very careful with my answer. If I were to say I missed her, it might put some awkward pressure on the moment, so I chose the side of levity. In my best macho voice, I said, "Cookin' is woman's work. Just give me a tree to cut down, or a bear to shoot."

"Well, it looks as though you managed to keep dinner from burning and get the table set, and I know you don't hunt."

She was right about hunting, but again I blamed the paper route. Seven days a week without a day off and I had to sleep after the morning route. "I may never get a chance to go hunting, but if a bear happened to come around here, you just watch and see how fast I can dial 911."

She brought all of the food to the table and filled my glass with ice. As she sat down, she put out her hand and asked me if I would bless the food. She said, "We don't want to take any chances with my cooking."

I hadn't even thought about this moment. I guess I knew we would say grace, but I hadn't thought about her asking me. Although it would have been appropriate to say something about her or her apartment, I kicked into the automatic mode of saying my dad's everyday blessing. As I reached out to hold her hand, I felt chills down my back. As I closed my eyes, the first thing I said to myself was 'Thank you God for blessing this moment' and then I said out loud, "Heavenly Father, bless this food to its intended use, and our lives in Thy service. We ask in Christ's name. Amen."

She said, "Thank you, can I get you anything else?"

I needed a minute, because I think I felt a tear in my eye, so I asked her, "Could you get a piece of bread for me and just fill my glass with water?"

Then she remembered, "That's right, you hate Dr. Pepper. I have Coke, if you prefer."

"No thanks, I just prefer water. I try to drink as much as I can."

She handed the loaf of bread to me and I placed a piece on my plate. As I began to spoon the hash onto the bread, she said, "Gross, you're going to have soggy bread."

I explained my actions, "My mother makes something similar to this and she calls it hash. We always put it on bread so it soaks up the gravy."

She was a little bit disgusted by the appearance but she said, "You fix it however you want it. I just hope it tastes all right."

I had already tried it by that time and I reassured her it tasted delicious. It had a slightly different taste but I'm sure she must have used different spices. It actually tasted better than my mother's hash, but I would never tell my mother.

After we finished eating, she cleared the table and told me to go sit down and turn on the television. As she washed the dishes, I sat down to see what was on TV. During the summer, just about everything was reruns, but they had started showing last year's shows of All in the Family to get ready for the new season in September. I asked her if she liked that show and she said she thought it was hilarious. She especially liked Archie. I didn't realize it at the time, but later, as I got to know her dad, I think Archie must have been patterned after him.

Archie wouldn't be on til 8:00, so I checked to see what was on Wonderful World of Disney. It was just some animal show, so I went to the kitchen to see if I could help. As I neared the kitchen Sheryl said, "I've got everything under control in here and I don't think we know each other well enough to be in this kitchen at the same time. Maybe if we were married for five years, it would be okay."

When she said that, I got another chill. I didn't know if it was the Holy Spirit or just Yvonne, but apparently Sheryl and I were not alone. I took the chill as a good thing, but I still was having some problems with our age difference. I guess I needed to focus more on Sheryl and less on 18. What was it Yvonne had said? Oh yeah, 'when it comes to love, throw out the rules' and 'difference in age doesn't mean anything'.

I guess I should just focus on the present and let the future happen as God sees fit. I decided to turn the discussion back to television. "What do you like to watch on TV?"

She stopped cleaning for a minute to look up at the ceiling, like the answer was printed up there. "Tuesday night was my favorite night last year with 'Happy Days', 'Laverne and Shirley', and 'Three's Company'. I also like 'Little House on the Prairie' on Monday because I read all of the books and I love Michael Landon. The only other show I really hate to miss is 'Donny and Marie' on Friday night."

"I will have to remember not to ask you out on a date on Friday night." I said.

She wasn't tripped up by the mention of a date with me, but was quick to add, "You'll just have to make it a TV date and we'll watch television and eat pop corn. 'The Friday Night Movie' follows 'Donny and Marie' and if it's no good, we could watch 'The Rockford Files'. I just love James Garner."

I thought I would try to see how far I could push this 'date' idea. "Okay, sounds like a plan to me, but this time, you come to my house and I'll fix dinner. You can bring the snacks, because I may not have what you like."

Without missing a beat, she responded, "Oh, you have what I like, but I'll bring the snacks anyway. I've been wanting to try out this new recipe called 'Puppy Chow'."

"That sounds good to me, because I'm all out of 'Milk Bones'." Actually Pat took them all with her when she took our dog, but I didn't think it would be appropriate to bring up the ex-wife.

She was quick to clarify, "It's not really dog food. It's good. I've tasted it and that's why I got the recipe. I bet you'll love it."

If I was going to be fixing dinner, I needed a little bit of direction. "Okay, I know you like Dr. Pepper, and we're having 'Puppy Chow' for snacks, so what do you want for the main course?"

"I thought YOU were the main course." She said as she patted my tummy.

There was another sexual innuendo. I didn't know whether to respond or not. Was she just kidding around or was she trying to entice me? I decided to return the suggestive comment and see how she reacted. "Oh, darn, I thought I would be dessert."

She didn't hesitate to answer, "If you're dessert then it doesn't matter what the main course is, because I'll be sure to save room."

She made it pretty clear she was interested in taking our friendship to another level. But was I prepared? I paused for a few minutes as I was going over my list in my head. The only item I didn't know about was whether she loved animals. Then I began to wonder why I put it on the list at all. I could certainly get along without a pet. I didn't know if I would be able to get along without her. We sat on the couch together watching television, and for awhile, she laid down with her head in my lap.

We had been good friends for about four or five years and we almost always hugged when we said goodbye. I was already contemplating our parting. Would a kiss be appropriate? I thought back on my previous relationships. Jane and I had known each other for several years before we kissed. Yvonne and I kissed just hours after our first meeting. Pat and I had known each other about a month. I decided that time was not the appropriate gauge for such a decision. What were my feelings towards Sheryl? I had always liked her. I had always respected her intelligence. She had a wonderful sense of humor. Now I was here on the couch with her, I felt more comfortable and complete than I had been with anyone since Yvonne. I didn't want to set my hopes too high, because I didn't know what her feelings were. To hell with age and uncertainty, I knew what I felt. For the first time since I had been with Yvonne, I was complete. I would definitely kiss her and if she kissed me back, it would be well worth the risk. If she pulled away or slapped me, then I would have to rethink our relationship.

As we continued to watch television, she made herself comfortable lying on my lap. Was she relaxed because she felt at ease with me or was she relaxed because she felt no threat from me? I know those may sound the same, but it's possible to feel totally at ease and relaxed with a husband and you can feel no threat from a brother or parent. Did she consider me to be husband material or brother material? She didn't hesitate to shower or change clothes with me so close. I didn't know if I could find out without putting my neck in the noose. If she really did think of me as a brother-figure, I would be putting our whole relationship in jeopardy by kissing her. On the other hand, if I didn't kiss her and she was thinking of me as potential husband material, she may think I saw her as a sister. It was so simple and uncomplicated with Yvonne. I needed a little bit more information. I needed to be serious. As she reclined on my lap, my right hand was touching her hair and I moved my left hand and placed in on her waist. "I certainly am glad you invited me to your apartment for dinner. It was nice of you to fix dinner and ask me to stay and watch TV. I've had a great time and I look forward to when we can do it again. I assume I haven't made you too uncomfortable. Have you entertained a lot?"

She held my left hand with both of her hands. She replied, "You're the first person to see this apartment besides family. I didn't want to entertain anyone else, and you make me feel very comfortable."

That was certainly good to hear, but it still could be misconstrued. I needed to probe a little deeper. "I thought you must be fairly comfortable with me, considering the first thing you did after I got here was to take a shower."

"How else could I show you I trusted you? I was naked and totally vulnerable. Neither the bathroom nor the bedroom doors have locks on them. Yet, I felt totally safe."

This might be my chance for total clarity. "You would have felt totally safe with your dad in the apartment."

She took my left hand in both of her hands and brought it to her mouth. I didn't know if she was going to bite it or kiss it. "Yes, I would have felt totally safe with my dad in the apartment, but I don't think of you as anything close to my dad." Then she softly kissed my hand and added, "I trust you to never do anything that would hurt me."

It appeared we were both trying to take this relationship in the same direction, and I wanted her to know I would never do anything to intentionally harm her. Again, I needed to be very careful with my word choice. "You're right; I would never do anything to intentionally hurt you. However, I am a man, and men have been known to do some pretty stupid things in relationships. I just want you to know if I ever did anything that hurt you, it could not be deliberate. It's just because, when it comes to relationships, I'm no genius."

"Don't worry," she said, as she gently kissed my hand again, "if you do anything wrong, I will be sure to point it out to you."

I thought I was clear on the direction we were going, but knew we should take it slow, so, as much as I hated to, I needed to leave. It was nearing eleven. We had already watched the news and Johnny's monologue. "I need to be heading home."

She bit my hand and said, "I told you I would let you know if you did anything wrong. I don't want you to leave yet."

It was reassuring to know she did want me to stay, but we both had work in a few hours and we would have more chances to take the relationship further. I slid out from under her and stood up. She stayed reclining where I had left her, and said, "Did I say you could get up?"

I moved toward the door, smiled, and said, "There's nothing I would rather do than stay here, but, unfortunately, I have to go on the route in a couple of hours and I really do need to get a little sleep." I was hoping she would get up and walk me to the door, so I could give her a kiss, but she hadn't moved yet. I didn't want to leave without a kiss, so I asked, "Do I get a goodbye hug?"

She got up from the couch and begrudgingly said, "Oh, I guess."

We had hugged hundreds of times before at MYF functions but they had been different. Those were hugs from one friend to another and usually with a bunch of people around. When we embraced this time, it was the first time we had done it while we were all alone. Normally, as she hugged me, she would lay her head on my shoulder with her face turned away from me. This time, she laid her head on my shoulder with her lips touching my neck. As we hugged, she kissed my neck and said, "Thank you for coming over."

When I relaxed my arms, she pulled her head back and looked at me. Then, I couldn't resist. I took the leap with no safety net. I kissed her passionately. I didn't want to stop and I would have loved to stay, but this was not the time. As our lips parted, she looked up at me and said, "Can I have another one?"

I smiled and said, "You can have all you want."

She said, "Don't make a promise unless you plan to keep it."

When I got home, sleeping was out of the question. My mind was whirling a mile a minute. So many thoughts were running through my head. I had to clear my brain and figure things out. I thought about my list. Sheryl topped almost every item on the list. I still hadn't asked her about pets and we hadn't discussed her opinion concerning glue in a relationship. I could handle it if she didn't want pets, but I was firm on the necessity of physical closeness. After wasting two hours in bed without sleep, the phone rang. The Star truck driver always called me to let me know when he was leaving downtown. I answered the phone, "Hey, are you on your way, already?"

There was a short pause and Jeff, the truck driver said, "Yeah, I'm leaving now."

I jumped out of bed and was on my way in minutes. The route was a blur. I don't even remember anything that happened. I know my mind kept drifting back to Sheryl. It was as if she was a combination of all of my previous loves, but different from them all. Maybe everything happens for a reason. Christy made me notice and appreciate girls. I needed to experience the relationship with Jane before I could have a successful relationship with Yvonne. Pat opened my eyes to help me realize which traits matter. For some reason, I couldn't think of anything wrong with Sheryl, except she was born too late. I can hear Yvonne say, 'When it comes to love, age doesn't matter.'

When I got home from the route, I was dead tired. I was not accustomed to going on the route without a nap. I didn't have any trouble falling asleep and didn't wake up until nearly noon. I woke up to the sound of the phone ringing again. I thought it would probably be my mother calling with an invitation to lunch before the afternoon route. I was still about half asleep when I answered the phone. "Hello."

I then heard the pleasing sound of Sheryl's voice, "Hi, you sound sleepy. Did I wake you up?"

I answered, "Yes, as a matter of fact, you did, but I can't think of anyone I would rather wake up to."

"I'm sorry for waking you up." She said, "If you want me to, I can call back later."

"No," I said, "It was time for me to get up anyway. What can I do for you?"

"Okay," she said, "I just needed to tell you something. I meant to tell you last night before you left, but I chickened out. You need to know that....I...really do like you a lot. I love spending time with you and I hope we can do it again, soon. I'm not certain you remembered, but I thought I should remind you I am a little bit younger than you. I don't think you should let it bother you, because it certainly doesn't bother me. I think when it comes to personal relationships, age doesn't matter."

I felt shivers down my back. I thought 'okay, Yvonne, I know you're here, now tell me what to say'. "I'm so glad you called. I wanted to call you, but I didn't know if there was a proper amount of time to wait before contacting you. The time I spent with you yesterday was perfect. The only thing wrong was leaving you. I wasn't able to sleep at all before the route, which is why I slept so late today. I really do like you a lot, too and I thoroughly enjoy every minute I spend with you, but I had forgotten you were younger. I thought you were around thirty. I can't wait until we can spend some more time together."

We didn't have to wait long to be together again. I invited her to my house for dinner that night. She stopped by her apartment to change clothes and make the 'Puppy Chow'. As soon as I got home from the route, I jumped in the shower. I told her I would leave the door unlocked so she could just walk in. When I got out of the shower, I hurried to get dressed. As I stepped out of the bathroom, I heard the unmistakable sounds of clanging pans in the kitchen. Sheryl probably wanted to make enough noise so I would be sure to hear her. She must have wanted to derail any potentially embarrassing moment before I got dressed. I stuck my head out of the bedroom door and yelled, "I don't know who's down there, but I hope you're fixing dinner."

She didn't come to the doorway, because she probably thought I wasn't dressed, but she yelled back, "I'm your ex-wife taking all of my cookware!"

Continuing the charade I said, "Take all you want, but it won't do any good, because you don't have any idea how to use them."

When I came downstairs, Sheryl was waiting for me with an ice-filled glass of Coke. She gently kissed me and said, "Hi, Honey. How was your day?"

I think I fixed a ham steak, macaroni, and corn, but I'm not sure. My kitchen was not large but it was long and skinny. To pass from one end to the other, we passed in very close proximity to each other. Each time we touched, the hair on the back of my neck stood up. As I was stirring the macaroni, she came up behind me and placed both of her hands on my back and gently kissed my neck. "I could get used to this," she said.

Just the slightest touch of her hand made me shiver. I had been with other women, but Sheryl was different. There wasn't a spark when we touched, because that would have been painful. It was more like a magnetic reaction. I can't be certain if she felt it, but when she touched me, my body was drawn to her. The hairs on my arm stretched to greet her hand. When our lips touched, I felt a passion that had been locked away for years. She told me to lie down and watch TV while she put the dishes in the dishwasher, but I needed to be in the same room with her. Finally, we went into the family room to watch television. She brought the 'Puppy Chow' and we snacked while the television blared. I'm not sure what was on TV. All that mattered was we were together.

We were nearly inseparable. The paper route required a great deal of attention even when I was resting at home. It was necessary to do several hours of bookwork each month. Sheryl quickly picked up the billing procedure. Working with her turned an onerous task into a bonding experience. If we did the bookwork at the dining room table, she took off her shoes and fondled my feet and legs. If we did the bookwork on the couch, she reclined with her head on my lap.

When we were together, we truly enjoyed each other's company. We could talk for hours on any subject. Well, I guess that's stretching it a little bit. We could talk on most subjects.

When I started reminiscing about the Kansas City A's, she just said, "I'll take your word for it, because that's way before my time."

And when she started gushing over Barry Manilow, I just said, "I'll take your word for it, because he's way after my time."

We shared a love of 50's and 60's music. I was a little surprised she seemed to love the same oldies I did. She was crushed when Elvis died. I wasn't crushed, but more disappointed. I believe he was a truly good person, who became a victim of his own popularity. I would have enjoyed watching him grow old and mature as an entertainer and singer like Frank Sinatra.

Along with our love of oldies music, and our enthusiasm for playing tennis, we also both thoroughly enjoyed watching the Grand Slam Tennis Championships on television. Chrissie and Jimmy were dominating the American tennis scene and Sheryl looked forward to, someday, seeing both of them play in person. We shared the dream of completing our own Grand Slam with visits to the U.S. Open in New York, Wimbledon, the French Open, and the Australian Open. She also said if Barry ever came to Kansas City, she would be there, no matter what. I didn't know much about Barry, but I figured if she was such a big fan, I should dedicate myself to learning more about him.

Sheryl had some allergies and it hurt me to see her suffer. During the fall, if she spent any time outdoors, she sneezed continually. She tried many over-the-counter drugs, but none solved the problem. She thought she might be allergic to animal hair, but she loved my cat, Tacky, and surprisingly enough, Tacky liked her. Tacky didn't like being around most people. The point about loving animals was certainly in her favor. She loved Tacky enough to endure potential allergic reactions.

Playing tennis together was special. When we kept score, I usually won, but it was certainly no rout. The set score was always close and we didn't always have time for a full match. Sheryl's serve was more accurate than mine and it frequently had more pace on it. She played with a 'no mercy' attitude and if I was out of position on the deuce side, she loved to hit the line on the add side. Occasionally, we played mixed doubles and we seemed to work great together. I actually preferred playing with her on my team instead of against her.

Going to movies or sporting events together was a time to be savored. Attending church services together was fulfilling. We bought groceries together, but most of them ended up at my house. I had a larger kitchen with more utensils. The only item on my list that hadn't been answered was the importance of glue, so we had an in-depth discussion about the physical expectations of a complete relationship, and I felt comfortable we were in agreement. We agreed before any relationship could be consummated, it was necessary both people were committed to the other.

One evening in September, Sheryl was suffering with allergy problems. She was trying to help me with some bookwork, but she had sneezed about fifty times. Every time she sneezed, I felt my stomach muscles tighten. I couldn't experience the pain and burning in the sinuses, but I actually felt the abdominal pain from her sneezing. Her nose would have made Rudolph jealous. Her eyes were puffy and watering. I needed to do something to help. I asked if she had any medication and she said she hadn't found anything that worked. We were nearly out of tissues, so I told her I would run to the drug store.

I explained Sheryl's symptoms to the pharmacist and he said she should probably go to see her doctor, because there were many new drugs that were very effective against allergies. He recommended an over-the-counter drug and I purchased it. When I returned home with the softest, lotion-coated tissues I could find and the best anti-allergy drug I could buy, I gave them to Sheryl. She read the fine print on the box of pills and agreed to give them a try. She relaxed on the couch in the living room and said she was going to try to read a book. After about thirty minutes, I noticed the sneezing had subsided somewhat. I thought perhaps she had fallen asleep, when she yelled for me. When I approached the couch, she patted a spot next to her and asked me to sit down.

In her best stuffy-nose voice she said, "It said on the box these pills may cause drowsiness, so I wanted to tell you something before I fell asleep." She wiped her nose and continued, "Thank you for going to all of the trouble to try to make me feel better. The tissues are very soft and I think the drugs might be working. You make me feel important and I just want you to know…I love you."

The words didn't follow a passionate kiss and didn't accompany a candle-lit dinner, but they came from her heart. I had devoted my life, perhaps without being fully aware, to making her realize in every way, I wanted her to know she was loved. As our relationship became more intimate, I felt this was the connection I had been praying for since Yvonne. I believed we were meant for each other, and hoped we would be together for the rest of our lives.

Every day I received a call from Sheryl while she was at work. For no reason at all, she would bring me a greeting card. She happened to be reading through the cards and one in particular made her think of me. Without my knowledge, she asked my mother for the recipe to salmon croquettes. Even though the smell of the canned salmon made her nauseous, she made them for me. She was willing to do anything to make sure I knew I was loved.

Neither one of us cared much about mushy 'pet' names. Sweetie, Puddin', Lover Lips, and Pooh Bear all sounded rather ridiculous. For the most part, we were just John and Sheryl. However, one day I asked Sheryl if she would mind if I called her 'Honey'. She made some joke about being as sweet as honey and I told her honey also had another characteristic most people didn't know about. Honey is the only food known to man, that apparently, doesn't spoil. I read something about honey being found in some ancient pyramids and after several thousand years, it was still edible. I told her when I called her honey I was not only thinking she was sweet, but I was also thinking she would be that way forever. Her romantic response was, "I wonder who the idiot was who tasted 4000-year-old honey."

After several months of constant togetherness, we frequently discussed the future and we always described it in the first person plural. Even though we felt we belonged together, I had not yet formally proposed to her. Our relationship was not immediately accepted by our families, mainly due to our age differences, but I believed her parents realized I truly loved Sheryl and I know my family accepted her. I planned to propose to her, but I would feel better if I knew her parents approved. Frequently, when Sheryl and I visited her parents' house, we would find her mother in the kitchen and her dad in the basement. Sheryl normally went into the kitchen to talk to her mother, and I went down to the basement to visit with her dad. I shared the ability with him to fix and repair just about anything. He was always working on some project when I found him in his shop.

"Hello, John." He said as I entered the shop. "I was just wishing I had another pair of hands. Come here and hold the other end of this pipe. It keeps turning on me." As he worked on the pipe, he asked me what we were doing. I told him we were planning to grab something to eat and then head over to my house to do some bookwork. "That doesn't sound like much fun." He said.

"It's not a lot of fun, but it's more enjoyable when we work on it together."

"Seems like you two have been together quite a bit lately." I smiled when he spoke and I was hoping to see a smile from him, but he looked very serious.

"Yes," I said, "we've been spending a lot of time together. That's kind of what I wanted to talk to you about."

"Mmm," he growled, "that sounds serious."

I normally was quite competent expressing my feelings, but suddenly I couldn't even remember my name. I gathered my thoughts and started to speak. "I…"

He interrupted me. "Are you plannin' on asking me if you can marry my little girl?"

The question called for an answer, but I needed to be very careful. "I love Sheryl and she loves me. I plan to ask her if she will do me the honor of being my wife, but first, I wanted to know if you would give us your blessing."

He stopped what he was doing and started to clean his hands. "I've already talked about this with Sheryl's mother 'cause we could tell you two were gettin' serious. At first, we were both totally against it because of the age difference, but it looks like you care about her and can make her happy. I don't know you real well, but you seem to be a nice young man. The only one I care about here is Sheryl. She's real special to me and I don't want to see her hurt. She's a smart girl and I think she can make the right choice. If she says she wants to marry you, then I think you should consider yourself the luckiest guy in the world and let me make one thing real clear, if you ever hurt her, you'll be the sorriest guy in the world. If my baby decides to marry you, then you will have our total blessing." He offered his hand to me.

After clearing that hurdle, I asked Sheryl to go with me to V's Italian Restaurant. I planned to ask her to marry me in the restaurant over a beautiful table with a romantic, candlelight setting. It was a wonderful meal and the setting was certainly romantic, but we talked about the paper route and her work and the impending holiday season, but I couldn't easily bring the topic to marriage. The proper moment never surfaced and after dinner we got up to leave.

I was committed to asking her on this particular night, so I asked her not to leave yet. We were both sitting in her car in the parking lot and when I took her hand, I'm sure she knew what was coming. I would like to say I created a beautiful, romantic speech that would bring a Marine to tears, but I didn't. It was very simple and to the point. I said, "I knew you as a friend for many years before I discovered I loved you as a woman. I know we have many challenges ahead of us. Someone once told me 'when it comes to love, throw out the rules'. I'm just going to speak from my heart about what I know. I know I love you. I can't promise I will never hurt you, because everyone has disagreements, but what I can promise you is I will never hurt you intentionally. I will always do everything in my power to provide for you and to make certain every day for the rest of your life, you'll know you are loved. If God chooses to bless us with children, I promise I will be the best father possible. I have no idea what the future holds for us, but whatever it is I want to share it with you. Will you do me the honor of being my wife?"

I thought she would answer immediately, but she didn't. She paused for a few minutes and looked out the window and then looked at me. I don't know if she was just trying to scare me, or if she was really weighing her choices, but those few seconds lasted an hour for me before she finally said yes.

She wanted a June wedding and the church was available on June 21, so she started with the wedding plans. It was my responsibility to deal with the rehearsal dinner and, of course, the honeymoon. I was consulted about all decisions, but as any smart groom would do, I agreed to everything.

I told Sheryl we should plan to take an unforgettable honeymoon, because it might be years before we got another vacation. The paper route had a way of being either an anchor in a storm or an albatross around your neck. I had not been on a family vacation with my parents since they started running the paper route. Sheryl had taken several family vacations, and visited many states. However, I always wanted to travel to Europe. I was anxious to visit France so I could actually communicate in French. I started checking with travel agencies and realized we could afford to take a three-week tour.

I also checked with my dad to see if he would be willing to drive the paper route for me while I was gone. He was almost seventy years old but the boys working for me knew all of the correct houses to deliver, so he would just need to drive the truck. Mother volunteered to take care of the billing and bookwork.

After many hectic months of photographers, caterers, florists, clothiers, printers, jewelers, and travel agents, the day finally arrived. It was a sunny, hot Saturday. The wedding went off perfectly. Sheryl was gorgeous. Her dress was stunning. I can honestly say I had never seen a wedding dress like it before and I have never seen another one since. I am certainly no dress designer and I don't know the correct technical terms, but in layman's lingo, it was white, the top was beaded and had a v-neck, and the bottom was straight-down with about a million pleats. I had never seen a pleated wedding dress before. It took my breath away.

The temperature neared one hundred degrees and the photographer wanted to take several outside pictures. We hurried out to take the pictures and then hurried back into the air conditioning. Dad said he would drive the route on Sunday morning since our plane was to leave around 8:00am. It was great to be able to stay home. I didn't get much sleep, but not for the reason you might think. I had been getting up by 2:00 every morning for so long that I just automatically woke up. I was awake for nearly an hour, worrying about Dad and waiting for the phone to ring because someone couldn't work. We were up early, putting the last minute items in the suitcases.

Our honeymoon was marvelous. The first stop was London. We managed to take a side trip to Wimbledon to see John McEnroe play a doubles match. Our next stop was Paris. It was truly incredible to speak French in France. We traveled by train through Germany to Lucerne, Switzerland. The train carried us through the breathtaking Alps to Venice. We boarded a ferry and were transported to Lido Island, which is a giant sandbar that protects the Island City of Venice from the waves of the Adriatic Sea. From there, we were shuttled to Florence, Italy. Following two days in this historic museum haven, we journeyed to our ultimate destination of Rome. After nearly three weeks experiencing the aura of Europe, we left Rome to return home.

While we were in our hotel in Paris, we met some tourists who just arrived from the United States. They told us people were dying in the Midwest from the oppressive heat. What I wouldn't find out until we returned home was every day since we had left Kansas City, the temperature had exceeded one hundred degrees. If that weren't enough of a hindrance to delivering the papers, Mother was admitted to the hospital on the day we left. She had gall bladder surgery and spent six days in the hospital. During that time, Dad delivered the papers in the morning, went home for a short nap, stayed with Mother until route time in the afternoon, delivered the afternoon edition, went back to the hospital to share evening meal with Mother, and then home to sleep for a few hours before it all started again.

Many people talk about the worst job to have in oppressive heat. I'm not going to say delivering papers was the worst, but it surely must rank in the top ten. The papers were delivered during the hottest time of the day. All paper trucks were different, but most were vans. My van was a full-size chevy. My seat was right next to the engine cover and even with insulation, the engine put out a great deal of heat. The windows needed to be open to throw the papers so there was no chance for air conditioning. Even if someone did try to turn on the a/c, the engine would probably overheat because the van rarely was able to go faster than twenty miles an hour. When the temperature climbed over ninety-eight, the air that came in the window was above body temperature, so it felt like a heater. We tried everything to keep cool. I regularly froze jugs of water for myself and my helpers, so the hotter the temperature, the more ice melted and the more cold water to drink. I also bought neck coolers, which are cloth tubes with some type of crystal in them that turns cold when wet. I just soaked them in water before going on the route and then we put them around our necks. I also had a small fan mounted on the dashboard that oscillated to keep a breeze blowing.

Dad was nearly seventy years old, and I knew it must have been very difficult for him. He said they considered calling us to let us know about Mother going into the hospital, but they decided not to, because they knew there was nothing we could do but worry. They didn't want to ruin our honeymoon with the problems at home. I was appreciative they didn't call us because I know I would have worried endlessly. We arrived back in Kansas City at about 10:00 at night and my parents met the plane. We were so excited about all of the European events, we barely gave them a chance to talk. Dad told me he had my van at his house, so he would go ahead and drive the route the next morning. When I asked if everything had gone okay, he told us about the heat and the hospital. I felt regretful they had encountered so much trouble. Dad said not to worry about it, because it was done and it wasn't that big of a deal. He reminded us, "The paper route is just like the farm, chores have to be done, morning and night. You just do what you have to do."

THE NEXT GENERATION

THE HONEYMOON GAVE ME A NEEDED BREAK FROM THE DAILY PAPER ROUTE GRIND. Sheryl and I shared a memorable time together away from the demands of the route and we knew our next vacation could be twenty years away. Within a few days, the trip to Europe was just a very fond memory. The summer continued to be dreadfully hot and humid, but the bright spot of the season was the Royals' success. They had a victorious season and capped it off with a trip to the World Series. They played the Phillies and weren't very competitive. It was very exciting though, just to be one of the two teams left standing at the end of the season. Sheryl had melted right into the pool of ink. She accepted the responsibilities that accompanied the route. She didn't need to actually work on the route, but was a great help with the bookkeeping.

We discussed starting a family soon, because I was already thirty-three. With all of the problems Pat and I had encountered, we thought it could take, at least, several months. We began trying around the end of October and by Thanksgiving, she was pregnant. Maybe my mother was right when she said God didn't ever bless my marriage to Pat with children. Within a year of Pat's marriage, she was pregnant and within six months of our wedding, so was Sheryl.

We looked forward to the impending birth with great anticipation. We had no idea if it was going to be a boy or a girl, and really didn't care, but we prayed for a healthy, happy child. I happily joined Sheryl in the pre-delivery classes and we approached the big event with all of the expected fervor. We turned one of our spare bedrooms into a nursery and put up new wallpaper. We stayed away from pink and blue and narrowed down name choices for either sex.

The answer to our prayers was a beautiful male child, born as a result of our love and God's blessing. I really didn't want to saddle a boy with my middle name. Even though I knew I was named for a beloved uncle, I constantly had to explain its origin. In biblical terminology, John meant love and Adam meant man, so we agreed on John Adam. To eliminate confusion, we decided to call him Adam. He joined our little family on August 19 and shared the same birthday as Sheryl's dad.

Another hot summer morning found me on the paper route as usual. It was a Wednesday, so the paper was a little bit bigger than normal and a little bit late arriving. The route was fairly uneventful, but when I finished the route and turned onto my street, I could hear someone playing the piano. As I pulled into the driveway, I noticed the front door standing open and Sheryl sitting at the piano banging out 'He Lives'. When I went inside, I asked her what was going on, and she said she was having contractions, so she was playing the piano to take her mind off of the pain. She said the contractions were pretty close, but her water hadn't broken yet, so she figured we'd have plenty of time, but we should head for the hospital.

Sheryl worked right up until Adam was scheduled to arrive, but he was comfortable in his current surroundings and chose to stay there for a while longer. Adam was actually supposed to arrive near the end of July, but after nearly three weeks, our doctor said we should plan to come in on Thursday, August 20 and he would induce labor. When we arrived at the hospital on Wednesday, the admitting nurse tried to tell us we were a day early and we told her it wasn't our choice. Sheryl was admitted by 8:00am and Adam was born by 10:20am. I have heard all kinds of war stories about women giving birth and I'm certain Sheryl must have experienced inscrutable pain, but she wasn't a wild woman. She didn't scream or use any profane language and she didn't threaten to have me castrated. She followed the directions of the nurse and I helped her as much as I could. I know I wasn't the first, and I'm certain I wasn't the last, but I couldn't keep from crying when I held my son for the first time. Adam's slow, laid-back approach to the birth process was indicative of his approach to the rest of his life.

There were a great many books available on the subject of parenting and I believe between the two of us, we read most of them. It is inevitable that a child will change anyone's life, but we tried to make the change as positive as possible. We shared all of the chores, except feeding, which Sheryl could only provide. Our plan was to acclimatize Adam into our life style, instead of allowing him to create a totally new life style for us.

We normally went to bed around 10:00 and watched the news in bed. Then I got up every morning around 2:00 to deliver papers. After the morning deliveries, I usually got home by 5:00-5:30 and then Sheryl was normally up by 6:00 to get ready for work. After she left, I slept until about 10:00. I ate lunch, went on the afternoon deliveries, and we both returned home around 5:30. After we ate dinner, we watched television, and were back in bed by 10:00.

Although most people told us we should have Adam in bed by 8:00, we decided to keep him awake until 10:00. Sheryl fed him and put him to bed while I watched the news. When I got up to go on the morning route, she got up with me and fed him again. They both slept while I was on the route and then when I returned home, she fed him again. He seemed to accept the routine and before long, he skipped the 2:00 feeding.

Sheryl had four months off work after Adam's birth. By the time she returned to work in December, she fed him at 10, slept until 6, fed him again, and then went to work. I was able to sleep til 10 and then Adam and I were both up for the rest of the day. At the age of just four months, he started going with me on the afternoon paper route. He sat in his car seat until I went by Caroline's house. She was a friend from church who agreed to watch Adam for a couple of hours every day from the time I dropped him off til Sheryl picked him up on her way home from work.

This routine seemed to work okay for us and Adam seemed to like it, too. When I woke up around 10am, I could usually hear him playing in his crib. If he happened to hear me moving around, he looked towards the door, watching for me to come pick him up. He was a very good baby and was very happy most of the time. Sheryl and I still enjoyed going out for a good steak dinner occasionally, and we just took him with us. He was very content to sit in a high chair and eat club crackers.

After about two and a half years, we welcomed another addition to our family. There was no problem conceiving her and the pregnancy went smoothly. Sheryl didn't have many of the problems associated with pregnancy with either child. The only predicament we experienced with our second child was she had her foot down in the birth canal, which didn't allow her to turn head down as the delivery drew closer. The doctor tried repeatedly to turn her, but nothing worked. Katie was as willful then as she would turn out to be later. He said the best and safest alternative was to have a Caesarian section.

Sheryl's due date was the end of February in 1984. We needed to pick a date for the birth and thought seriously about choosing the 29th. The only drawback to that date was we were afraid Sheryl might go into labor before then. We decided on the 23rd. The delivery happened with no difficulty and I was fortunate to witness both methods of child birth. There was a little disagreement about our daughter's name. Sheryl wanted to name her Katie Scarlett, but I was a little concerned Katie might be teased about her middle name, so in keeping with the Gone with the Wind theme, we named her Kaitlyn Tara and called her Katie. We decided our family was complete and felt if we could manage to raise two children without encountering major crises, we should truly consider ourselves blessed.

After Katie was born, we decided Sheryl should quit work and be a stay-at-home mom. My route had been gradually dwindling in size and potential income. With the obvious reduction in family earnings, it became necessary to increase the financial prospective of the paper route. After a few months of negotiations with Susan, the Star's zone manager over Eastern Jackson County, she handed me a marker and told me to draw the boundaries I wanted for my route. The route directly north and east of mine had become available and she told me after I had decided what I wanted, she would split the rest among the other neighboring carriers. By increasing the boundaries, I also added about four hundred customers to my route. With those additional customers, I increased my gross income by about 50%, without incurring too many additional costs. It took me about thirty minutes longer to complete my deliveries.

DAME BLAMES JAMES FOR FRAME'S FLAMES

FINDING CAPABLE, WILLING HELP HAS ALWAYS BEEN A MAJOR PROBLEM IN THIS BUSINESS. Times have changed and most people don't want their children to work until they are 16 years old. I have found by the time an employee reaches 16, he gets his driver's license, and drives himself to a better paying job. My only hope was starting an employee under the age of 16 and keeping him after he started driving. There were certain benefits to working on the paper route. Helpers only worked two 3-hour shifts and the rest of their day was free. They had all of their evenings free to do homework or just play.

I was definitely looking forward to the time Adam would be able to work full-time. I knew my parents were fortunate to have Bill and me working for them at the same time. The only relatives I had who were willing to help on the route were Sheryl's niece and nephew, Scott and Dawn. Scott was old enough to handle rolling and throwing the papers but Dawn was still a little young. She could help out on Sunday, by assembling the Sunday paper for resale. Scott turned out to be one of my best workers. He was the fastest roller and he was very quick to learn new changes. I only needed to tell him once when we had a new start or a vacation stop.

Scott worked for me for several years, but when he turned 16, he bought a car. Once he had a mode of transportation, he became very difficult to find. I asked him to notify me if he was not going to be at home, but frequently he forgot. In order to allow him to make more money, I had eliminated the rest of my helpers and paid him double-pay to work by himself. He lost interest in school and dropped out. I was usually able to find him for the afternoon deliveries, because that was during his sleep time. The morning deliveries, however, coincided directly with his play time. I normally left home a little early for the morning route, because I knew I would probably have to go searching for Scott. It was a normal occurrence for me to go to four or five houses looking for him. I'm certain there were times when I went in the front door of a house, Scott went out the back door. Alcohol, drugs, loud music, and sex were common at all of these locations. The young people were not the least bit shy about their activities. There were many times when I walked in on teenagers drinking, smoking pot, and having sex. As long as I was not a cop or a parent, they didn't even slow down. On those occasions when I couldn't find Scott, I did the deliveries by myself. After the first time, Scott and I had a serious talk about responsibility and trust. The second time, I hired another helper. I still allowed Scott to work, because he was excellent help and he was family.

In the course of time, I hired many helpers, but most didn't last. However, there were three that withstood the test of time. Jason worked for me for several years and was a very good, dependable helper. Jim lasted for several years and was also very dependable. The third helper, who actually worked for me, off and on, for over twenty years, was Brian.

One afternoon when I stopped in at 7-11, I saw an old friend there. Kirk, in addition to being a high school friend, was the one who introduced me to my first wife. I told him I was constantly in need of help on the route, and he said he had a son who might be interested in making some extra money. I never turned down an offer from anyone, so I wrote down the boy's name and phone number. Kirk said he and Phyllis and divorced shortly after their son's birth. Pat and I attended their wedding and went to visit Phyllis when Brian was less than a year old. She told us then she and Kirk had split up. When I called Phyllis, she was thrilled with the prospect of Brian working for me. She said he could use the money and the paper route might help teach him about responsibility.

Brian was usually good about being home when he was scheduled to work, but one afternoon when I went to pick him up, he was not home. He was too young to drive, so I searched the area and didn't find him. Scott happened to be working that trip so I just decided to go on and let Scott work by himself. After about twenty minutes, we spotted Brian walking down Winner Road. I pulled over to ask him where he had gone and why he hadn't called me. He just said he wanted to go uptown and play some video games and he figured if he didn't work, I'd just use someone else. I told him I didn't have a huge list of potential helpers and I depended on him to show up and work. I told him dependability was a sign of maturity and if he could not be dependable, he would always have a hard time finding employment. I think it may have been the first time in his life anyone really needed him.

From that day on, he was very dependable. I told him I didn't care what his reason for not working; I just needed to be notified when he couldn't be available. The biggest drawback with Brian was waking him up. When he first started working for me, I called Phyllis right before I left home and she woke him up to be ready by the time I got to his house. After a couple of months, Phyllis told me she was afraid Brian was going to be forced to quit, because waking him was causing too much conflict between them. I wasn't aware she was having so much trouble waking him up. I would do just about anything to avoid finding new helpers, so I told her if she wanted me to, I would wake him up. She gave me a key to the house and showed me where Brian slept. I needed to leave home a little bit earlier in order to allow time for the process. I arrived at his house, unlocked the front door, and quietly entered his bedroom. I stood in the doorway and said "Brian" in a little more than a whisper. He didn't move. I moved closer to his bed and again said "Brian, it's time to get up." This time, I spoke a little louder and still no movement.

"You'll probably have to shake him." Phyllis appeared in the doorway behind me.

I reached down and grabbed his shoulder and shook him. Then in a normal voice, I said, "Brian, come on, it's time to get up." He rolled over with his back to me.

"Okay, you've got him moving. Just keep talking to him." Phyllis was coaching from the doorway.

I continued to talk to him and ask him questions. If he didn't answer, I shook him again. Eventually, after about ten minutes, he sat up on the side of the bed and growled, "All right, dammit, I'm up." I turned to walk out of his room and Phyllis had already disappeared. When I went into the living room, she was standing there waiting for me.

"Do you think you want to go through that every morning?" She asked, as she headed back to her bedroom.

I followed her to the door and said, "You don't know how difficult it is to find dependable help. I would do just about anything to keep from having to find a new employee. One time when I was looking for Scott, I had to interrupt two kids having sex to ask them if they knew where I could find him. They told me he was in the kitchen, but by the time I got there, he was gone."

It took me a minimum of ten minutes to awaken Brian on the mornings he worked. There were times when it took thirty minutes. One time he fell asleep on the couch in the living room. After unsuccessfully trying for nearly thirty minutes to awaken him, I picked up the back of the couch and dumped him on the floor. He jumped up ready to fight. As he entered High School, Brian decided he wanted to attend school in the Independence School District, so he moved in with his dad. While he was living with Kirk, all I needed to do was pull in his driveway and honk my horn. A light came on immediately and Brian came out in less than five minutes. He said if his dad just opened the bedroom door, it woke him up. I think he was just not as comfortable at his dad's house as he was at his own house. I've had nearly a thousand employ-ees, but never any that could sleep as soundly as Brian.

Once Brian was awake and in the truck, he was a great person. We talked a great deal. He was always interested in my opinion and asked for my advice concerning many different situations. Scott just wanted to turn the radio up louder. Brian did a lot of growing up on the paper route. Not long after he started working, a friend of mine had a baby and Brian said, "What did they have, or can they tell yet?" He was extremely serious because someone told him if it is a boy, sometimes it takes several days before the penis grows out. I explained to him although that may happen in some members of the animal kingdom, humans are almost always born as either male or female. I suppose he may have watched too many cartoons, because he thought it was possible to be going 100 miles per hour and make a ninety degree turn. I then gave him the lesson on centrifugal force. I went about 25 miles per hour and made a sharp turn. When he nearly fell on the floor, he understood. He really didn't have a very close relationship with his dad, so he considered me as the father-figure in his life.

Brian loved to play the guitar and was a member of many bands during the time he worked for me. He really loved music and might someday be a famous rock star. One day when he was talking about his cousin, Mark Stark, I told him rhyming words was excellent practice for song writing. I told him if Mark Stark owned a park, it would be called Mark Stark Park. Then we decided if there were no lights in the park, it would be the Mark Stark Dark Park and if Mark had a deep suntan, it would be the Dark Mark Stark Dark Park. If there happened to be a narcotics officer in the park, he would be the Dark Mark Stark Dark Park narc. If that officer was supposed to sound like a dog if he saw a criminal, it would be a Dark Mark Stark Dark Park narc bark. If that officer happened to be having fun in the park and pretended to see a criminal, it would be a Dark Mark Stark Dark Park narc bark lark and if you happened to hear that bark, you could say Hark, a Dark Mark Stark Dark Park narc bark lark. We enjoyed seeing how many rhyming words we could string together and still make some sense. I think our longest string was fourteen words that started with old gold. It was always a little more challenging when we included homophones like bold/bowled, crude/crewed, hail/hale, pear/pair, and of course, coarse, to, too and two.

We did whatever we could to make the time more enjoyable. It was on one of those boring winter mornings when we discovered a house on fire. The snow started to fall on the previous afternoon and finally tapered off about the time we started the morning deliveries. The streets were not cleared yet and most yards were covered with a three to four inch blanket of soft snow. We put the papers in bright orange colored plastic bags so the customers would be more likely to find them.

As I approached Maywood, I happened to notice the house just south of the intersection was on fire. I turned the corner and pulled into the driveway. There were tracks left in the snow from several vehicles, but no vehicles in the driveway. The people across the street were subscribers, so I told Brian to go over and wake them up and ask them to call the fire department. I grabbed my flashlight and as I got out of the van, I observed there were three or four different sets of footprints leading up to the house. There were three distinctly different large sets of prints and one very small set that looked as if it were made by a small person. However, there were no sets of prints leading away from the house. I was certain there must be someone still inside. As I reached the front porch, I rang the doorbell and pounded on the front door. There was no response, so I tried the door and it was unlocked. I opened the door and yelled to see if anyone was there. There was still no response. I shined the flashlight around, but didn't see anyone. I tried the light switch, but the lights didn't work. There were several candles burning in the living room. I looked through an opening and noticed more candles and a kerosene lamp burning in the dining room. The flames seemed to be mainly in the rear of the house which looked like the kitchen. There was a hallway to the left, so I went down the hall while continuing to yell. No response. I opened one door and it was the bathroom, but it was unoccupied. I looked across the hall and opened another door. That room was empty also. I was beginning to think I was risking my life for nothing. I opened the last door and shined my light inside. There was a girl on the bed. She wasn't moving, but there weren't any flames in that room, just a lot of smoke. She was naked except for a pair of white bobby sox. I ran to the bed and shook her. She was still alive, but I didn't know if she was just asleep or passed out from the smoke. She pushed me away and said, "Not again!" and tried to roll over. She was a small girl but I would guess she was in her late teens or early twenties.

I rolled her onto her back and shook her again. "Wake up," I said, "the house is on fire and you need to get out of here."

Her speech was slurred, so I figured she was either drunk or on some type of drug. "Oh all right," she said, "but make it quick."

I looked around and saw a pair of sweat pants and a sweat shirt on the floor. There was also a pair of small sneakers that appeared to be about the same size as the foot prints coming in the front door. I heard sirens in the distance, but I couldn't wait. I needed to get her out of the house. I threw the sweats and shoes on top of her and wrapped her in a blanket. She was starting to cough, but still unaware of her dangerous predicament. The flames had spread to the bathroom and the other bedroom, but I still had a clear path out the front door.

She was struggling, but I tried to reassure her she would be okay. I carried her out the front door and around to the back of my van. Brian saw I was carrying someone, so he opened the back door. As I placed her in the van, she pushed the blanket away and Brian observed our new passenger was a naked, young female, he said, "Whoa, it looks like you won the prize. Are there any more like that still in the house?"

"No," I told him, "I think she was the only one." Then I turned to the girl and said, "I'm not sure if these were your clothes or not, but I thought it would give you something to wear."

"Yeah, they're mine." And to Brian's disappointment, she quickly put on the sweats and shoes. "Who are you?"

"I'm just the paperman," I said. "I was driving by and saw the flames. I noticed there were several sets of foot prints going in the front door, but I didn't see anyone else in the house."

She looked around and said, "Where's James and his buddies? The car's gone; they must have gone to get some more beer."

The fire truck turned the corner onto Maywood and stopped about a hundred feet south of the house beside the fire hydrant. As the firemen went running past me, one of them stopped and asked if there was anyone else in the house. I told him I had been through the house but didn't see anyone else. He asked if it was my house and I explained I was the paperman and noticed the flames from the corner. I told him my employee had gone across the street to call for help while I searched the house and the only occupant I found was the young girl sitting in the back of my van. Two police cars arrived from different directions at about the same time.

The fireman turned toward one of the cops and said, "He's the paperman, she was in the house. He got her out and we're searching to see if anyone else is inside."

I knew many of the Independence cops, but didn't recognize either of the two on the scene. I reiterated the events for the cop, who scribbled down highlights of my account and then he asked, "Who are you? I need your name, address, phone number, and social security number."

I gave him the information he requested and asked if I could leave. I explained we were in the middle of deliveries and I needed to hurry up and finish before 5:30. The girl was sitting on the back bumper of my van talking to the other cop. As I approached, she stood up and hugged me. She said, "Thank you, I think you probably saved my life."

"You're welcome." I said, "I don't think I did any more than anyone else would have done under the same circumstances. I'm just glad I happened by at the right time."

The policemen let me go and told me if they had any further questions, they would contact me. I did hear from an arson investigator a few days later. He said the house was apparently being used as a party house. It was unoccupied and the utilities were turned off. He had talked to all of the parties involved and decided the fire was probably an accident, brought about by a combination of candles, kerosene lamps, kerosene heaters, and beer. The reason I didn't observe any footprints leaving the front of the house was because the three guys left by the back door. Apparently, one of the guys was named James and he knew the people who owned the house. He occasionally brought his girl friend and other people over to the house to party. The power was off and they used kerosene heaters to heat the house. According to their statements, the heater in the kitchen was on a footstool. When the men left to go get more beer, it must have fallen and started the fire.

There is no way of knowing how long the fire may have burned, if I hadn't seen it. That young lady would probably have perished. I'm not saying that for any personal acclaim; I'm saying it for newspaper carriers everywhere. We are the eyes and ears on the street. Policemen can't be everywhere and firemen usually wait until they are called before they leave the fire station. Between about 2am and 6am, newspaper carriers travel down almost every street in nearly every metropolitan area. If it ever became necessary for every house and building in the entire metro area to receive a message in a very short time, the newspaper delivery agents would be capable of handling that task.

DIVORCE RATE REACHES 50%

NEWSPAPER CARRIERS CONTINUE DELIVERING THE DAILY NEWS IN A SIMILAR FASHION TO THE WAY IT WAS DELIVERED OVER A HUNDRED YEARS AGO. The method of transportation has changed from foot, to horse-drawn, to gas-powered vehicle, but the basic principle is the same; pick up the printed news, distribute it to the appropriate customers, and collect payment from the customers. It all sounds very simple and basic. However, the financial ethics of the average person has undergone a metamorphosis. Up until about 1950, most transactions were on a cash-only basis. If a person wanted to buy something, but he didn't have enough money, then he just didn't buy it. Sometime during the 50's or early 60's, banks began offering checking accounts. It was possible for a person to just write down on a piece of paper, who he wanted to pay, how much he wanted to pay that person, and when he wanted the amount paid. These checks were a modern-day form of IOU. It didn't take very long before unscrupulous individuals began to write checks when they had no money in their account.

When my parents started in the newspaper business, most financial dealings were still transacted by cash. If a person really wanted to have the paper delivered to his house, he would contact the newspaper or the carrier and ask for service to begin. He knew there would be a charge for the service, and he had every intention of paying for it. Most subscribers paid for their delivery service and would never have even considered shorting the paperman. On the other hand, there were more and more people who wanted to get something for nothing. Some people took advantage of the trusting individuals and companies who were willing to accept checks for payments. People could subscribe to the paper and wait for their second billing. Carriers generally trusted people to pay for the service. By the time the customer received his second notice, he could send in a check as payment even though the checking account was empty. When the carrier actually knocked on the door of the deadbeat, he realized he was not going to be paid for the service he provided.

I had been involved in the newspaper delivery system when it was a trusting relationship. The customer trusted the carrier to deliver the paper and the carrier trusted the customer to pay for the service. When my parents delivered the paper, they normally collected payments from one hundred per cent of the customers. The percentage had dropped to around ninety-five by the mid 80's. That may not sound like a huge drop, but paper route profit is a very small margin, generally only about ten percent. With the additional customers I had obtained, I was still able to get by.

Every year, the Star analyzed each carrier's performance and decided whether to renew the contract and whether the carrier deserved a financial increase. If the carrier had not fulfilled the Star's expectations, his contract could be cancelled. The carrier was expected to meet certain service criteria and make efforts to increase circulation. If a carrier had too many missed papers, he could lose his route. If a carrier didn't make solicitation attempts, he could lose his route. The Star usually had circulation contests once or twice a year. For every new subscriber the carrier could acquire, the Star paid a bonus. The Star paid each carrier a delivery fee and a collection fee. Those fees were a negotiable part of the contract.

Most carriers operated with a contract that allowed them between 5 and 10 percent collection fee. In other words, the carrier paid the Star between 90 and 95 percent of the gross amount of charges owed be the customers. Whether the customer paid or not, the carrier still had to pay the Star. For example, if the cost of the paper was $10.00 per month and a carrier had 1000 customers, then the potential gross monthly income from the customers would be

$10,000.00. If that carrier was operating with a 92 percent collection fee, then the carrier was required to pay the Star $9,200.00. The absolute most a carrier could pocket while operating under that fee, would be $800.00 per month if every customer paid. By the time you calculate the costs involved with billing, such as postage and printing, that potential profit is reduced to about $600.00. It is extremely difficult to maintain a 100% collection rate, so for most carriers, that potential $600.00 per month is just an unattainable dream.

The delivery fee the Star allocated for each route was based mainly on the difficulty of delivery. On some routes, the carrier might travel 30 miles and deliver 1000 papers. On other routes, a carrier might travel 100 miles and only deliver 300 papers. If any agent demonstrated he was an excellent, conscientious carrier, who had very few missed papers and consistently worked to increase the circulation on his route, then the Star deemed it possible for that agent to receive an increase in delivery fees. I worked hard to maintain excellent delivery standards and participated in all of the circulation increase opportunities. As a result, every year, I was given an income increase.

The formula the Star used to calculate delivery fees would be too difficult to explain, but in simple terms, each carrier was paid a few pennies for each paper he delivered. Over a period of ten years, my daily delivery fee was raised from six cents per paper to fourteen cents per paper. However, during that same period of time, my circulation dropped from nearly 1200 to about 800 customers. The area I was responsible for delivering was considered a socio-economically depressed area. There was no place on my route where there could be any new home construction. As a result of the flood in 1977, over 200 homes had been removed and could not be rebuilt because they were in a flood-plain. Many of the customers who lived in that area were either dying, or moving into larger, nicer homes. The people who replaced those customers were low-income renters and if they did agree to subscribe to the paper, they rarely paid for it. All of these factors caused the business to suffer financially.

Finding boys or girls who were willing to work on the paper route had always been a problem, but it was becoming more difficult. Parents didn't want their children going to work at 2:00 in the morning. They felt it was too dangerous and the obvious lack of sleep was detrimental to their schooling. I tried to hire people who were older. I discovered many people who needed extra money, so I started hiring men and women who had full-time jobs to help me with the morning deliveries. The route didn't take very long and most of my helpers went straight from the route to their full-time job. Then I used teen-aged helpers for the afternoon deliveries. The older workers were more dependable than the younger ones, but they didn't seem to last as long.

I continued to struggle with the employee problem and watched my route income dwindle away. With Sheryl not working, the whole burden of bill-paying rested with the paper route. I did everything I could to increase the number of customers and decrease the amount of expenditures, but it felt like a losing battle. I cut back to just one helper per trip, except Sunday. I paid my helper the same amount of money per trip, but I took over all of the throwing. I threw all of the papers on both sides. During the week, I could throw the left side customers out the left window and the right side customers out the right window. On Sunday, I threw all of the papers with my left arm. In order to throw the right side, I had to throw the papers over the top of the truck with my left arm.

Bill had a route in the same part of town I did, so we picked up our papers at the same location. If the papers happened to be late, we sat and talked. He was having the same problems with helpers I had. He even did his route by himself occasionally. One afternoon while we were waiting for the Star truck to arrive, he asked me, "Why did you decide to divorce Pat?"

He caught me off guard but I didn't mind telling him anything about that time in my life, so I said, "The main reason was because she had been with another man, but we had been growing apart for several years. Our priorities had changed and she decided she didn't want to have children and she wanted to sell everything we owned and move to California."

"I didn't know she had been with someone else." He said, "How did you find out?"

"I really didn't see any reason to mention all of the sordid details when we divorced, but she told me about it, so I know it happened. According to her, it only happened once and it was with a guy she knew in high school. You know she worked at a bank and she couldn't leave work until her drawer balanced. Sometimes she didn't leave until an hour or more after she was supposed to get off. One afternoon, I called to see if she was going to leave on time and Alice, the head teller, told me she had already left. After about an hour and a half, she got home. I asked her why she was so late and she said she couldn't get her drawer to balance. When I told her I had called and talked to Alice and I knew what time she left work, she broke down and told me the whole story. Apparently, this guy had come into the bank and didn't even know she worked there. After talking for a while, he asked her if she would like to meet him after work to talk about old times. When they met, they did more than talk."

"Wow!" he said, "Why didn't you tell me? That must've been terrible to deal with."

"Yeah," I said, "it was difficult to handle, but the great thing was that I didn't have to explain anything to my family. They just all accepted my decision without needing to know the details. Why are you curious now?"

He seemed a little uncomfortable and finally said, "Things aren't very good between us and I don't know what to do. The one thing I don't want to do is leave the kids, but I've heard it is worse to stay together just for the kids. What do you think?"

I had no idea what to say. Luckily, Pat and I never had children, so it was just her stuff and my stuff. All I could say was, "I don't know what to tell you, but I'm sure counseling would probably help." Bill always felt he was not as smart or as accomplished as others, and felt he was unable to make the wise choice. I wanted to help him but I really didn't know what to say. It was a decision he needed to make for himself. If I told him what to do and it turned out to be the wrong decision, I didn't want him to blame me for leading him astray. I didn't know if he had already talked to anyone else, or if I was the first one, so I asked, "Have you talked to Bob about this?"

"No," he said, "I know what he'll say. He and Earline both think she is great and he would just try to convince me to stay with her. They only know her public personality. They haven't been around here enough to know what she's really like. You can talk to him about this if you want to, but I'm not going to yet."

"You may be right," I said, "but remember, Bob is not just a minister, he's your brother. Love and support from family members is not something you should have to work for. You don't have to earn it or maybe you don't even deserve it, but it should be as automatic as breathing."

"I hope you're right," he said, "but I just know how they act. Whenever they visit, they act as if I don't exist and they treat her the way I would like to be treated."

As we both finished loading the papers in our trucks, I went over to Bill and said, "I don't have any answers and I'm not qualified to give any advice, but I will always be here if you just need someone to talk to."

He got in his truck and said, "I don't expect you to tell me what to do, but it helps just to have someone to talk to who knows what I'm going through."

That evening when I got home from the route, I called Bob and told him what Bill had said. I also told him I didn't know what to say, but I certainly didn't want to say the wrong thing. I believe Bob gave me the best advice I had ever received when he said, "Whatever you do, don't give him advice. Just reinforce his decisions. If he says he wants to stay with her, support his decision. If he says he wants to leave her, support that decision. Be sure he understands that he is the only one who can make the decisions and you are just there for support. You were right to suggest counseling. That should be their first step."

I felt much more at ease after I talked to Bob. Before I spoke with him, I felt a real burden. I desperately wanted to help Bill, but I was confused. I didn't want to say the wrong thing. I needed to be very careful with my choice of words, so Bill wouldn't consider them advice. Bob gave me very simple instructions and I followed them to the letter.

Bill spoke to me many times after that and I always felt very comfortable that I knew what to say. There was no pressure to give wise counsel; all I did was support whatever he said. Some days, he would say, "I just can't leave the kids. Whether I'm happy or not, I can get by. I just can't imagine living any kind of a life without my kids."

I responded by saying, "If you decide to stay together, I will support that decision 100%. Whenever we are with the two of you, I will kid around with her and she will never even know that you and I discussed this topic. Sheryl and I will do whatever we can to support you."

On other days, Bill might say, "I just don't think I can handle it any longer. She just puts me down and makes me feel like everything is wrong with me. Whenever we're together, I just feel worthless. If it weren't for the kids, I'd already be gone."

I responded by saying, "If you decide to separate, I will support that decision 100%. If there is anything I can do to help, just let me know."

Bill told me what happened when they first went to see a psychologist. Sherry wanted to know how long it would take before they would be okay. The psychologist said before they could have a happy marriage, both of them needed to take a positive approach to the relationship. He wanted to work with them separately. He said Bill needed to like Bill before he could possibly learn to like anyone else. They continued with the counseling sessions for quite a while. Usually, they went separately, but once in a while they attended together and even as a family. Sometimes Bill would relay things the counselor had said, but I never asked, because I didn't feel like it was any of my business.

The paper route again offered stability. Every afternoon Bill and I were brought together at the same location. We were given the opportunity to sit and talk. If we were not brought together, we probably would not have talked nearly as much. He rarely called me and only came by my house once to talk. I guess he knew if he really wanted to talk to me, he would see me every day at the paper drop. As the months progressed, I could see a change in his personality. He seemed to be more decisive and proud of his ability to make decisions. Perhaps, for the first time in his life, he felt confident in his own capacity to make important choices by himself. Bob had certainly given me the necessary tool to be Bill's support system.

After several months of counseling and soul-searching, Bill told me he was going to move out of his home. It was through tears he told me he couldn't handle the constant degradation any longer. I'm not sure if I would have been strong enough to do that. By that time, I had two children, and I am certain I would not be able to leave them. He told me he would definitely need some help, and I told him I would help him any way I could.

With my divorce from Pat and Bill's divorce from Sherry, our family had equaled the national average of fifty percent. The people who say divorce is the easy way out have, obviously, not experienced it. There is nothing easy about divorce, especially when children are involved. All I could do was to support Bill and make certain he understood that I fully accepted his decision to remove Sherry from our family. I would like to say that everyone in the family totally supported Bill, but I can't. Bob and his family thought that it was possible to support both participants equally. When the participants are friends or acquaintances, that might be possible, but when one of the divorced persons is a family member, it's just not possible. Bill saw every item of support for Sherry as a stab in his back. He said, hopefully, some day, they might realize just how much they hurt him. He said the only way they would ever understand was if they were confronted with divorce in their own immediate family. Then he felt certain they would totally support the blood relative and not the in-law. Maybe then, they would realize how abandoned he felt.

IT WAS THE WORST OF TIMES,
IT WAS THE BEST OF TIMES

IN A CONSTANT EFFORT TO MAINTAIN HELPERS ON THE PAPER ROUTE, I TRAV-
ELED MANY MILES TO PICK THEM UP. I hired Alan when he lived in the apartment complex on the route. It was very convenient to pick up my helpers just
a few blocks from the start and end of the route. However, after about three
months, his family moved north of Truman Road by Noland. That was a little
further to travel, but he was a good worker and a fast roller. I was willing to
travel great lengths to keep from hiring new help. After about six months at
that location, he moved again. The move took him north of 24 Highway and
about five miles east of 291. I was driving more miles to pick him up and take
him home than I was driving while actually on the route. Luckily, gas was
not terribly expensive and it was worth the cost of gas to continue using him.
Even though the price of gas skyrocketed to over $2.50 per gallon in 1980, it
had come back down under $2.00 per gallon in 1985. The price at Quik-Trip
was $1.79 per gallon. It was costing me about five to six dollars per trip in
gasoline just to use Alan.

One morning, as I was going north on 291 to pick up Alan, a car was approaching from the opposite direction. The car veered into my lane and as I

swerved to the left to miss him, he swerved back into his own lane and ran me off of the road to my left. Fortunately, there was no ditch, so I just drove through the grass. There was a concrete driveway that ran perpendicular to the road and as I hit the pavement, my door flew open. I braced myself with my left foot on the door well. I noticed a fire hydrant in front of me and, as I swerved to my right to miss it, I slammed the door shut to keep from hitting the hydrant with my door. As I came to a stop, I got out to investigate the damage to the truck. The other driver just continued to go south on 291. He must have been either drunk or sleeping because he didn't even slow down for the red light at 23rd Street. A quick walk around the truck revealed no vehicular damage, but my left foot sure did hurt. I looked down and saw blood on my left shoe. I took off the shoe to examine the extent of damage. My sock was bloody by my toes and there was a hole, through which, I could see my toes. When I reached down to touch my toe, I realized it was not connected to my foot. I slipped my shoe back on in order to keep the toe from getting lost. Fortunately, the Medical Center was just east of 291 on 23rd Street, so I got back in the truck and drove straight to the emergency entrance. I was in a great deal of pain and this was definitely the worst of times. When the doctor examined my foot, he said he would be able to reconnect the toe, but I would probably lose the toenail. I told him to do whatever he could, but I needed to hurry, because I had to deliver the morning paper. He said he would need to deaden the area in order to sew the toe back on, but he wouldn't give me any other painkillers, so I could still drive. It took nearly an hour to clean and disinfect the area, and to sew the toe back in place. He bandaged it heavily and told me to try to keep my weight off of that foot for at least a day. He did give me a prescription for some painkillers, but told me I couldn't take them if I was going to be driving. I knew the papers were going to be in and set off on the ground for me, so I hurried to pick up Alan. I told him what had happened and he said for me to stay in the truck. He would load all of the papers and get out for me at the stores. I did get out at 7-ll, because my left foot was starting to throb. I guess the local anesthetic was wearing off. There wasn't any place open to get the prescription filled, so I just bought Extra Strength Tylenol and took three of them. After a short time, the pain began to subside. By the time I returned home, I told Sheryl what had happened and she told me I should have called her from the hospital and she could have run the route. I told her if it had been my right foot, I probably would have called her, because I wouldn't have been able to drive. In the end, my toe stayed attached, but I did lose the toenail.

This was one of the few experiences with doctors and hospitals in my life. Since I was discharged from the Navy in the late 60s, I had only seen a doctor twice. The first time was the year I turned 30. Every spring, I pulled all of the poison ivy from my North property line. Since I was not allergic to it, I bundled it all up and put it in a trash bag. Apparently, my body changed when I turned thirty, because I had a terrible allergic reaction to it. In addition to a severe rash and uncontrollable itching, the rash had spread into my mouth, neck, nose and other more tender areas. I went to the emergency room and they gave me a shot and some lotion to put on the rash. I never touched poison ivy again. I didn't realize I was only equipped with a thirty year warranty.

The second time I visited a doctor was when I hurt my back. I was shoveling snow and my lower back got really sore. I stopped shoveling because it was time to go on the paper route. When I picked up a bundle of papers, I heard something snap in my back. My left leg went numb, and I fell down. After the route, I went to our family doctor and he said surgery was the only alternative. I was not looking forward to surgery, not to mention I'd have to find someone to run the route, so I went to my parents' doctor and he said I should be put in traction for two weeks. I knew I couldn't do that, because, again I'd have to find someone to run the paper route.

Then I went to my friendly neighborhood chiropractor, who was also a longtime friend from church. He said if I promised to be a nearly perfect patient, he could fix the problem without surgery or traction. I visited his office three times a week and spent the rest of the time sitting. It was too painful to lie down. When I tried to sleep, I had to prop my head up and put a pillow under my knee. Whenever I rode in the car or truck, I had a rolled up towel behind the small of my back. At the time, Adam was four and Katie was one. Sheryl drove the paper route for me, but I still did the billing and paperwork and stayed home with the kids. After about three weeks, I began driving the route again. I never spent a night in a hospital since I was dismissed at the age of three days, nor was I anxious to, but I was thankful Sheryl was able to help me when I needed it. My helpers, at the time, rolled and threw all of the papers, so she only had to drive, but she was all too willing to give the responsibility back to me.

After about three months of picking Alan up at his mother's house, I went to get him one morning, but he wasn't home. His mother didn't know where he was, but she told me her other son could probably help. She called him for me and he said he could use the money, so he would be glad to help. I asked her where her other son lived, and his address was just about a block off of my route. When I arrived at his house, he was sitting on the front porch waiting for me. He turned out to be a very good worker. He couldn't roll quite as fast as Alan, but he was consistent. Doug had a regular job during the day, so he couldn't work in the afternoon, but he was willing to work every morning. After about a week, Alan showed up at Doug's house. He had a long story about girl friend problems, but was going to be living with Doug and he wanted to work on the route. They took turns working for about six months until Doug obtained a new job in Lee's Summit. When he moved, Alan moved with him and I was again left without help.

Since I didn't have anyone to help me, I usually rolled most of the papers before starting the route and then I rolled the rest of them while I was driving. I loaded up the papers and headed straight for the apartments. It only took about ten minutes to deliver the apartments, but it was a well-lit area and there were frequently people moving about, so I used it as a place to roll papers. As I was rolling the papers one morning, I heard someone ask me if I needed any help. When I turned around, I saw a teenage girl. She said she could use the money if I could use the help. I was worn out from rolling all of those papers every morning and every afternoon, so I asked her if she would be able to work everyday. She said she could, if I could pick her up at home. I figured there would be a catch and she probably lived in Kansas. I asked her where she lived and she said she lived near 27th and Crysler. Perfect! I went right by there on my way to start the route and again on my way home. I soon discovered she was only 15 years old and was visiting a friend at the apartments. Her name was Stephanie and she said her boyfriend (the one she had been visiting in the apartments) worked for the Star. He worked in the mail room and was one of the culprits responsible for stuffing ads in our papers.

During the time Stephanie worked for me, she moved three times. While she lived with her mother, I couldn't call her because they didn't have a phone.

Stephanie just told me to knock on her bedroom window and she would get right up and get ready. As soon as I knocked, she turned on the bedroom light and I went back to the truck to wait for her. She was certainly not shy. All of the curtains and shades were open and the light was on so it was easy to see she slept in the buff. She apparently didn't like underwear, because she just slipped on a pair of shorts and a t-shirt. Her mother objected to her life-style, so Stephanie soon moved in with her boyfriend. I didn't mind because he lived in the apartments on the route. Since he had a phone, it was very convenient picking her up. I called her before I left home and she was waiting for me at the curb when I got to the apartments. After living there for a few months, she had a fight with him. She didn't tell me exactly what the argument was about, but she did say it had something to do with him being responsible for stuffing too many ads in the papers.

She couldn't go back home, so she moved in with her aunt. Her aunt lived a little further away but still not out of my range. Her aunt had a phone, but didn't want to be awakened in the middle of the night, so I couldn't call her. Stephanie was sleeping in the basement, so I just knocked on the basement window and she was out in a few minutes. She managed to live with her aunt for almost a year before being asked to leave. She said her aunt was an old fuddy-duddy who complained every time she brought a boy home with her. Her third move was closer to the route. Her best girl friend was living with a guy in a big house just about a block east of Noland Road. Stephanie thought she would live with her friend for quite a while; that didn't work out either. Apparently, the guy tried to make a move on Stephanie and she said she didn't want to spend another night there. She had made up with her original boy friend who worked at the Star and she said she was going to move in with him. That would be fine for her, but not for me. He had moved to a different apartment north of the river in Gladstone. She wanted to continue working on the route, so I tried calling her and she drove to meet me at the bundle drop. That worked for a short while, but she soon tired of driving that far everyday and, once again, I was left without help.

Finding and keeping competent help was a major challenge in operating the paper route. There were only a limited number of people available to help. Most helpers were in drastic need of money, but few maintained a consistent residence. Their life style was transient and they had few, if any, ties.

Although some helpers stayed with me for many years, most only lasted a few months. The route was purely a means of obtaining a few dollars to get by for a short time.

The paper route was my life-blood. It was not just a job; it was a way of life. I really didn't think much about delivering papers every morning and afternoon. The route had become more like eating or breathing. It was just something I did everyday. Many days passed without incidents and during those days, I certainly felt fortunate that I could make a living doing such easy work, although every time I found myself without help, or with a broken down truck, or with a sore back, I yearned for a desk job.

In order to keep my focus centered, I enjoyed other areas of interest. Sheryl and I were very active in our church and took a great deal of pleasure in church activities. Our Sunday School class was called the Gabriels, a name that was chosen after a great deal of discussion because it seemed to fit most of the members in the group. We certainly made a lot of noise, verbally, supportively, administratively, and financially in the church. As a group, we were nearing forty years old, but still felt like we were in our 20s. Some of us played on the church softball team, went on river canoe trips, and played volleyball with fervor. During the winter, we played indoor volleyball and, a sport I had never heard of before, called wallyball. It was volleyball played on a racquetball court. There were no boundaries. Balls were in-play off of the walls. Sheryl and I were also deeply involved in other church organizations. She was a very active participant in the womens' organization and I was very active in the men's club.

The single biggest event for the men's club was Santa-Cali-Gon. The city of Independence was established long before Kansas City. It was the jumping-off point for early western expansion. The three main trails to the west coast began in Independence. The Santa-Fe Trail left Independence and headed southwest toward what would become Santa Fe, New Mexico. The California Trail headed straight west through the Rockies to California. The Oregon Trail took a northerly path to the great northwest. Every year, over the Labor Day week-end, the city of Independence commemorated that heritage and hosted a large city-wide celebration. There were hundreds of craft tents, live performances, and every type of food one could imagine, even some food beyond imagination. In 1976, as our way of paying tribute to the early travelers to the west, four men from the Gabriel Sunday School Class, myself, my brother Bill, Jim, and Craig, decided to open a food booth selling Buffalo Burgers. We did not want to exploit the buffalo, but there was a buffalo ranch in south Missouri where we could purchase buffalo meat. All proceeds from the weekend sales were to go directly into the men's club treasury. We didn't make a large profit, but we recognized the potential. That first weekend in '76 Bill, Craig, Jim, and I were about the only ones to work. There were a few others who helped, but the four of us were there from open to close every day. Aspiring to reach financial possibilities, not only the men's club, but the entire church, had taken on the responsibility of making the Santa-Cali-Gon venture a success. The profits moved into five digit territory and were a nice addition to the church's income.

In addition to our limited physical exercise in Gabriel class activities, Sheryl and I also did our best to keep fit by playing tennis. Neither of us could threaten the pros, but we enjoyed the time together and we were fairly evenly matched. A less strenuous sport, but one equally enjoyed, was watching professional sports on television. We never missed watching one of the Grand Slam Tennis matches, Chief's football, or Royals baseball. I met several of the Royals while I delivered papers by the Stadium Complex. Some of the players chose to live at the hotel near the Complex where I delivered papers. On several occasions, I met, had dinner with, or celebrated with many of them. I even went out to play golf with Darrell Porter, former Royals catcher, once.

I loved baseball. I loved the history of the game and had high hopes for the future of the game. I loved playing shortstop and pitcher on my Little League team, the Salisbury Hills Cardinals. I loved listening to the Kansas City Athletics baseball games. I loved watching the rookie get a game winning base hit, and the veteran dig deep for one more leg-shaking run to first base. I loved the suspense of a bottom of the 9th, tied game, with the strategy exhibited as each team tried to out-maneuver the other. Pitchers had to pitch until the game was over – throw the ball and everyone got his chance to be the hero. There was no manipulating the clock, or taking a knee. 'Cuz it ain't over 'til it's over.

Since their inception in 1969, the Royals had been more competitive than the A's. With the A's, the fans in Kansas City never expected to see the home team in the post season, but the Royals had become consistent winners. In just their third year of existence, they finished in second place. From 1975 through 1985, they never finished below second place. During that time frame, the Royals won their division seven times and won the American League pennant twice. The Royals were definitely a power in the American League, but couldn't seem to go all of the way. For those eleven years, they had been an exciting, winning team. After growing up listening to the A's on the radio, I finally realized my dream of having a winning team in Kansas City.

In 1976, the Royals won their first of three straight Division Championships. However, the hated Yankees stopped their run to the World Series. After a second place finish in 1979, Whitey Herzog was fired and Jim Frey was chosen as new manager. He managed to take the Royals back to first place again. This time, with the help of a George Brett home run, the Royals vanquished the impotent Yankees in three straight games. Unfortunately, the Royals were the ones who lacked the potency to win it all. They lost to the Phillies in six games. I wondered if I would ever see my home team win the final baseball game of the year.

Even though the Royals returned to the playoffs the next season, 1981 will always be considered by baseball fans as an embarrassment. My beloved baseball heroes had spit in the face of the fans by going on strike. These men seemed to have lost touch with reality. Even though the owners were actually blamed for causing the strike, as a fan, I saw men who were being paid millions of dollars to play a game they loved, walk away from the sport. Even though some may claim victory, everyone associated with baseball was a loser in 1981, and the biggest loser was the fan. If the players and owners really wanted to make amends with their fans, they should have played the remainder of the season for free. By that, I mean no admission price. All of the fans could enter the game without paying. Season ticket holders could sit in their guaranteed seat, but they would be refunded the amount paid for the tickets. The owners and players could still share in the proceeds from concessions and broadcasting revenue. The season resumed, but no one really cared. Attendance was down everywhere and fans turned their backs on baseball. I had a difficult time forgiving baseball.

Probably the most exciting event to occur in baseball over the next couple of years involved the Royals and Yankees. George Brett was kicked out of a game for using too much pine tar on his bat which has become known worldwide as the famous pine-tar incident. That incident helped to reignite the interest in baseball. People who had given up on baseball were intrigued by the antics of the performers. One by one, the loyal fans found their way back to the arena.

With Dick Howser as the new manager, the Royals returned to the top of the American League in 1984. Again they were thwarted in their drive to a World Series, but this time, the villains were the Detroit Tigers instead of the Yankees. After such an exciting season in 1984, the team seemed poised to go all of the way in 1985. I was hopeful this would be the year I could finally experience the thrill of victory instead of suffering the agony of defeat. The Royals managed to win their division for the seventh time in ten years. They were challenged in the playoffs by the Toronto Blue Jays. After falling behind Toronto three games to one, the Royals had their backs to the wall and were facing elimination in each of the next three games. One loss would have ended their season. The boys from KC managed to escape elimination and won all of the remaining games to get a second shot at the World Series. The American League Championship Series was only a precursor for the events to follow in the World Series.

Once again the Royals fell behind three games to one, this time to their cross-state rivals, the St. Louis Cardinals. The '85 Series may not have been the most watched nation-wide, but just about every television set in the state of Missouri was tuned in each of the seven nights. Most of the games were uneventful except for game 6, which was played on October 26 in Kansas City. There are many differing recollections of the game, but I was at both games and have the scorecard to prove it. St. Louis fans would forever claim the umpires gave the series to the Royals, or they could even be more vindictive and claim the Royals stole the series. Those are the cries of desperation from people who really don't know what they're talking about and just want someone to blame. The blame lies at the feet of their own team.

The infamous play the Cardinal fans scream about happened at first base in the ninth inning. Jorge Orta rolled a grounder to Jack Clark at first base. Clark flipped the ball to the Cardinal pitcher, Todd Worrell, covering first base. The umpire, Don Denkinger, called Orta safe. All replays show he missed the call and Orta should have been out. This is where recollections by Cardinal fans get a little cloudy. That wouldn't have been the third out to end the game. If it had been, I could certainly understand their angst. It would have been the first out. The Royals next batter was Steve Balboni, who hit a harmless pop foul over by the Royals dugout. Darrell Porter and Jack Clark converged and both watched it fall harmlessly between them. If the Cardinal fans want to blame somebody, how about Porter or Clark? Given a reprieve, Balboni hit a single to put runners at first and second. Orta, the guy Cardinal fans didn't think should be on base, was then erased on an attempted sacrifice bunt by Jim Sundberg. The next play, like the foul ball to the first base side, commonly is forgotten by Cardinal fans. Darrell Porter was charged with a passed ball, allowing both runners to advance to second and third. With Hal McRae at the plate, Whitey Herzog decided to intentionally walk him to load the bases for Dan Iorg. Iorg looped a single to right field. Cardinal right fielder, Andy Van Slyke picked up the ball and threw on target to Porter who missed the sliding Sundberg. Game over, Royals win 2-1.

The poor mistreated Cardinals were not the only victims of questionable umpiring in game six. Most St. Louis fans forget about the play in the fourth inning. Frank White was called out on an attempted steal of second base. All replays showed the umpire missed that call also. The next hitter for the Royals, Pat Sheridan, hit a single to the outfield that would have easily scored White. If that call had been correct, the Royals may not have even needed to bat in the bottom of the ninth. The major difference in the game was the Royals were given a bad call by an umpire and continued to play ball. The Cardinals received a bad call and fell apart. After the missed call in the ninth, the Cardinals missed an easy pop foul, allowed a passed ball, and missed a tag at home.

Take all of the questionable calls and mistakes into consideration and then remember, it was only game six. Both teams started out on even footing in game seven. The Cards had the same opportunity as the Royals to take the Series. The Royals sent their ace, Bret Saberhagen to the mound to face the Cardinals ace, John Tudor. The Royals continued their attack and won easily 11-0. Saberhagen spaced out five harmless hits to win a complete game. In addition to losing the game, the Cardinals also lost their cool. The umpire that had missed the call at first base on the previous night had moved behind the plate for game seven. Herzog continually baited Denkinger until the frustration finally boiled over onto the field. In the fifth inning, already trailing 9-0,

Herzog brought Joaquin Andujar into the game to try to stop the onslaught. After giving up a run-producing single to Frank White, Andujar and Herzog were both ejected from the game for disputing the strike zone. Believe me, I understand their frustration. After watching the A's lose year after year, and then the Royals get so close but not quite able to win the last game of the season, I had felt disappointment for over 30 years. But this was definitely the best of times for me. I didn't need to explain why or blame anyone else. The Kansas City Royals had become the World Champions in 1985. They became the first team to ever come from a 3-1 deficit in the League Championship Series, and a 3-1 deficit in the World Series to win the title.

The Cardinal fans are left to deal with the 'what ifs'. What if Vince Coleman had not been injured in that freak automatic tarpaulin accident? What if either Darrell Porter or Jack Clark had caught that easy foul pop-up? What if Whitey Herzog had come out in that ninth inning to settle his team down? What if Darrell Porter had not missed that passed ball? What if Porter could have applied the tag on Sundberg? What if Major League Baseball's winningest team had hit better than .185 in the World Series? What if they had scored more than just 13 runs in the seven games? What if they had faced some other team that didn't have Danny Jackson, Charlie Leibrandt, Bret Saberhagen, and Dan Quisenberry? I've always heard if: 'ifs and buts were candy and nuts, we'd all have a Merry Christmas', so I'd like to wish a Merry Christmas to all of those St. Louis Cardinal fans who felt the exasperation of getting so close and not winning the final game of the year.

MADAM, I'M ADAM

BILL AND I PICKED UP OUR PAPERS AT THE GROCERY STORE NEAR 27TH AND CRYSLER, ALONG WITH THREE OTHER CARRIERS. Most of the time, we just met the Star truck out in the parking lot, but if it happened to be raining, the driver put our papers up next to the building under the canopy. After leaving our location, the driver went on to another location and left papers for six additional carriers. In an effort to reduce the number of Star trucks and neighborhood bundle drops, the Star decided to open distribution centers. It was the Star's plan to eventually have just five or six locations around the metropolitan area where all 400 carriers would pick up their papers. They leased a building on 23rd Street just east of Crysler and 24 carriers were assigned to pick up their papers at that location.

There were advantages and disadvantages to the distribution center plan. The main disadvantage was, on some occasions, some carrier was going to be the eightieth truck in line to load his papers. The main advantage was the papers should arrive earlier, or at least that was the theory. It would only seem logical that it would take less time to load 5 or even 10 trucks at the Star's loading dock, than it would 40 or 50. Another advantage of the distribution center was that many carriers would meet in the same location, which would present the possibility for information and idea exchange. One piece of information that would be an invaluable part of this network was a list of potential helpers. It was from one of those additional carriers that I got the name of my next helper.

Stuffy had experience working for another carrier, but the carrier gave up his route and Stuffy was left without a job. His real name was Bill, but he couldn't say a sentence without adding 'and stuff' at the end—thus the nickname. It's always nice to have someone with experience because they should be able to handle the work on the very first trip. Bill's first trip with me was no exception. He easily handled all of the rolling and I even had him throw some of the right side. The next trip, however, was a bit of a letdown. Stuffy couldn't keep his eyes open. He could get out of the truck at 7-11, get something to eat, get back in the truck, and be asleep before I pulled out of the parking lot. I adjusted my mirror so I could watch him and I know he sometimes rolled the papers with his eyes closed. When his hands stopped moving, I yelled at him to wake him up. His answer was always the same, "I'm awake!" Sometimes, I waited until I needed to turn the corner, and as I turned, he nearly fell out of his chair.

I found out the reason he was so sleepy was because he was holding down three jobs. He worked for me from 2:30-5:30am, then he went to work at a tire store and worked there from 7:00am til 5:00pm, and then he went to work at an Arby's Restaurant until about 10:00pm. His responsibility at Arby's was to empty all of the days' grease into a big tank and take all of the garbage and put in the proper receptacle outside. Apparently cleanliness was not a requirement for the job he did at Arby's because he sometimes came to work on the route with wheel grease still on his arms from the tire store. Since he was probably asleep before he got in bed, a shower was an unnecessary diversion. He frequently came to work on the paper route smelling like a combination of garbage, day old grease, and tires.

Most of my other helpers refused to work with him because they couldn't stand the odor. I really didn't notice it, because I sat next to an open window. Stuffy was certainly not the smartest or the cleanest helper to work for me, but he was one of the most dependable. The only real problem I ever had with him was keeping him awake. From time to time, when Stuffy couldn't work for me, his daughter or his brother worked in his place. Stuffy's daughter, Bobbie Jo, was a competent helper, but she really didn't want to work. She enjoyed having the money, but she didn't like the hours. Stuffy's brother, David, was a very capable worker, but he had many physical limitations. Muscular Dystrophy and colon cancer were just two of David's medical issues. He also had a colostomy. He never complained about any of his ailments, but he loved to talk. There were occasions when I just had to tell David to be quiet because, when his mouth was moving, his hands stopped moving.

The Star didn't stay in the building east of Crysler very long. When their lease was up, they moved into another building on 23rd Street just west of Crysler. We continued to use that building for a couple of years and then we were combined with about 25 more carriers and put in a building near Independence Center. The new building was quite a bit larger and was meant to be the loading station for all of the metro area carriers who had routes located south of the Missouri River, east of I-435, north of Hiway 50, and west of Oak Grove. There were a total of about 50 routes in the building. About 35 of them were home delivery carriers and about 15 were single-copy carriers. The new location was very convenient for me. After we had moved into our new house, I was less than five minutes from the substation.

There was a constant turnover in truck drivers who brought the papers out to us from the Star. With the substation system in place, the Star only needed about ten drivers instead of the previous 40-50. The Star had implemented a new means of notifying the carriers about press-time and departure of trucks. They used a telephone recording system which was intended to be updated every fifteen minutes during a press run. Obviously, the system could only be as efficient as the person responsible for updating information. Only about one or two days out of a month was the system utilized perfectly. Frequently, there would be an hour or more between updates. That could mean the presses had shut down or it could mean the person responsible for the updates had taken a break or a nap. It took between 18 and 30 minutes for the driver to travel the distance between the Star and our substation. Sometimes, the driver stopped to get a sandwich and a drink on his way. There were several occasions when the driver was confused and took our papers to the wrong substation. By the time he got to us, over an hour passed since he left the loading dock at the Star. Every morning when I woke up, the first thing I did was call the Star recording and find out how the papers were running. As soon as our load left the dock, I left home. I went to the substation, loaded my papers, and then went to pick up my help. As I drove, I rolled a few papers so I could deliver them on my way.

Adam was already in school and Sheryl stayed at home with Katie during the day. We purchased a vacant lot with plans to build a new house. I had been looking for a lot for several years. After the paper route in the mornings, I drove around Independence to see if there were any available lots with a view of the Eastern horizon. I loved to watch the sunrise and wanted to have a house where I would be able to have an unobstructed view. After dealing with water in our basement, it was equally important to find a location that was high as possible. I found the perfect lot, but it was in a rather high-end neighborhood. We weren't sure whether we would be able to build a house that would fit into the neighborhood. I had been hoping to build a house for several years and I had drawn up a potential floor-plan. The first floor was mainly for entertaining and the second floor the private family bedrooms. I wanted the kitchen and dining room on one side and an office, a bathroom, and a small multi-functional room on the other side. In the middle would be a two-story entryway and great room surrounding a large two-story brick fireplace and chimney.

Our old house was almost paid off and we had very good credit, so we secured a construction loan to pay for the new house. One of my former employees owned a construction company and he agreed to help me with the construction. Whenever anything needed to be done, he would tell me how much it would cost for him to have the job done and if I could get it done for less, then I would do it. Professionals did the hard stuff like excavated for the basement, poured the concrete, installed the insulation, hung the sheet rock, and put on the roofing materials. I helped with the rough-in. I took care of the painting, carpeting, wiring, plumbing, and trim work.

I spent many hours working at the new house. After the route in the morning, I went straight to the house to do whatever needed to be done. Then I usually went home for lunch, took a short nap, and then went on the afternoon route. The only possible way that we could afford the new house was for us to do as much work as we could. We received help from many family members. Bill helped me a great deal, especially with the plumbing. Sheryl's mother also helped us with the painting and clean-up. From the time the hole was excavated for the basement, until we actually moved in, was a little over a year. We still hadn't finished the landscaping and the exterior painting, but the house was livable.

We could see William Yates Elementary School out our back door, but Adam was required to ride the bus. Our new home was on a very quiet cul-de-sac. Most of the yards appeared to be perfectly manicured, lush green carpets. My yard was never the showplace of the neighborhood. I couldn't afford to pay a professional to cut, weed, and manicure the lawn. Even though most of my neighbors had underground sprinkler systems, my philosophy was 'if God wants to water the yard, I won't try to stop Him'. I was not an ardent environmentalist, but I really hated to use any chemicals on my yard. I was always afraid the kids would be poisoned.

A drive through our neighborhood showed the dandelion was the number one enemy of homeowners. If it had been possible, the poor, defenseless yellow flower would have been forbidden in the confines of our housing addition. My yard remained a haven for the unfortunate, vulnerable wild flower. There were times my yellow ground cover appeared almost as lush as the neighbors' deep, green grass. The survival of the dandelion is rather amazing. For at least the last fifty years, homeowners, lawn professionals, and chemists have labored endlessly to eradicate the species completely. It is necessary to protect and pamper grass seed. In order for it to grow and mature, it must receive constant care and coddling. I suppose if I could discover some beneficial use to the dandelion, I could become a millionaire. Even though my yard would never be a showplace, I managed to mow it and cultivate it enough to keep it from becoming an embarrassment.

Adam enjoyed going on the route in the afternoon, so he worked whenever he could during the summer. Everyone knew him at the substation and he learned most of their names. He was somewhat enthralled by the fact that his name was part of a very popular palindrome. Whenever he met a new woman, he would always offer to shake her hand and say, "Madam, I'm Adam." Some of the women recognized the palindrome and others would just say something like, "Aren't you formal?" He just looked at me and smiled, because we knew something she didn't. He shared my love for letters and loved to play word games with homophones and rhyming words. He also enjoyed figuring out the meaning of a rebus. When a board game called 'Whatzit?' became available, he just had to have it. The game was a contest to see who could be the first to interpret the rebus. He loved to play the game, but no one wanted to play it with him, because he always won. We later found out he had read through all of the cards and knew all of their meanings. However, palindromes were the most intriguing to him. He found out there were regular palindromes and also palindromes of words. In order to actually say something that made sense, the word palindromes were much easier. In order to make sense out of a true palindrome, it was much easier when it was short.

There was a girl in Adam's class at school whose name was Hannah Chastain. She was a good friend of Adam's and they were in the same classroom several years. She was a very nice girl and we always kind of hoped someday they would get married. Hannah's mother, Julie, was the maid of honor in our wedding. I think one of the reasons why Adam was so interested in Hannah was because her name was also a palindrome. He constantly tried to maneuver her name and his name into a long palindrome. That was the trouble with palindromes, they took time and usually a pen and paper to originate. Rhyming words and homonyms could be rattled off at any moment. Sometimes, Adam would create a palindrome and then wait for an opportunity to insert it into normal conversation. His challenge was to use a palindrome without anyone knowing it.

Each substation had a warehouse foreman whose responsibility was to assist the carriers and be certain each of them received the correct number of papers. The foreman at our substation was a guy named Ron and he was probably the best warehouse foreman we ever had. The papers were assembled in bundles at the end of the press line at the Star building and then placed on large wooden or plastic pallets. There were usually around 60 or 70 bundles on a pallet, and ten to fifteen pallets on a truck. One of the responsibilities of the warehouse foreman was to unload the delivery truck from downtown and distribute the proper number of papers to each carrier. Ron was very efficient at his job. He allowed four carriers to load at the same time, but he watched each carrier carefully to make certain they didn't take too many or too few bundles. Even though most carriers were very honest and very careful, anyone can make a mistake and if Ron thought someone had made a miscount, he made them recount their bundles. One of the carriers, a woman named Norma, usually ran her route by herself, and since she didn't have a set way to load her bundles, she frequently miscounted. She just tried to count the bundles as she put them in her van. If anyone spoke to her while she was loading, she lost track. While we waited for the papers to arrive from downtown, the carriers and the warehouse staff sat and visited. Sometimes, I walked to other carriers' trucks and sometimes they came to my truck. If the weather was inclement, we frequently went inside the warehouse and waited.

One rainy afternoon, Adam and I were sitting in Ron's office chatting as we awaited the arrival of the Star truck from downtown. Ron and I were discussing the problems of delivering papers to the customers in the rain and Adam rather abruptly changed the subject.

"The rain kind of makes everybody hurry and that's when they make mistakes." Adam said and then he turned to Ron and continued, "You'd better watch everybody twice as close today, to make sure they don't miscount their bundles."

"Yeah," Ron answered, "I wish everyone stacked their bundles like you guys do. It's much easier for me to recount and they probably wouldn't be as likely to make a mistake."

"Do you think some of them might take an extra bundle just because they're selfish and don't care about anyone else?" Adam asked.

"Maybe there's a couple that might try to steal a bundle, but most of them just can't count." Ron said.

Norma had just pulled up outside, but it was raining pretty hard, so she stayed in her van. Adam pointed to her and said, "She will probably miscount."

Ron shook his head and said, "No, she will probably be okay as long as she is at the end of the line. As long as no one talks to her, she counts okay."

Ron turned to call the Star to see if our truck had left downtown. As soon as he hung up, he said, "Our load still hasn't left yet."

I started to say something about late papers, but before I could say anything Adam continued with his train of thought, "You don't think Norma is selfish, do you?"

"No," Ron said, "I think she's just careless."

Adam hesitated for a few seconds like he was trying to decide what to say, and then he said, "Norma is as selfless as I am, Ron."

Ron looked at him with a puzzled glance and said, "Yeah, I think she's a good person."

Adam just smiled and looked at me for confirmation. I was a little confused by his choice of words, but I just smiled and nodded at him. Then I turned to Ron and asked which load was the last to leave. He said our load should be next, so we headed out to the warehouse to get ready to load up the papers.

Once we were back in our truck, Adam asked me, "Did you figure that out?"

"Did I figure WHAT out?" I was still a little confused.

"Ha-ha!" Adam said, with an air of accomplishment. "You didn't catch it either. I know Ron didn't catch it. That was a palindrome. 'Norma is as self-less as I am, Ron'."

"You're right I didn't catch it. I just thought you were a little crazy. I wondered why you chose to use the word selfless."

I grabbed a piece of paper and printed the palindrome on it. While Adam was loading the papers in our van, I went over to Ron and gave him the piece of paper. "I think you were a little confused by Adam's choice of words. This is what he said. It's a palindrome."

"What's a palindrome?" Ron asked.

I explained, "The letters can be arranged first to last or last to first and it says exactly the same thing. Just stick that in your pocket and check it out after everybody is gone." He was all business and I knew he wouldn't want to take time out while he was watching carriers load their vehicles. As I pulled out of the substation, I noticed he was reading the note.

The challenge was on. I would not rest until I could come up with a palindrome Adam would not recognize.

I really enjoyed it when Adam went on the route with me. He could help me load the bundles and then he could begin rolling as soon as we left the substation. Adam continued to help me during the summer and occasionally during the year, but I didn't want him to experience the same restrictions I felt when I was in school. He was a really good helper. He was a fast roller and he had a great memory. He learned all of the throws on each side of the route. He liked working on the afternoon trips, but the morning trips were just as much of a pain for him as they were for everyone else. I was aware of the potential pitfalls of working every day, so I limited his trips. He worked nearly every afternoon trip and about half of the morning trips. I needed him to work on both Saturday and Sunday mornings, so the only school mornings I used him were Tuesday and Thursday. I adjusted his schedule so he could work on any days school was not in session, which meant he worked on just about every school holiday.

The Star had been discussing the possibility of discontinuing the afternoon delivery of the paper. Those discussions had been ongoing for several years, but the main drawback seemed to be they would lose some sort of accreditation by the national newspapers organization. Apparently, they were allowed to wear some sort of special feather in their cap by producing a newspaper twice-a-day. Since the circulation of the afternoon delivery had decreased substantially, the big shots downtown finally agreed to discontinue the afternoon publication of the Star. Wednesday, February 28, 1990, was the last afternoon delivery of the Star. Starting on Thursday, March 1, I felt semi-retired. The morning edition of the Star was called the Times and it was totally discontinued on that date. The Star went from an evening paper to a morning paper.

With the elimination of the afternoon paper, my weekly gross income was cut, but after eliminating the afternoon expenses, my net loss was about twenty dollars a day. It was well worth it to be free of the afternoon delivery. By eliminating the afternoon route, the mileage I put on my van was nearly cut in half. I only needed to find someone to work seven trips a week instead of twelve and my days were open to do whatever I wanted to do.

Adam had heard Sheryl and me talking about our reduction in income and one morning on the route, he asked me if we were poor and if we would need to sell our house. That was the first time he had ever really seemed concerned about money. Sheryl and I were not independently wealthy, but we were successful. We had been able to build the house of our dreams, which came with the mortgage of our nightmares.

My dad had not ever talked to me about assets and liabilities. That's a lesson I had to learn on my own. When I was a child, I was happy. I didn't have the fanciest bike in the neighborhood, but it met my needs. I wore hand-me-down clothes, but I didn't care, because they were new to me. We didn't go out for ice cream very often, but when we did, it was a real treat. We couldn't afford to buy things from the Ice Cream Man, but I loved the grape ice cubes my mother made in the freezer. I wanted to give Adam some financial guidance, but I knew it needed to be simple and trustworthy. It needed to be advice he could remember and also something he could follow.

"No," I said, "we're not poor and we're not going to sell our house. We are making less money now with just one paper a day, but I have a great deal more free time to spend with you and Katie. Someday, if our house becomes more valuable to someone else than it is to me, I will sell it. Building our house was a goal I had set a long time ago. When that goal became reality, we celebrated, because we had conquered a target. You should always set goals. Set goals. Set lots of them. Set short range goals that are attainable, so you can celebrate when you reach them and set long range goals that are more difficult to attain so you can continue to be motivated. Define what success means to you, so you will know when you become successful. Define what rich means to you, so you will know when you become rich. Just remember money can be a very powerful commodity in your life, but be very careful to make it your servant and not your master."

"I know what my first goal is." He said, "I want to get a Nintendo."

"Okay," I said, "just find out how much it will cost you and then decide if you are willing to spend that amount. What effect will that expenditure have on your long range goals, like college or a car?"

"Oh yeah," he said, "I want to get a car as soon as I'm 16."

I saw the opportunity for motivation. "Your goals may require more money than you can make by just working on the paper route. You may need to get another job to increase your income. Just always remember to set goals and make money your servant and not your master."

Since there were no more afternoon trips, Adam's opportunity to help was drastically reduced. I still needed his help on weekends, but he was only able to work one or two trips during the week. The excitement had worn off and the paper route had become a burdensome chore to be accomplished. If the morning paper had been eliminated, I am certain he would have had a different sentiment. It had become very difficult to wake him up for the paper route. Those first mornings are but a hazy memory now. Before he started going to school, he woke up easily and jumped out of bed to get ready. Frequently, he was in my bedroom, dressed, and ready to go before I could get dressed.

As he got older, the preparation time took longer. Occasionally, he would go back to sleep and I would have to wake him up for a second time. I understood the frustration my dad felt when he tried to wake me up. I tried to be patient with Adam, but I'm certain my frustration showed through on many occasions. I viewed our interaction on the route as irreplaceable bonding time. It gave us an opportunity to spend time together to chat and become friends. Some dads occasionally take their sons hunting or fishing, but I was able to spend quality time with my son several times a week. Not only were we creating the opportunity to become good friends, but I seized the chance to discover who he was becoming and he welcomed the chance to discern how I had achieved my identity.

Adam loved to hear stories about my adventures on the paper route. He especially liked hearing the story about finding the dead body in the apartments. The only problem was he feared the same circumstance would happen to him. I only had one very small set of apartments on my route, and he always hated to run them. I constantly assured him he would be okay because I never actually left the complex. I let him out, drove about a hundred yards, let out the other helper, and then backed up to pick him up. He only had to deliver about twenty papers. Most of the time, his trek through the apartments was uneventful. One afternoon, he was running through the apartments and when he got back to the van, he said, "You're not gonna believe what just happened."

I smiled and said, "Did you find a dead body?"

He just looked at me in disbelief and said, "I just went into that last door and when I went up the steps, I noticed the door for Apartment C was open."

I interrupted because I was a little afraid he might have seen a man and a woman enjoying a personal moment on the couch. "You didn't see anything you shouldn't, did you?"

"No," he said, "nobody was doing anything they weren't supposed to do. There was a whole bunch of people in there and one guy came to the door to get the paper. When I handed it to him, he said, 'Thanks, Adam.' And then he turned around to a woman and said 'Hey, look who our paper boy is, it's Adam.' Then she came to the door and said, 'Well, Adam, I'm certainly happy to see you are our paper boy.'"

I was a little confused, also, "Did you recognize them?"

"No," he said emphatically, "I've never seen any of them. How did they know me?"

Just then, I looked in my rear view mirror and realized he was wearing his baseball cap from his little league team. In order to help the coach learn all of the players' names, he had given them caps with their names on the front. "If

I had gone in that door wearing that cap, they would have called me Adam, too."

He took off his cap and looked at the big 'Adam' across the front. "So that's it! I couldn't figure out how they all knew me, but I didn't know them."

Adam's only other adventure in the apartments happened on a morning trip. Some of my helpers just strolled slowly through the apartments, but Adam always ran. I don't think he was running to impress or please me, he just wanted to hurry up and get it over with. These apartments are laid out with eight units in each building. There were four apartments in each door. It was possible to run through the basement between the two doors, but he was too afraid someone might be down there, so even in the rain, he ran outside. On this particular morning, he was almost done. He had gone in the last door. He had to go up six steps, drop a paper in front of Apartment E and then go up six more steps to a landing, and toss a paper up to Apartment F. As he dropped the paper in front of Apartment E, he hurried to run up the next flight of stairs and stepped on something. At first, he thought it might be a blanket or pillow, but suddenly realized it was a man. As Adam stepped on him, the man groaned. He repositioned himself on the stairs but didn't wake up. Adam gently put the paper on the steps and ran out of the building. That was as close as he ever wanted to come to finding a dead body. Even though he swore he would never run the apartments again, he gave in and ran them when it was his turn. However, he was very careful. He always looked where he was going and watched where he was stepping.

I was generally able to find sufficient help on the route so Adam didn't have to work every day. Even though I enjoyed working with him, he got to the point he really hated being awakened for the morning trip. He constantly asked me when I was planning to retire, so he could quit working on the route. I wished he appreciated the opportunity for us to spend time together, but he placed a higher value on a full night's sleep. Once he was up and he realized working on the route was inevitable, he usually managed to make the most of the situation. The two to three hours of driving around in the same van gave us the chance to discuss many topics. Sometimes, parents spend very little time with their children. Even though they live in the same house, they rarely sit down one-on-one to discuss anything. One, or occasionally both, parents may see their child for a few minutes in the morning, but that time is usually wasted on logistical questions that can, and usually are, answered with single syllable responses.

"Come on, it's time to get up."

"Hurry up, or you'll miss your bus."

"Did you get your homework done?"

"Did you brush your teeth?"

"Did you put on clean socks?"

"Did you put your dirty clothes in the hamper?"

"Hurry up, if you don't have time for breakfast, at least, eat a Toaster Pop-Up on the way to the bus."

"I'm doing the laundry today, so when you get home, you need to put away all of your clean clothes."

"Hurry up, here comes your bus."

Unfortunately, the communication is one-sided and does not reflect the love and concern most parents feel. The verbal exchange in the afternoon is generally very similar to the morning exchange. So much time is wasted on logistics. After a brief encounter at the front door, the child frequently grabs a quick snack, heads for a television, and is not seen again until supper. If the family is fortunate, they will have the luxury of sitting down at the table together and eating the evening meal as a family unit. Regrettably, many families eat separately and adjourn to their own areas of interest with very little face-to-face communication. Too many parents don't take the time to get to know their children and then are surprised by their children's actions.

Sheryl and I did not claim to be perfect parents, but we decided when we first got married, we would do everything we could to make certain our children knew, every day, they were loved and important. The paper route gave me the chance to spend one-on-one time with Adam and Katie. For those three hours every day, I could talk with them and find out their interests and their ideas. In 1990, when the Star eliminated the afternoon paper, I could be home every day when they got home from school. In an ongoing effort to make them feel important, I asked questions that required lengthy responses, and I listened to those answers. I know that may sound obvious, but many parents ask their children how their day went, but really don't listen to the answer. I made it my business to know all of their teachers' names and whether they were liked or disliked. We were a little worried about who Adam and Katie would choose as friends, but soon found out our concerns were unwarranted. When kids have a good set of values, they generally tend to choose friends with the same set of values. We could not have done any better at choosing their friends if we had taken applications and triple checked references. Sheryl and I both made it very clear to Adam and Katie their friends were always welcome in our home.

We decided if we were going to make our home a 'hang-out', then we would have to make it a place where all of the kids felt welcome. We remodeled the basement to give them a place to call their own. We put up sheet rock, put black and white tile on the floor, and installed a suspended ceiling to absorb some of the noise. We put in a kitchen table and chairs for playing cards or table games. We already owned a pool table, but added ping-pong and foosball tables for their entertainment. We put in a bathroom and a full kitchen for their use. The kitchen was always stocked with a variety of soda pop, pizza, sweets, and snacks. If we were home, we left the front door unlocked. We told all of Adam and Katie's friends they should consider our house their home-away-from-home and they were always welcome. They didn't need to knock. If the front door was locked, then we were not home. If the front door was unlocked, they could walk in without knocking. On one occasion, we were out doing some running around and Adam received a call on his cell phone. The person calling was his good friend, Doug. Doug said he was sitting in our living room watching television. He walked in the front door, but soon found no one was home. He said he didn't want to leave the house unlocked, so he just sat down and waited for our return.

For a period of about five or six years, there was a constant procession of young people coming in our front door and heading down to our basement. We knew most of them, but once in a while, one would cautiously enter and look confused. We introduced ourselves to them and tried to make them feel comfortable. I think many of them were surprised that we remembered their names. We took the extra effort to find out something unique about each one who entered. We wanted all of them to know this was not just a place to hang out, but a place where they felt important and cared about. Adam knew a pair of twins whose names were Jared and Jordan. I think they were amazed we could tell them apart. Although we encouraged most of the young people to call us John and Sheryl, many of them preferred to call us Mr. and Mrs.

Morrison. We were tolerant of those names and realized the young people were not trying to be formal, just respectful. Those were the kind of friends Adam and Katie chose.

THROUGH THE VALLEY OF DEATH

I IMAGINE MY PARENTS WERE PROBABLY JUST AS CONCERNED ABOUT MY CHOICE OF FRIENDS AS WE WERE WITH ADAM AND KATIE'S. Perhaps that's why they made church such an important part of our lives. Going to church and knowing Jesus were paramount in directing the path my feet would follow. Religion was just as important in both of my parents' lives when they were young. My mother was raised in a Christian home. Grandpa and Grandma Parrish went to church every Sunday and were active in all areas of the church.

Even though Grandpa Parrish died at the age of 76, Grandma Parrish lived to be 100. Grandma had a very close relationship with God. She seemed to know Him as a friend and she spoke to Him often. Since I never knew either of my dad's parents, and my mother's dad died when I was just 10 years old, Grandma Parrish was the only real grandparent I had the opportunity to know as an adult. I always looked forward to her visits. She was very intelligent and she loved to work the crossword puzzles. She told me those puzzles were what kept her mind sharp. I can remember how frustrated she became if she couldn't recall a certain word. She told me repeatedly the words were in her brain, but sometimes there was so much clutter up there she couldn't find them.

As Grandma passed 90 years old in a virtual trot, reaching 100 seemed like a foregone conclusion. Just like her father, who lived to be over 100, she was very active. She really hated it when she, for her own safety and for the safety of those with whom she shared the road, quit driving. The key to her car was the key to her freedom. She loved to visit her children and grandchildren. When she gave up the key to the car, she depended on others to come to visit her. She wasn't able to cook for herself, so she left her beloved Norborne and moved into John Knox Village in Lee's Summit. My sister, Barbara, lived the closest to her and visited frequently. It was through those visits Barbara decided to be a volunteer and help other elderly occupants. When she discovered the feeling of fulfillment she received, Barbara decided, after the age of forty, to become a registered nurse.

I led a busy life, and the paper route called me home every day, but I still made certain to visit Grandma on special occasions. Whenever I visited, she always wanted to know what was going on in my life. She always made me feel special. That feeling of importance was something I hoped to instill in my children someday. I always offered to do anything to help her, but she rarely had any requests. She said if she really needed anything, all she had to do was press a button, and someone would be right there to offer assistance. One of her normal requests was for me to read scripture to her. It had become too difficult for her to read the small print.

On a cold day in October, I stopped by for a short visit on my way to Lee's Summit to buy a part for my truck. Since I would be passing very near John Knox Village, I decided to take advantage of the opportunity and let her know I was thinking of her. We always had a big celebration for Grandma's birthday, but she said, even though she appreciated the thought, she loved to remember others' birthdays and anniversaries. I wanted to get a card for her, but her birthday was in June and it was still about three weeks til Halloween. I didn't remember the date of her anniversary, but I did remember Grandpa Parrish's birthday was some time in October. I didn't recollect the actual date, but I hoped it hadn't passed. I made a quick stop at Osco and bought a 'Thinking of You' card. I just wrote a short note about remembering that Grandpa Parrish's birthday was approaching and I was thinking of her. She loved to receive cards and had many displayed in her small room. She was amazed I would go to all of the trouble to find a card, write a personal note, and come by for a visit in commemoration of her husband's birthday, especially since he had been dead for over twenty years. She said she felt guilty because she had forgotten it was approaching. That made me feel guilty because I was just on my way to buy a part for my paper truck and I wanted to bring her a card.

Grandma made the past real to me. I loved to hear the stories of life in this country when she was a little girl. I explained to her I was on my way to buy a heater core for my paper truck and she told me if I couldn't get the heater fixed, I could always do what her father had done when she was a little girl. She said during the winter, her dad would place two or three bricks next to the fireplace early on Sunday morning. Then, when it was time to go to church, he took the bricks and wrapped them in a blanket and placed them on the floor of the carriage, so she could keep her feet warm on the way to church. When they arrived at church, he took the bricks and placed them next to the wood stove to heat them up for the return trip home.

As much as I loved listening to her stories, I knew I had several hours of work to do on the van to repair the heater. I apologized for the brevity of my stay, but promised to stay longer on my next visit. She reached for her Bible and asked me if I had time to read a short scripture. I really needed to leave, but told her I would try to always find time for God's word. I asked her what she wanted me to read and she said the twenty-third Psalm. I said, "Why do you want me to read that? You and I could both recite it from memory."

She said, "Just do an old lady a favor and read it to me."

I was in a hurry so I started reciting it before I found it in the Bible. "The Lord is my shepherd; I shall not want...." As I was reading, she shut her eyes and listened intently. "Yea though I walk through the valley of death, I will fear no evil: for thou art with"

She laid her hand on the Bible and said, "Do you know that I think you just said the most important word in the Bible?" I quickly scanned the last few words. Could it have been righteousness, death, or evil? How could one of those be the most important word in the Bible? She could see I was frantically searching for the right word. Then she said, "THROUGH, you walk THROUGH the valley of death. Death is not an end. You don't walk into it and stop. You can't walk around it. There is no way to get to the other side without walking through it. We are on this side of the valley and eternal life is on the other side. In order to receive eternal life, I must walk through that valley. At my age, death is a constant presence. I just want you to know I feel reassured, knowing there is something on the other side of that valley and I am looking forward to walking through it someday soon. Don't mourn for me when I die. Rejoice in knowing I have passed through that valley of death and I am waiting for you on the other side."

I certainly am thankful I decided to stop by and visit with Grandma Parrish. I think I learned more in that one afternoon than I learned in a lifetime of Sunday School and sermons. She lived to see and surpass 100 years old, and I still cried at her funeral, not because I was sad for her, because I knew she had passed through the valley, but I was sad for myself because I would miss her.

I never knew my dad's parents. I know they went to church regularly. My dad told me his family never missed a Sunday at church, and every evening before dinner, each of the family knelt down behind his or her chair, and his father said a prayer. It was a different prayer every night and each of the family members was mentioned. Those prayers were apparently answered because Grandpa and Grandma Morrison raised four good Christian sons. One of those sons, Kirk, was a Presbyterian minister and a dedicated missionary to the Congo in Africa. He spent most of his adult life in Africa helping others to know the same message he had been taught. Unfortunately, his life was cut short and he died of emphysema at the age of 67. The second son, S.B., was also a devout Presbyterian, but couldn't get the necessary education to become a minister. He did, however, devote his life to working in the church. He was the only Morrison son who was able to make a living as a farmer. I fondly remember spending many summers at the farm of Uncle B. and Aunt Clara. He was an elder in the Presbyterian Church and worked tirelessly as a Sunday School teacher and active member of the Men's Organization. S.B. died when he was 77. Lewis was the third son of the family and his twin brother, James, died at birth. Lewis, an ordained Presbyterian minister, devoted his life to that ministry. Lewis was the first of the Morrison brothers to die. He died suddenly of a massive heart attack in his home, while playing with his beloved granddaughter, Kathy. He was only 52 years old. My dad was the youngest of the Morrison brothers and he lived the longest.

Like his brother, S.B., Dad didn't have the opportunity for a college education. He said he lacked the intelligence to make it, but the main barrier was financial. He knew he couldn't afford to spend money on college when he needed every penny to support his wife and children. He said he was lucky because he managed to find a job. He would tell you he was fortunate, because he managed to have enough left over after the bills were paid to build a new house and help send his children to college. True to Grandpa Parrish's guidance, Dad would be quick to point out he really enjoyed running the paper route and so he would certainly consider himself to be truly blessed.

Just like his brother, Lewis, Dad also experienced heart trouble. Great advances were being made in the medical field. In 1962, when Lewis suffered his heart attack and died, there was very limited knowledge about heart disease. Through vigilant medical check-ups, Dad found out he had some blockage around his heart. He was easily tired and unable to perform even small amounts of exertion. He said his biggest struggle of the day was to walk from the bedroom to his chair in the living room. The doctor recommended he have open-heart surgery. The process called cardio-arterial-bypass was being accomplished quite frequently. Apparently, arteries around the heart become clogged and blood cannot be pumped through them. To fix the problem, doctors open up the chest, expose the heart, cut out the blocked artery and replace it with a good artery from the leg or groin area. The more blockages the doctor can repair, the more blood can be pumped effectively. Dad was able to endure a quadruple bypass. During the surgery, his heart stopped beating and the doctors used electric shock to restart it. We could see the two large bruises where the treatment was administered. After the surgery, he was able to resume most normal activities. Within six months, he was in the back yard, splitting fire wood with an axe.

Dad and Mother went to St. Louis to visit Aunt Carolyn as often as possible. Mother loved to visit with her little sister, but it was difficult to find a time when Aunt Carolyn was home. She loved to travel and we called her a social butterfly. On one of the visits to St. Louis, Dad encountered a problem with his bowels. When he attempted to go to the bathroom, there was an obvious problem and substantial blood loss. They hurried back to Independence and checked into the hospital.

The surgeon informed Dad there appeared to be a tear in his colon. The only way to repair the tear was to open his abdominal area, remove the damaged section of colon, and suture the two remaining sections together. That part of the surgery was successful. However, when the surgeon opened up the abdominal area, it was apparent a cancerous tumor had grown too large and split through the wall of the colon. The cancer spread to most of the other internal organs. He could visibly recognize there was cancer on the spleen, stomach, and liver. He said nothing else could be done, so he just closed him back up. Even though Dad took chemo for a short time, it was painfully obvious he would pass through that valley very soon.

No one in Dad's family ever lived to be eighty years old, so when he reached that milestone, we threw a large party for him. With the cancer, every day was a gift. I took the opportunity to videotape an interview with Dad to seize the memories while I had the chance. With a lot of help from Barbara, Bill, and Bob, we put together a video tribute to Dad. It included a historical listing of all Morrison relatives from Robert Morrison, who was a linen draper in Ireland before coming to Bucks County, Pennsylvania in America, in 1767, to Meghan Judeman, Dad's great-great-niece who was the youngest Morrison at the time. She was born in 1990 and Dad celebrated his eightieth birthday in June of 1991. Shortly after his birthday, Dad welcomed a new granddaughter, Rebecca, and a new great-granddaughter, Kelly, to the family.

Dad managed to survive in his battle over cancer until December, 1992. As Christmas approached, I told him he couldn't die, because it would ruin everyone's Christmas and besides, I had already bought him a present. He said he didn't expect to get much use out of whatever it might be. Dad and Mother came to our house for Christmas Day. Everyone opened presents and ate a huge Christmas dinner. At Dad's age and living with his medical situation, there was really nothing he could use, so I gave him a bookmark. It only cost fifty cents and had the twenty-third Psalm on it. I relayed the interpretation Grandma Parrish had told me. Since the heart surgery, tears came easily to his eyes. He said, "Maybe I CAN use this."

The next day I went by to see how he was doing. He was sitting in his chair napping when I arrived. We chatted for a few minutes about all of the previous day's activities and then he said, "So, is Christmas over with? Would it be okay if I died, now?"

I didn't really know how to respond. On the one hand, I wanted to tell him 'No, you can't die yet, your anniversary is next week.' But on the other hand, I knew he was worn out from fighting the cancer. He just wanted to lie down and rest. I didn't want to lose him, but he was exhausted. He looked at me with those clear, blue, watery eyes asking me for approval to pass through the valley. With tears in my blue eyes, I said, "Dad, I don't want to lose you, but I love you and I know you are worn out. If you need to rest, then it's okay to shut your eyes and rest. If you wake up on the other side of the valley, tell Grandma Parrish 'Hi' for me."

Later that night, he became unable to speak and Mother called to say he was worse. When I arrived, he was still unable to speak, but he looked like he wanted to say something. I stayed for a couple of hours and then I needed to leave to go on the damn paper route again. I went into the bedroom and told him it was paper route time and I needed to leave. He still had that look on his face like he wanted to say something. I told him I knew he would probably like to go along with me on the route, but I already had enough help lined up and he had already worked his share of trips. Now it was time for him to rest. Again, I reminded him I loved him and I would be back as soon as I finished the route. It was a Sunday morning, so I promised him I would bring him a paper and read Peanuts to him.

When I finished the route, I called to see how he was doing and Mother said he was still holding on, but she called the church and Karen Sue, one of the associate ministers at our church, was on her way. I arrived at Mom and Dad's house and went straight into the bedroom. Karen Sue was already there and when I arrived, we all gathered around Dad's bed while Karen Sue offered a prayer. I really don't remember the words she said, but during that prayer, Dad passed through that lonesome valley.

TIME MARCHES ON

DEATH DIDN'T AFFECT THE PAPER ROUTE. The demands were constant; every day without a break. I missed Dad and was disappointed Katie never really knew the real Grandpa Morrison. By the time she was born, he had already experienced several health problems. He had been very ill for most of his last three or four years. Adam spent a great deal of time with Grandma and Grandpa. Almost every afternoon from the time he was four months old until he started first grade, he went with me on the afternoon trip. He loved to visit and followed Grandpa everywhere. When Dad poured a new sidewalk in front of his house, he put Adam's handprints in the concrete. I would frequently find Dad out in the backyard swing pitching to Adam. He would hit the ball back toward Dad, and then run the nonexistent bases, pretending to be any one of the several Royals he could name.

Without the afternoon route, Adam and Katie were both able to pursue extracurricular activities at school. They were both very interested in band. From the time they were able to walk, we put them on the piano bench and encouraged them to play. After hours of practice, numerous lessons and one very patient piano teacher, they both had achieved proficiency on the piano.

From that fundamental understanding of music, it was a fairly simple transition to other instruments. Adam enjoyed playing the trumpet, and Katie preferred the clarinet, but Adam possessed the uncanny ability to play almost every instrument he picked up. He also learned how to play the guitar with help from Kent Brauninger, a long time family friend. Katie wanted to be in the drum line, and she chose to play the bells, chimes, and vibraphone, but her personal favorite was the marimba.

Blue Springs High School Band offered varsity letters in four areas, Marching Band (which began practicing a month before school started), Pep Band, Concert Band, and Jazz Band. Each area had very strict criteria. In order to receive a varsity letter, many requirements had to be met. Adam was the first, and still only, student to receive all four varsity letters for all four of his high school years. During his senior year, he was chosen as one of the Drum Majors, i.e. student leader, of the band. It was a wonderful opportunity and honor for him.

The school enjoyed a very active and demanding band. During every other year, the band traveled to various parts of the country to perform in special events. Adam had the opportunity to travel to Hawaii during the summer between his eighth and ninth grade to perform in the King Kamehameha Parade, but we felt he was too young to make the long trip. Sheryl and I were new to the band program and were totally unaware of the professionalism and integrity that were paramount in the planning of the entire Blue Springs High School road-trip organization. If we had been aware of that fact prior to the trip, we would have allowed Adam to participate.

Any band-parent will tell you it is usually very difficult to pick out a son or daughter among the hundreds of band members all dressed alike. We were extremely fortunate when, as a sophomore, Adam marched in the Orange Bowl Parade. The band was only on the television screen for a few minutes. During that time, there were three or four different views of the entire band and a couple of close-ups of individual members. Adam happened to be one of those close-ups. With all of the nearly 200 young people in the band, Adam was singled out on national television. The cameraman gave the entire country an up-close look up Adam's nose. The group also took a side trip to Jamaica, where Adam went parasailing. It was a wonderful experience for all of the band members and a marvelous memory Adam would always treasure.

When Adam went to the Orange Bowl, Sheryl and I didn't feel we could afford to go. It was difficult enough just to pay his way. The paper route had a death-grip on me and I couldn't possibly leave. Sheryl was working at a new job and, even if we could have afforded it, she couldn't get away either.

When Adam was a Senior, and Katie was a Sophomore, the Golden Regiment Marching Band from Blue Springs High School had a chance to march in the Rose Bowl Parade in Pasadena, California. That was a very prestigious opportunity for a high school band. There were only three or four high schools in the entire country were invited to perform. Since Adam was one of the Drum Majors, he had the privilege of marching with the other three Drum Majors out in front of the band. Katie continued to play the clarinet for concert band, but she played the marimba in the Drum Line for marching season. While the band was field marching and going through their formations, the Drum Line stood at the sideline and accompanied the band. The students who played stationary Drum Line instruments could not perform in a parade. Therefore, Katie and the other drum line members carried the banners in front of the band. There were fifteen students who each carried a letter or space to spell out BLUE SPRINGS, MO. Katie carried the R, and as such, was the center alignment person. We could not have scripted a better situation. As band-parents with two children marching in the Rose Bowl Parade, both of them were easy to pick out.

Sheryl, Adam, Katie, and I had never had a family vacation. Sheryl accompanied Adam and Katie and the youth group from church when they went on summer work camps, but I had never been able to attend, because of the paper route. We realized this would probably be the last, and probably only, chance we would have to all go on a 'family vacation' together. The cost for the students to go as a group was around $1100.00 each. That amount covered all costs including air fare, room at a four star hotel, all meals, and admission to all events, including Disneyland and Universal Studios. Fortunately, the school made it possible for families to reduce that cost by helping in fundraisers. Sheryl and I both did as much as we could do to bring the price down. With the reductions we had earned, we were able to pay for both Adam and Katie. However, there was no way we would be able to raise enough money for Sheryl and me to go.

Sheryl was working for an attorney at the time and she told him about our predicament. He asked her how much it would cost for her to be able to go. She told him the school was charging $1100.00 per person. He made out a check for that amount and told her to have fun. With the help from David, our financial concerns were eliminated. Now the only problem was finding someone to run the paper route for me for those eight days. It had been eighteen and a half years since I missed a day working on the route. My last day off was the day Sheryl and I returned home from our honeymoon in Europe.

I discussed the situation with, Chris Cronk, my District Representative from the Star. He knew it had been nearly twenty years since I had a day off and he also knew this would probably be our last opportunity to take a vacation as a family. He agreed to run the route for me if I would make him a throw-book. I had never used a throw-book, because I knew all of my throws by memory. It took nearly two weeks of non-stop effort to get the book ready for him to use. Every address on my route was listed in the book and notations were made to denote customers. After I completed the book, Chris went along with me on the route to make sure he understood my system. Corner houses were the main problem. Sometimes we threw the paper in the front and sometimes we threw it at the side. He knew finances were tight for us, so he said he would not charge me anything to drive and throw as long as I supplied him with a vehicle to use and furnished him with helpers to roll all of the papers.

I discussed the situation with my helpers, and they understood the importance of being available on their assigned days to work. I gave Chris the keys to my old reliable van and even left him the keys to my '92 Aerostar. It was my back-up in case the van broke down. It was also equipped with four-wheel drive, so I told him to use it if there was any threat of ice or snow. With Chris to take care of the route, and with the financial help from David, we finally had the opportunity for a family vacation. The school needed all reservations made and payments received before December 1, so Sheryl and I were not part of the school group. We bought our own airline tickets and when we arrived in Los Angeles, we booked our own transportation and housing. My cousin, Frank, lived just a few blocks from the airport so we rented a vehicle and went by his house to visit with him. We had even hoped we might be able to spend a couple of nights at his house. I had been trying to call him for a couple of weeks before we left Kansas City, but he never answered. When we arrived at his house, no one was home. The woman next door came out and, after she found out who we were, she said Frank was out of town on business and she was watching his house. He wasn't expected home for two weeks.

The band group was staying in a very nice hotel, just a few minutes from the airport. Sheryl and I went by the hotel to visit with Adam and Katie for a few minutes. They didn't have long to visit, because the band was dining at Medieval Times. It was a really exciting restaurant where some of the employees put on an Arthurian type of show with horses, lances, and jousting. The kids loved the part where they ate with their fingers. Sheryl and I decided not to attend the performance, because we still had not located a hotel. We drove around for a couple of hours and found a Super 8 not too far from the band hotel. The only problem was we could only stay there for four nights. The hotel had already been booked to capacity on New Year's Eve for Rose Bowl participants. We took what we could get and booked our reservations through noon on New Year's Eve. Then we figured we would find something for the last three nights.

Once we found a place to sleep, we decided to do some sight-seeing. With Sheryl driving and me navigating, we drove around Hollywood and Bel-Air. We chose La Cienega Boulevard as our main north-south corridor. We didn't take time to stop anywhere, and mostly looked around. We didn't have a great deal of time, because the band was going to go to Manhattan Beach the next day and we wanted to meet them there. We tried to avoid the freeways and, with the help of a map, managed to become familiar with the LA area.

The next morning, we were up early and went to McDonalds for breakfast. We went to Manhattan Beach where we met up with Adam and Katie and headed for the beach. Adam had seen the Atlantic when he went to the Orange Bowl, but it was Katie's first view of the ocean. Adam had a girl friend, and most of his time was spent with her. The beach area was not too big, so he was always in sight. He and his buddies built mammoth sand castles and Katie just played in the water with her best friend Mallory. We had lunch with both of them and Sheryl did a little souvenir shopping. After spending most of the day at the beach, the band had a little free time and then went to the local high school to have one last practice before the parade. Sheryl and I did some more sight-seeing and went shopping for some things Adam and Katie wanted.

The next day, while the band went to Disneyland, Sheryl and I went to see some more sights. We had lunch at Johnny Rocket's in Hollywood and sat just a few bar stools away from Jack Lemmon. We thought it was Jack Lemmon, but since we had never seen him in person, we weren't absolutely certain. I asked our waitress if it was really him and she told us he had lunch there almost every day. I told her I wanted to pay for his lunch. She said that would be fine and she would tell him we were paying. She went over and spoke to him and he turned and waved to us and said 'thank you'. When she presented us with Mr. Lemmon's ticket, I paid it and asked her if she could ask him to sign it for us. She took the ticket to him and gave him a pen. He wrote something on it and stood up to leave. He walked past us, said 'thanks' again, and said he got the tip. When she brought the ticket to us, he had written 'Thanks for lunch, Jack Lemmon'. After souvenir shopping on Hollywood Boulevard, and driving past celebrities homes, we headed south to Anaheim to meet up with the band at Disneyland. They were scheduled to march through Disneyland at 10:00 PM. We were not interested in the rides; we just wanted to watch them march.

We met the band at Universal Studios the next day and spent the whole day with Katie and some of her friends. We spent a little time with Adam, but again, Heather took priority. We rode most of the rides and had dinner with Katie and Adam at the Hard Rock Café in Universal Studios. We had a great time and were totally worn out by the time we left. This was to be our last night at the Super 8, so we needed to spend some time looking for a new place to stay. The desk clerk told us we could check back after 6:00 PM to see if there were any no-shows.

We spent most of the next day, New Year's Eve, looking for a vacancy. We called many hotels before leaving the Super 8, but were not fortunate to find another room available. We drove from one end of Hollywood Boulevard to the other, but every room was taken. We found ourselves in Santa Monica and checked all of the hotels there. While we were there, we walked down the Santa Monica Pier. We were both totally surprised to find there was a carnival permanently located on the pier. There was a roller coaster, other rides, and many games of chance. I totally impressed my favorite girl with my strength and agility by winning a stuffed lion.

We headed south past Venice Beach, Marina Del Rey, and Loyola University. We went back to the Super 8 but there were no vacancies. We decided to go back to the hotel where the band was staying and spend the evening with Adam and Katie. The band director and the other adults decided to allow the students to have a New Year's Eve party and celebrate the New

Year at 10:00 PM, which was midnight in Blue Springs. As we were nearing the airport, we saw a small hotel with a vacancy sign on. It was very small and there were three guys out in front on motorcycles. It appeared this could be our only option, unless we slept in the rental car. Sheryl didn't want to get out of the car, so I went in to find out how much it would cost. At that point, it really didn't matter what the charge, if there was a room available, we would take it.

As I entered the office, there was no one behind the desk. It was a very small, dark lobby. A large fish aquarium took up most of one wall. Along another wall, there was a small table with a chair on each side. On the table were several magazines. I didn't take time to peruse all of them, but I noticed the one on top was 'Big 'Uns'. Right beside that were a 'Penthouse' and a 'Stud'. The desk was just a counter with a ledger book, a small bell, and a display case that held about a dozen porn tapes and a collection of condoms. I could hear sounds coming from the room behind the desk. It sounded like a porn movie. I didn't want to interrupt the drama, so I waited until there was a lull in the action. It sounded as if the participants in the activity were satiated, so I hoped the desk clerk would be in a good mood. After a few seconds of silence, I hit the bell on the desk. I could hear two voices, one male and one female, whispering loudly. The female said, "You go!" Then the male replied, "No, it's your turn, you go!" The female responded, "Oh, all right. It's probably just one of your buddies wanting to use the phone." There was a short pause then the male said, "Don't button up your shirt. Give 'em a little peek."

As the young lady appeared from the back room, she was wearing a pair of men's boxer shorts and she was putting on a man's shirt. As she entered the lobby, she was just putting her right arm in the shirt. She was in her twenties and had a very nice figure. Her hair was a dirty blond, which was probably just the color of the week. The top of a tattoo was protruding from the left side of the shorts. I couldn't make out any words but it appeared to be the top of a red heart. Over her right breast was the word 'White' and over the left breast was the word 'Chocolate'. She didn't seem to be in a big hurry to close her shirt when she confronted a stranger. I guess she figured since I had already seen them it didn't really matter. She asked, "What can I do for you?"

I skipped the obvious response of 'you've already done quite enough' and said, "Do you have any rooms available?"

She just pushed a registration book toward me and said, "Do you want it by the hour or all night?"

I took the pen in my hand and said, "How much is it?"

"It's twenty bucks for an hour and fifty for all night." She said as she pointed to the display case, "We also have tapes for rent or condoms if you need them."

That was about twenty-five dollars cheaper than Super 8, so I said, "I think we will need it for the whole night."

She just smiled and said, "Check-out time is noon. Will you be done by then?"

As I finished filling out the info, I handed her the money and said, "We'll be gone early, because we need to be in Pasadena by 9."

She glanced at my name and address and said, "Oh, are you in town for the parade?" She shifted her weight to her left side and placed her left thumb in the top of the shorts, pulling them down enough to uncover a little more of the red heart.

"Yeah, we just need a place to rest our head for the night." I answered and then I pointed to the heart and said, "Nice tattoo."

She quickly inserted her right thumb and pushed down the shorts to expose another tattoo and the fact that she was not a real blond. The other tattoo was on her right side and it was a pair of dice. She was very proud of the tattoo and she said, "Get it? Pair of dice, paradise?"

I smiled and said, "Cute!" Then, as I turned to walk to the door, she pulled the shorts up and held the shirt together with one hand and said, "When you leave tomorrow, just leave the key in the room and lock the door behind you."

I went to the car and as I got in, Sheryl said, "That sure took a long time. I thought they knocked you over the head and those guys on the motorcycles kept looking over here at me. Did you get a room?"

I handed her the key and noticed at the same time she did, it was for room number one. She said, "While I was sitting here waiting and looking at this place, I realized how much it looks like the 'Bates' Motel' from 'Psycho'. Now you come back with the key to room number one. That's creepy."

"If it's any consolation," I said, "the clerk didn't look anything like Norman Bates. At least the one I met didn't look like him. The clerk was a girl, but there was a guy in the back room with her when I rang the bell. I guess that could have been Norman."

"Don't laugh." She said, "This place really looks sleazy."

"Don't judge it without actually viewing the elaborate adornments of the luxurious accommodations." I said, "Let's go in and check it out."

As we entered the room, she said, "How much did this cost?" I told her fifty dollars. She looked around a little more and told me I'd gotten taken. I didn't mention we could have gotten it by the hour. The room shared a wall with the office and I remembered it was the wall with the aquarium. However, the office was very small and the rest of our bedroom wall and our bathroom wall must have shared the wall with the back room of the office. The room was just a little bit bigger than the bed. There was a nightstand on each side of the bed and I asked Sheryl to look and see if the Gideons had been there. As she opened the drawer, she said, "Unless the Gideons quit placing Bibles and started placing porn, then they haven't been here." She pulled out a couple of magazines similar to the ones in the office.

I opened the drawer and found the Gideon's Bible in the stand along with another collection of porn. I reassured her the Gideons had been there and left a Bible, but she said, "Somehow, that doesn't make me feel any better." She had tip-toed into the bathroom, and whispered, "Do you think they can hear us?"

I put my ear to the wall and heard the unmistakable moans and groans of the porn tape. I said, "I really don't think they're too interested in us. They have their own show going on."

Sheryl placed her ear to the wall and said, "Gross, do you think that's a tape or is it in person?"

I said, "I don't know, but it sounds like the tape playing when I was in the office."

Sheryl whispered again, "Let's get out of here. I need to go to the bathroom, but I'd rather use a Port-a-Potty!"

When we got to the car, we realized we needed to stop by a store for supplies. Since the band was going to have a New Year's Eve party, I assumed she wanted to pick up some balloons and decorations. When she came out with a rather large bag, I reminded her the band chaperones had probably bought there own supplies, she said, "I just thought it would be nice to have some balloons and noise-makers for Adam and Katie and their friends. While I was there, I also picked up a pair of sheets and some germicide for our suite. I'm not about to lie on those sheets. I'd be surprised if they even wash them between customers."

We arrived at the band's hotel and Katie was in the lobby with some friends. We chatted for a little bit and Sheryl gave her the balloons and noise-makers. Sheryl told Katie about our lodgings for the night and Katie wanted to see the hotel. I told Katie she was too young to even drive in the parking lot at this particular location. We stayed at their hotel for all of the festivities and the countdown at 9:59. The students were allowed to celebrate for a little while, but they all had to be in their own rooms by 10:30. Bed checks were to begin then and all of the students' rooms would be taped shut by 11:00. They had a 6:30 AM wake-up call and needed to be on the bus by 7:30.

Sheryl and I reluctantly headed for our luxurious honeymoon suite. When we arrived, there were about twenty motorcycles in the parking lot and the 'No Vacancy' sign was lit. I noticed the girl I had dealt with outside the office door and I said, "Looks like we got that room just in time. No vacancy now."

"We still have a couple of rooms available, but I just put up the sign so we wouldn't be bothered." Then she pointed to the guys in the parking lot and said, "We'll probably need to put some of them in a room, if they get too drunk to drive."

Once in our room, Sheryl took out the new sheets and spread them over the entire bed and pillows. She had bought a second sheet for us to cover up with. She refused to take off her clothes. She was certain there were peep holes in the bedroom and the bathroom and made me check behind one picture for any suspicious holes. I didn't think I would be able to sleep in my clothes, so I took off everything but my underwear and undershirt. Jokingly, I reached my hand under her shirt and said, "How about a little New Year's celebration?" I knew there was no chance for any playing around, but I just thought I'd see what she said.

She grabbed my arm and pushed it away saying, "The only celebration you're going to get is a handshake or possibly a quick kiss."

I gave her a quick kiss and said, "No matter how many New Year's Eves we may spend together, this will probably be the most memorable."

The motorcycles were constantly revved up and there was a lot of yelling, but we got as comfortable as we could, under the circumstances. Sheryl was asleep in a few minutes, and I think I might have even dozed off when all hell broke loose. It sounded like Fireworks Friday at the Royals' Stadium. Sheryl woke up and I jumped out of bed to look out the window. Apparently, the motorcycle riders didn't want to invest in actual fireworks, but they had their own arsenal of guns to celebrate with. There were several minutes of shooting guns in the air and even target practice on street signs and empty beer bottles across the street. It was after 12:30 when we heard the last salvo, followed closely by the roar of motorcycles, which, fortunately, faded into the distance. There was a little bit of yelling and profanity followed immediately by total silence. The silence was almost eerier than the gunfire. It didn't take long before Sheryl was snoring, but I think I slept with one eye open all night.

We were up early the next morning to head to Pasadena. After carefully avoiding the broken glass in the parking lot, we escaped our own version of the Bates Motel with our lives and most of our belongings. Sheryl decided to leave the sheets as our thanks for the comfortable accommodations. Just so they wouldn't try to use the sheets without washing them, I squirted a little bit of sun tan lotion on them. Adam had given us the essential parade information. He told us where the band would begin, where they would march, and where they would end up. I checked the map and we found a place to park near the end of the parade. We cut across Pasadena on foot to Colorado Boulevard and then we headed west to meet up with the band. Adam told us what float they would be following, so we could have a little warning. We weren't too worried about missing the rest of the parade, because, before leaving Independence, we had set our VCR to record the entire parade on one channel and asked friends to record the two other channels. Our reason for coming to California was to watch both of our kids march in the Rose Bowl Parade and we were not going to miss the opportunity to witness as much of them as we could.

As we turned south on Orange Grove, we watched for a while, because that was very near the beginning and we were able to sit right on the curb. We knew the band hadn't passed yet, because we met some parents wearing Blue Springs shirts. We sat and watched for a while and then we heard the unmistakable cadence of the Golden Regiment's drummers. We stood and cheered as they approached. Adam saw us, but he was all business. He didn't smile or acknowledge our presence. However, Katie saw us, smiled, and waved with her fingers, as she was holding the R in BLUE SPRINGS MO. We walked along with the band up to the corner where they turned onto Colorado Boulevard. As they headed down the long straight-away, we hurried along on the sidewalk. We heard another roar from the crowd as the band passed one of the reviewing stands. Most of the parents and chaperones told the band leader where they would be sitting, so at the prearranged moment, Adam and the other Drum Majors signaled the band to play the Wildcat Fight Song. There were enough Blue Springs fans in the stands to scream out the words to the cheer.

Realizing the band members were not accustomed to marching over five miles in winter uniforms, the adults scheduled a parent to drive along parallel to the parade route in a van. In case any of the students fall victim to the heat and exertion, one of the accompanying adults was prepared to help the stricken party to the cool confines of the waiting van. The heavy long-sleeve wool uniforms were ordered for the cold November nights in Missouri, not the hot sunny days in California. There were five students who were unable to complete the rigorous journey. Although those students were embarrassed to be unable to handle the demands of the day, the adults were remarkable at comforting them and making them feel better. The adult sponsors also planned ahead and set up a refreshment center in the park near where the parade was to disband. Once Sheryl and I reached the street where our car was parked, we left the band and headed north. We crossed over to the park and helped the other parents prepare for the bands' arrival. In about thirty minutes, the hot, exhausted troopers staggered off of the street and collapsed in the grass. By the time they hit the ground, most of the students had already removed their hats and jackets. Water was readily available for everyone and after a short recovery period, nearly three hundred starving teenagers engulfed the chow line. After resting, refueling, and cooling down, the resilient teenagers were ready to board the bus for the next adventure.

The band was given free time in the afternoon and we asked Doug Watts, the band director, if we could take Adam and Katie with us. He said we were welcome to spend time with our kids, but they needed to be in the hotel for bed check at 10 PM. Again, Adam opted for staying with his girl friend instead of coming with us, but Katie was happy to join us. We wanted to show her some of the highlights we had already seen and explore some new ones. The itinerary included a close-up view of the Hollywood sign, a view of some celebrities' homes, a journey down Hollywood Boulevard, a chance to buy authentic Hollywood souvenirs, a visit to Graumann's Theater, a quick snack at Johnny Rocket's in Beverly Hills (with the hope of seeing another celebrity), a snapshot of the Post Office at Beverly Hills, 90210 (this was exclusively for Katie), a drive down Santa Monica Boulevard to the Pier, a stroll down Venice Beach, a scenic excursion down Hiway 1, and concluding with the panoramic view along Vista Del Mar. Katie thoroughly enjoyed the activities and all three of us had a great deal of fun together. We only wished Adam could have been with us, too.

While we were helping to set up the food in the park, Sheryl shared our situation at the 'Bates Motel', perhaps with a little embellishment, with one of the other parents. We had known Linda for nearly ten years. Her son, Matt, was a classmate of Adam's in elementary school and we all loved to watch the video of Adam saving Matt from rolling off of the stage during an Earth Day production at William Yates Elementary School. Matt was encased in a large papier-mache globe and, when he lost his balance, he was rolling off the stage, and Adam came to his rescue. Even though Matt would probably have escaped serious injury, the world was headed for certain destruction. Linda said she 'owed the world, or at least, her son's life to Adam' and she insisted we join her in her hotel room for our last night in Los Angeles. She stayed in the same hotel as the band, and shared a room with her mother. She suggested we stay in their two-room suite which had plenty of room for us to sleep. Since we were in no position to find other accommodations, we were very thankful for the offer.

We enjoyed the beautiful weather in Los Angeles, but, all too soon, it was time to return to reality. I stopped for a minute outside the airport terminal and told Sheryl I just wanted to bask in the warmth for another minute before we plunged back into the deep freeze in Missouri. When we returned to Kansas City, I found our '98 Chevy mini-van under about a foot of snow. I received another jolt of reality and for the first time in several days, I worried Chris may have had some trouble. Fortunately, this van was also equipped with all-wheel drive, so navigating the snow-covered roads to Independence was no problem. When we returned home, I contacted Chris and he said everything went smoothly, but he was glad he had the Aerostar to drive after it snowed.

MISS DEPENDABILITY

THE VERY NEXT MORNING, I FELL RIGHT BACK INTO THE PAPER ROUTE RUT LIKE NOTHING HAD EVER INTERRUPTED THE FLOW. I used the throw-book for the first couple of days so I could learn all of the changes. The route was becoming more and more difficult for me to handle physically. My back and my shoulders were constantly bothering me. My right shoulder was hurting so much I couldn't even raise my arm. In addition to having a roller, I had to use someone to sit in the passenger's seat and throw the right side. The additional labor cut into my profit, but I couldn't deal with throwing both sides by myself. After resting my right arm for about three months, I was able to begin throwing the right side again.

The profits from the route were not large enough to justify buying another truck, so I suffered with the same van for a long time. My old '86 Chevy one-ton van had nearly 400,000 miles on it when I called the junk yard to come pick it up. I had replaced the engine once, the differential once, the transmission four times, the radiator twice, the heater core three times, the power steering pump once, the gearbox once, hundreds of tires, countless brakes, several ball joints, and probably every other part on the truck at least once. Just about the only factory part still on the truck was the steering column. Luckily, I was able to make all of the repairs by myself. I probably would have been out of the business much sooner if it had been necessary for me to pay a mechanic to do my repairs.

In addition to the physical hardships, the route was wearing on me mentally. It seemed like every trip was a challenge. I guess I didn't handle it like I did when I was younger. When I was 25, I changed three transmissions in one day. The original one quit working on the morning route and I couldn't afford to buy a new one, so I bought one from a junk yard. The replacement transmission didn't have reverse, so I took it back to the junk yard and exchanged it for third. Finally, just in time for the afternoon route, I had the truck running again.

Maintaining employees was a constant source of frustration. When one helper quit, or managed to get fired, a replacement was frequently hard to find. I depended on friends and relatives when I couldn't find anyone else. Adam helped me by referring friends from school or Boy Scouts. Some worked out and some only lasted a trip or two. David was involved with Adam in both areas. He didn't work for an extended period of time, but was available when I needed him. He lived in our neighborhood, so picking him up and taking him home was convenient. I would have enjoyed having him work for several years, but he was a social butterfly and involved in many activities.

Customer satisfaction was difficult. People expected perfection. Most complaints were insignificant and about issues out of my control. The biggest complaint was always delivery time. Customers didn't realize it, but I felt the same way they did. I always wanted the papers to arrive earlier. Even though I listened to the customers, there was very little I could do about their concerns.

When the Star hassled me about something, I just did what I needed to do in order to appease them. If there was a problem with a customer, I took care of the problem. If there was a problem with my account, I fixed it. If the corporate office decided that it was imperative for all carriers to obtain new subscribers, I knocked on doors and called potential customers until I obtained the target figure.

As I increased in age, I decreased in aggressiveness. I avoided working on the truck until it was an absolute necessity. I took a lot of stuff from helpers I would not have taken when I was 25. It was still necessary to appease the Star, but most of the customer calls were handled by the Star directly. I constantly struggled with one aspect or another of the paper route. Finding helpers was consistently one of my major concerns, followed closely by keeping my van running. I had learned many years ago it was imperative I should have a back-up truck. If my main vehicle didn't start or broke down on the route, I needed another vehicle to deliver the papers. It seemed the break-downs were happening more and more frequently. I needed help so often the tow truck driver was on my speed-dial list.

Adam graduated from high school and began working at Dick's Sporting Goods store. He put in so many hours at Dick's that I couldn't count on him at all to help on the route. Katie worked occasionally, but usually only on Sunday mornings to help throw the right side. If Katie happened to be unavailable, I could usually call her best friend, Mallory. She was David's sister and living in close proximity to my house was a bonus. Even though Mallory was sixteen years old, she was about the size of a ten-year-old. She didn't let her small stature interfere with her work. She listened to me when I gave her instructions on how to throw the heavy paper by holding on to the top of the plastic bag and slinging it like a Frisbee. She usually managed to throw the large Sunday papers over the ditch and up into the yard.

With the difficulty finding help, I lowered my standards. At some point in the past, if a helper wanted a job working for me, he, or she, had to convince me they deserved the job. I had previously used teenagers to help on the route, but more and more parents didn't want to take the risk of having the child work in the middle of the night. Almost all carriers had decided to only hire adults as helpers. Most of the adults willing to work during the middle of the night for a couple of hours were not highly qualified individuals. Stuffy had not worked for me for a few years, but he had worked for several others carriers. There were several people who were available to work and regularly hung out at the substation waiting to see if anyone needed helpers. There was one married couple who worked for several carriers, but not for me. It seemed like when they were looking for a job, I had dependable help, and when I needed help, they were working for someone else.

The husband had a debilitating skin disease and was unable to work at a regular job. The wife was legally blind and unable to work at most jobs. They were both drawing Social Security, so they couldn't make too much money or they would lose their Social Security. One morning, I noticed Chris was sitting at the desk in the substation and Donna was not there. I asked him if he missed his ride and he said Donna was helping another carrier, but he didn't have anyone to work for. It looked like my current helper was not going to show up, so I asked him if he wanted to help me out. He said he never turned down a chance to make some extra money, but he didn't know if he would be able to roll fast enough to make me happy. I told him there was only one way to find out, so he jumped in and started to roll. I wasn't certain if he would be able to roll fast enough, so I went to Quik-Trip first. I went in to get something to eat and drink and he stayed in the truck to roll. After just a few minutes, I went back out to the van and when I opened the door, a bunch of papers fell out. I told him when the paper bin in front was full, he should start putting papers under the table in the back. He started putting papers in the back, but he didn't slow down. He managed to keep me in papers, but he was not the fastest roller I had ever employed. He worked hard and wasn't lazy. Either Chris or Donna worked for me for about three years. Sometimes Chris would work, and sometimes Donna would work. If neither had other employment, they both worked for me. I paid them the same whether one or both worked, but it was a shorter, easier trip if they worked together. They probably would have still been working for me, but they got a better offer from another carrier. I paid more than most carriers, because I had one of the biggest routes. It was a choice route. I delivered over a thousand papers in less than two hours.

When they left me, I nearly gave up the route. My arms, shoulders, and back were not in any kind of condition to load, roll, and throw all of those papers. I used some family members to help out for a while and then one of the other carriers said he knew of a girl looking for full-time employment. He said his route was too small and he could only use her three or four days a week and he couldn't afford to pay her very much, but she was a good worker and very dependable. When I talked to her on the phone, I told her I wanted someone who would be willing to work seven days a week. I explained I delivered over a thousand papers and she said she had never rolled that many before, but she thought she could handle it. She worked full-time at O'Reilly's but wanted a night job, so she could make more money. She worked five, and sometimes six, days a week for O'Reilly's from 8AM to 5PM. I didn't think she would last long working at both jobs. I just hoped she would prefer working a couple of hours during the night, to eight hours a day.

Aimee's first trip was on a Sunday morning. I had never started a helper on a Sunday before, but I didn't have a choice. Adam was available to help so I thought if she had any trouble rolling her share of papers, he could pick up the slack. I told him ahead of time our objective was to finish the route as soon as possible. If that meant he had to roll some of her papers, then I expected him to do it without complaining. The morning went flawlessly. I noticed Adam taking some papers from Aimee's side to roll, but I couldn't tell how many. Aimee hardly said a word, but consistently did her job. Most of the helpers that have worked for me have enjoyed chatting while on the route, except for Stuffy, who couldn't stay awake to chat. She had a very serious expression on her face and I thought perhaps, she might have been angry. When we finished the route, I told her she had done a great job and the daily trips would be a breeze compared to Sunday. She apologized for not being able to roll all of her own papers because she was not accustomed to my set-up. Adam told me later he only rolled one of her bundles.

Aimee was a very sweet girl and she was about the same age as Katie. She shared an apartment with another girl. She didn't have a car, so I had to drive to her apartment everyday to pick her up for the route. She didn't live too far away, so I didn't really mind. I had driven much further for less qualified help. During her first week, she gradually rolled faster and faster. After only a couple of weeks, she bought a car. It wasn't very dependable transportation, but she usually made it to my house. She became one of the best helpers I ever had. She told me it took her a little time to get accustomed to my set-up in the truck. She had never worked with a table and it was much more convenient than balancing the papers on her lap.

Every morning when I woke up, I called the Star to see how the papers were running. As soon as our load was close to leaving the Star, I called Aimee to tell her to get up and head to my house. She was very consistent. It took her about 12 to 15 minutes from the phone call until she parked in front of my house. She still didn't have much to say, but when I did talk to her, she said she really liked working on the paper route, but she hated working at O'Reilly's. She didn't work behind the counter. Her job was to drive a little pick-up truck from her retail store to the main warehouse to pick up parts. I hoped she would hate working at O'Reilly's enough to quit and just work for me, but she said she needed the money. I called her every morning around

2:30 AM and she was usually back to her apartment by 5:00. Then after a short nap, she had to get up and be at O'Reilly's by 8 AM. Frequently, she even held down a third job. She worked hard, was always looking for a way to make more money and rarely turned down any opportunity for employment.

The trips on the paper route were surprisingly quiet. Sheryl always said I could carry on a conversation for hours with a blank wall, but Aimee was certainly a challenge. I tried to find topics that might be of interest to her, but her responses were minimal and usually mono-syllabic. There were occasions when I could actually carry on a conversation with her, but it was normally at the end of the route when she was getting out of the truck. When I asked her about her silence, she said I shouldn't take it personally. She said she was just very tired and needed to concentrate on getting her job done. I know how difficult it can be to work seven days a week, so I offered to give her a day off once in a while. She said she preferred to work everyday. She was afraid if she took a day off, it would be too difficult to get up after sleeping all night.

People have repeatedly asked me how I could possibly work for years at a time without taking a day off. I have always told them the same thing. Going on the paper route is not really like going to work. It's more like eating or sleeping. I just do it everyday without thinking about it. My dad said that's the way it was on the farm. Everyday, you get up, milk the cows, collect the eggs, feed the animals, do the chores, milk the cows, and go to bed. It might have been different if it took eight hours to deliver all of the papers, but since it only took about 2-3 hours, I never really felt like I went to 'work'. I just drove around in the van chatting with the helpers as I threw the papers. It never seemed like a job. I was glad Aimee felt the same way.

It was so refreshing to have a helper who was willing to be there with me everyday, no matter how hot or cold, no matter how wet or dry, no matter how late or early. However, when the papers were about four hours late one morning, Aimee did say she might need to call her boss at O'Reilly's to tell him she would be a little late. I treated Aimee the same way I would have treated Katie. She was like a second daughter to me. I tried to make her as comfortable as possible. During the winter, when the temperature dropped below freezing, I turned on the propane heater I had installed in the back of the van. I kept a second bottle of propane at home in case the bottle in the van ran empty. Aimee never complained about being cold, so I had to ask her if she wanted me to light the heater. Since I threw both sides out of the front of the van, both front windows were rolled down. That created a strong draft of very cold air. In order to protect her as much as possible, I hung a quilt from the ceiling directly in front of her. It blocked most of the frigid blast and the heater supplied warm air from the back of the truck. I was constantly concerned about her comfort, but when I asked her, she reassured me she was fine.

The occasions were increasingly more frequent when the van broke down. Sometimes, if it was a minor problem, like a flat tire or overheating, I could fix the trouble in a few minutes and we would be on our way. I always carried a hydraulic jack, a spare tire, a gallon of coolant, a can of brake fluid, a can of steering fluid, a couple of quarts of oil, a roll of bailing wire, and some duct tape with me in the truck. If it happened to be a major breakdown, I would call Sheryl first, so she could get up and drive out to pick me up. If I needed a tow truck, that would be my second call. During all of the commotion, Aimee never said a word, she just kept rolling papers. If it was necessary to tow my truck home, then she rode with me and when we arrived at my house, she got back in the truck and started rolling while I moved the rolled papers from the van into my back-up vehicle. When she finished rolling, she could get in her car and go home.

Over the years I had used nearly a thousand helpers. Some of them only worked for one trip. Adam and Brian worked off and on for twenty years. The ones who couldn't handle the work or the hours didn't last very long. There were those who could handle the job and the hours, but I just couldn't handle them. Aimee was as near as I could possibly get to having a perfect helper. She had become a very fast, consistent roller. She never complained about anything. Even when she was too sick to go to work at O'Reilly's, she came to work for me, because she knew I was counting on her. If I had known she was sick, I would have made her take the day off, but she didn't tell me until a few days later. She was certainly the most dependable helper I had ever used. Whenever I interviewed a potential helper, I stressed the importance of dependability. As long as my helper showed up for work, I could deal with just about anything else. There were a few occasions when I had to take Scott home because he was too drunk to work. I had to take Carrie, Brian's girl friend, home a few times because she got car-sick every trip she worked. But Aimee missed very few trips.

During the nearly four years Aimee helped me, there were only three occasions when she didn't work. After only working for about three months, she asked me if it would be okay for her to take off a trip, because she had promised a friend that they would have a birthday party. I wanted her to know she could certainly take a day off if she wanted, and if I could know in advance, so much the better. It was a Saturday morning, so Adam was able to help and the route was handled without a problem. Aimee would have probably been better off if she had worked. The birthday party got a little out of hand and Aimee ended up in jail. Apparently, one of the guys at the party had become very obnoxious and Aimee warned him to shut up. He didn't shut up, so she punched him. The police were called and everyone at the party received a free night's lodgings at the local lockup. Most of her family and friends didn't believe me when I told them Aimee never said a word on the paper route. They all said she was very talkative and outgoing.

Aimee didn't even ask for another day off. She worked every day without a break. There were times she came on the route and didn't feel good, but she never requested a sick day. There were several occasions I felt guilty for having her work. She came on the route, no matter how she felt. When I recommended she stay home and try to recover for a day or two, she just said, "If I stay home, I won't feel any better, but if I work, at least, I'll make some money."

She dated a guy from O'Reilly's for quite a while. She said they decided to get married, but she didn't tell me when. One morning after the route, when she was getting out of the truck, she mentioned she and Mike Jones had gotten married the previous weekend. I scolded her for not telling me because Sheryl and I would have loved to attend and I would have given her the next morning off. She said she appreciated the thought but she needed the money. The next day, I gave her a congratulatory card with a gift in it. I gave her a bonus every year for Christmas, but much to my embarrassment, she always had a gift card for each member of my family. She really was like one of our family.

After a few months, Aimee told me she was pregnant. On the outside, I bubbled with excitement for her new experience. On the inside, I worried she would probably quit. I didn't know how I could possibly run the route without her. I certainly did not look forward to trying to find a replacement. Not only was she an excellent helper and unfailingly dependable, but I considered her to be a close friend. I didn't mention the possibility that she might have to quit when she had a small baby to care for.

During the next few weeks, we dealt with morning sickness. The first time she had nausea, she said she had eaten Mexican food for dinner. When the nausea returned the next morning, I told her she was probably experiencing morning sickness. On Sheryl's advice, I took some saltine crackers and 7-up on the route each morning. Nothing really seemed to help, so I just kept a stock of peppermints in the van. After the nausea, she liked to have the peppermint to suck on to get the bad taste out of her mouth. Every morning for about three months, Aimee was nauseous and generally threw up. Even though she normally had some warning and I was able to stop the truck for her, there was visible evidence on the side of the truck right beneath her window. Going by the car wash became a normal stop for me after the route. I was still fearful she was going to quit. Why would she continue to work everyday knowing she was going to get sick? One morning after she had been sick, I asked her if she was going to be okay, she replied, "I'll be fine when this stupid morning sickness stops. I just feel bad for causing a problem with the paper route."

I reassured her that the paper route would be just fine and she had nothing to feel sorry about. I was only concerned about her health and her pregnancy. I hesitated to suggest quitting the route, but I thought it might be the best thing for her. With great apprehension, I suggested, "Do you think you might be better off not working on the paper route?"

I looked at her in the mirror and she actually stopped rolling and looked at me. Her voice seemed to quiver a little when she said, "Don't you want me on the route?"

I pulled the truck over to the side of the road and put the transmission in Park. I turned around and looked at her and said, "Aimee, let me make this clear. The last thing I want is for you to quit. I don't know how I could run the route without you. If you quit, I'll probably have to quit, too, but the most important thing right now is your health and the health of your baby. If you feel that you need to quit, I'll understand."

She started to cry when she said, "I really like working with you on the paper route. I don't want to quit. I think of you and Sheryl and Katie and Adam as my family. I appreciate you putting up with all my morning sickness and if you don't mind, I'd like to keep working."

I told her, "Aimee, you can work for me as long as you want. If you decide you must quit some day, I'll deal with it."

No more was ever said about quitting. She continued with the morning sickness for about three months, and I drove the cleanest truck in the substation. She had no trouble handling her responsibilities on the route. Her chair was bolted to the floor, so it became necessary to move it back a few inches from the table as her tummy grew. She still helped stack the bundles of papers everyday. She still rolled all of the papers at a very consistent pace, so I never had to slow down. If she experienced any problems with the job expectations, she didn't tell me. She just, very quietly, accomplished the task.

The Thanksgiving Day paper had historically been quite large. Most retail businesses placed ads in the paper for, what had become known as, Black Friday. The day after Thanksgiving was the busiest shopping day of the year. Advertisers wanted to put their ads in the hands of the buying public on Thursday so the bargain hunters, Sheryl heading the line, could map out their strategy for shopping on Friday. I had always hated the Thanksgiving Day paper. Even though the Star published a paper 365 days a year, most holiday papers were small because most stores were closed. Since the paper was generally the same size, or bigger than a Sunday paper, I always needed additional help on the route. Adam had worked just about every Thanksgiving since he was five years old.

Aimee was capable of handling most Sunday papers on her own, but since Dick's was going to be closed on Thanksgiving Day, I asked Adam to help out rolling. Katie said she would go along to help throw the right side. The pregnancy didn't seem to slow Aimee down. She was still able to roll faster than I could throw on a daily trip and, normally, she had no problem keeping me stocked with papers on Sunday. However, that day, Aimee seemed to be rolling slower than usual. I asked her if she was feeling okay and she said her stomach was hurting. She had not been bothered with morning sickness for several months, but she thought she must have eaten something that didn't digest well. Luckily, Adam was able to take up the slack, and help her roll her papers. Normally, they both roll about five hundred papers each. Adam said he rolled nearly seven hundred and Aimee only rolled about three hundred. When she got out of the truck, I told her she should probably go to the hospital and check to make certain there was no problem with the baby. She said she would go home and go to bed, but if her stomach was still hurting when she got up, then she would go to the hospital.

Sheryl was up early preparing something to take to her sister Terry's for dinner. Since we had the most room to entertain, we frequently had two family celebrations for Thanksgiving and two family celebrations for Christmas at our house. Generally, Sheryl's side of the family arrived around eleven or twelve for the big holiday dinner at noon and they would leave around four, which gave us time to run the dish washer, put away the left-overs from the noon meal, and put out the food for the Morrison side of the family. My family members started to arrive around five and we were ready to eat the big holiday meal by six. All together, we generally served about twenty-five at noon and about thirty at six. Even though we continued that plan for Christmas, we got a break for Thanksgiving. We traveled to Terry's house for Thanksgiving dinner at noon and then on to my brother, Bill's, house for another big dinner at six.

We were just finishing our dinner at Terry's house when I got a call from the Medical Center in Independence. I knew it must be Aimee and I prayed there was no problem with her pregnancy. The person on the phone was Ashley, Aimee's sister. She said Aimee had continued to have pain in her abdominal area, so they took her to the hospital to be checked out. Apparently, her appendix was inflamed and she was having surgery to have it removed. Six months pregnant with an inflamed appendix and she still worked all of the way around the route without complaining. She just felt a little stomach ache. Ashley reassured me everything with the pregnancy was okay, but she didn't know when Aimee would be able to work again. I made a few phone calls and managed to get the route covered for the rest of the weekend, but I was a little bit concerned about Sunday. Adam said he could work, but he had to go in to Dick's at noon. Katie said she could go along and Sheryl said we might as well make it a family affair and she would go, too. The plan was for Adam and Katie to start out rolling while I threw the left side and Sheryl threw the right side. If there was a problem with them rolling too slowly, I would help roll papers while Sheryl drove and threw the left side.

Brian and I managed to get around the route without any trouble on Friday morning. He planned to help me on Saturday morning, also. About noon on Friday, I received a call from Aimee. She said she was home and ready to work on Saturday. I couldn't believe she wanted to work so soon after surgery. I appreciated her dedication, but I really thought she should take off another day. I told her I already had Saturday covered with Brian, but if she felt okay, she could help out on Sunday. She said she would probably be a little sore, but she wanted to work. She had some pain pills and they relieved most of the discomfort. When I informed the family they were off the hook for Sunday, they were all very happy, but couldn't believe Aimee was willing to work. Adam said he would leave his phone on the nightstand just in case I needed help. Sheryl was already planning to go along to help throw, but if Aimee needed any additional help, she would be happy to help her. The Sunday paper was fairly small because most of the ads had been in the Thursday paper. Aimee managed to keep up just fine. I stopped the truck a couple of times to move bundles up for her, because she was having trouble reaching them and pulling them forward.

If anyone could possibly have any doubt about Aimee's dedication to me and the paper route, that question would be answered in a couple of months. I had been concerned she might quit during her pregnancy, but she squelched that apprehension decisively. My next area of anxiety would come after the baby was born. How could she possibly work at O'Reilly's, take care of a new baby, and continue to help on the paper route? As the due date approached, I asked her what her plans might be. Her mother-in-law was going to stay with her for a few weeks after the baby was born. Grandma Jones was anxiously looking forward to having a new grandchild and said she would be thrilled to do whatever she could to help out Mike and Aimee.

Aimee could not have planned the birth any better if she controlled it. We just finished the Sunday morning deliveries when she said she had felt some small contractions while on the route, but she didn't want to tell me, because she was afraid I would worry. She said the contractions may not mean anything, but she would let me know if she needed to go to the hospital. I knew we were rapidly approaching her due date, so I had already made plans for Brian and Adam to fill in during Aimee's absence. Later in the afternoon, I received the call saying Aimee had given birth to a very healthy boy. She had already told me if she had a boy, they were going to name him Michael after his daddy. If she had a girl, they were going to name her either Abigail (and call her Abby) or Addison (and call her Addy). Aimee had three sisters and their names were Ambra, April, and Alexa.

When Aimee had her appendectomy, she took off work for two days. When she gave birth, Aimee needed a full four days until she called me and asked me if she could come back to work. I told her again, I appreciated her dedication, but I felt she should really take off for a full week. I didn't want her to work on Sunday, so I told her if she felt up to it, she could start helping again on Monday. She was ready, willing, and able to resume her paper route activities just one week after giving birth.

Being a new mother didn't mix well with two jobs. It wasn't very long until Aimee started to mention she hardly ever saw her son. She was very appreciative of her mother-in-law, but she wanted to be with Michael more than just a couple of hours in the evening. Again, I thought she might be wanting to quit the paper route, but she quickly reassured me she loved working on the route because it was easy and she only needed to be away from home for a couple of hours during the night while he was sleeping. Aimee didn't like working at O'Reilly's but she needed the money and the insurance because she was already planning the next addition to their family

BIRTHS: ABIGAIL JONES

FINANCIALLY, AIMEE AND MIKE FELT THEY COULD AFFORD ANOTHER CHILD. They were renting a duplex, but constantly scoured the classified ads looking for a house to buy. They were hoping to find a small home that needed some fixing up. Mike and his dad were capable of handling most of the required repairs. Their duplex was costing them as much as a mortgage would cost. With Aimee's indefatigable drive, she always found a way to supply more than her share of necessary income.

The income from the paper route was dwindling. The costs of running the route were skyrocketing. Fuel prices topped $3.00 a gallon and the petroleum based plastic bag prices had more than tripled. With no rate increase from the corporate office, my net income was reduced by more than half. The paper route had always paid the bills, but I needed more and more help from Sheryl. Fortunately, her income was sufficient to make up for most of my losses. There were many concerns with operating the paper route, but the income had always been consistent.

I had not taken a day off of the paper route for sickness in over fifty years. I took a thousand milligrams of Vitamin C every day to help prevent catching a cold and I took four hundred milligrams of Ibuprofen to keep my arms from falling off. There were definitely days I would have called in sick, if I could, but I didn't have anyone to call. When I had a cold, I just went on the route anyway. If I happened to have stomach issues, I just made several rush trips to the nearest bathroom. I hadn't seen a doctor in over thirty years and was blessed with overall good health, but my body was feeling the strain of fifty years times 365 days a year, or nearly twenty thousand days in a row without a day off due to sickness.

The constant stress on the muscles and bones had taken a toll on my body. My arms had thrown over thirty million papers. My back had lifted around twenty million pounds. On Sunday morning, May 6, 2007, my left arm reached its limit. The paper was one of the biggest of the year because of the Mother's Day ads. I almost completed the day's deliveries when I felt a sharp pain in my left shoulder. There was no way I could throw one more paper with my left arm. I pushed a few papers out of the left window with my right hand, but depended on Sheryl to throw the rest for that trip. I knew I was not going to be able to throw the next day, so I paid Brian to drive and throw the left side while I threw the right side. By the time I paid Aimee and Brian, I wasn't left with much of a profit.

Aimee never let me down. She continued to work every day without any thought of taking a day off. She quit working at O'Reilly's so she could spend more time at home with her new baby. With her new found free time, Aimee didn't need as much help from her mother-in-law. After helping me on the route, Aimee was able to go home and get a nap before her husband left for work. She loved spending the time with Michael and watching him grow.

She had a difficult time sitting around the house, so after only a couple of months, she began to look for another job. A friend told her the federal government was hiring people at their Lee's Summit office. She applied for the job and was hired to work three nights a week, Thursday-Saturday, from 4PM-2AM. She was able to get to my house by 2:30 to start the route. The new job not only paid well but offered great insurance coverage. Perhaps I was a little paranoid, but again, I worried she might quit. When I confronted her with my concern, she assured me she would not quit helping me.

The new job worked out perfectly with the route. I called Aimee every day as usual, except on Friday, Saturday, and Sunday. On those days, she came straight from work to my house. If the papers happened to run early, I went to pick them up with Brian. On a couple of occasions, when the papers were about an hour early, Brian drove and threw the left side while I rolled and threw the right side until Aimee arrived.

Everything was going along smoothly until one morning she was nauseous. She said she had eaten tacos for dinner the night before and it had apparently upset her stomach. I asked her if there was any possibility it could be morning sickness and she reassured me there was no chance. I assumed from her certainty she knew what she was talking about. The nausea wasn't consistent or long-lasting so we both figured the tacos were the problem.

About three months later, when we were heading back to my house, after Aimee had finished rolling the papers, she said she had something she needed to tell me. Those were very scary words. Immediately, I assumed she was going to quit. It didn't take long for her to squelch that fear.

She spoke slowly, "You know I told you I was nursing Michael. My sister told me you can't get pregnant while nursing a baby. She was wrong. A couple of weeks ago, I felt some weird fluttering in my stomach. It felt the same as it did when I felt Michael move for the first time. When it didn't stop, I decided to go to the doctor. She confirmed I am pregnant."

"Congratulations." The feelings were sincere but my sentiment was obviously not exuberant. "How far along are you?"

"The doctor wasn't certain, but thought about 5-6 months, around Thanksgiving, but don't worry, I won't quit."

I appreciated her determination, but silently wondered how she could manage to continue working on the route with two small babies. Her dedication to me and the route never ceased to amaze me. If it were humanly possible, Aimee would do it.

There were four main concerns with operating a paper route—income, help, vehicle, and health. Since the income from the route had always been consistent, finances had not been a major concern. Due to the increasing costs of operations and the lack of increase in income, the business was not meeting my expectations. The second concern was a dependable helper. Aimee virtually eliminated that concern. The third was having a dependable truck. Even though my old van was on life-support, I was generally successful keeping it on the road. The fourth concern was good health. My health was something I had taken for granted. Whether I was feeling great or in excruciating pain, I had to go on the paper route.

The first concern to cause a major problem was reduced income from the route. My net income decreased by over fifty per cent. The route paid the mortgage and the utilities, but that was about all. I always depended on the corporate office to increase my rate to offset expenses, but there had been no financial help in over seven years.

The second concern to cause a severe problem was my truck. The truck had over 400,000 miles on it and still managed to start every morning. I was certain I could fix any problem that might arise. I thought I could trust my van, even though it was leaking oil and transmission fluid. It had been leaking power steering fluid, until I replaced the steering gear box. The radiator had been leaking, until I replaced it.

On an otherwise uneventful morning, we finished the route and I turned on Lee's Summit Road to head home. The van had finished its responsibilities for the day, but couldn't muster enough strength to make the trip home. The death was sudden. Even though it had been losing oil for nearly a year, I checked the oil level daily and constantly monitored the oil pressure. The cause of death was officially listed as a 'thrown rod', but I'm sure it was just old age. I couldn't bear to send it to the junk yard, so I donated it to a friend who said he would fix it up and just use it to take people to church on Sunday. My only recourse was to drive my back-up vehicle on a daily basis.

The third concern was my health. I had never missed a trip for illness and I was certain I could trust my body to stand the strain, but it became necessary to go to the doctor to have my left shoulder checked out. Since I hadn't seen a doctor for over thirty years, he thought I should have a general physical – and, as it turned out, he was right. He prodded and poked just about every part of my body, and what he couldn't reach he used technology to see. Medical procedures have become a great deal more specialized than when I last visited a doctor. This doctor could tell my blood pressure was a little high and my cholesterol was a little high, but he said he could control those problems with some medication. He could see my back was injured in the sciatic area, but he said it would take a rather serious surgery to fix it. He could see my shoulder was injured, but he wanted me to get an MRI just to evaluate the extent of the injury. He could see there was blood in my stool and he referred me to another doctor to get a colonoscopy. He also discovered there were hard spots in my prostate gland and he referred me to yet another doctor for evaluation.

The MRI was the next stop on my medical journey. My assignment was to lie perfectly still for forty-five minutes while this huge camera that sounded like a locomotive took pictures of the inside of my shoulder. The results were sent to my family doctor, who called me to tell me he was referring me to another specialist to evaluate my shoulder. I could see this was destined to become a big circus, so I started keeping a very precise journal.

The first specialist I visited was the orthopedic specialist. He said the MRI showed a great deal of damage to the rotator cuff in my left shoulder. He explained the cuff was made up of several sets of tendons connecting the muscles to the bones. Two of my tendons were partially torn and one was totally severed. The only way of regaining full use of my left arm was to have surgery. He prescribed pain pills and a non-steroidal anti inflammatory drug. The drugs covered up the pain but I felt certain surgery was inevitable.

The next specialist I visited was the gastroenterologist. He was to perform the colonoscopy. The colonoscopy was the easy part. I was knocked out with anesthesia, so I didn't feel a thing. The difficult part was the preparation. The doctor sent me a very explicit list of directions to follow precisely before the colonoscopy.

In short, the directions told me to purchase a bowel-loosening aid. I'm not going to give the name of the product because I'm afraid it could fall into enemy hands and be used against us as a means of chemical warfare. I think the prescribed dose was one tablespoon in 24 hours, but my doctor's instructions informed me I was to drink about five gallons in two hours. Ask anyone who has had a colonoscopy and they will certainly echo my words when I say the inside of the colon had to be spotless. The only comparison I could think of was a story my dad once told me about flushing a car's radiator. 'Put a hose in the top. Open the valve on the bottom. Turn the water on full force and when the water comes out as clean as when it goes in, the radiator is clean.' I can tell you for a fact my radiator was clean.

On the day of the colonoscopy, the medical staff required another person pick you up, because it's unsafe to drive after the anesthesia. As soon as the procedure was completed, the doctor usually made an appearance to relate any pertinent information. When I began to wake up, the nurse asked if someone was coming to pick me up. I told her my son should be there any minute, but they could call him if they wanted to be sure. I had told him to pick me up by 10:30 and it was only a little after 10. I was a little concerned as to why the procedure didn't take as long as they had expected.

Shortly after Adam arrived, the doctor came into my room. He said he hadn't been able to complete the colonoscopy because he encountered an obstruction. He showed me full-color pictures of the obstruction and described it as a donut-shaped lesion. Apparently the hole in the center was too small for his scope to pass through. He took a biopsy of the lesion to ascertain if it was cancerous. He would contact me as soon as he received the results.

My mind instantly flashed back to my dad. He had a tumor in his colon that had grown too large and split through the walls. The tumor in my colon was donut-shaped and grew from the outside, inward. If the opening in the center was too small for his scope to pass through, then how could waste pass through? Suddenly, I became afraid to go to the bathroom. What if the waste passing through the center of the tumor pushed it outward and ripped the walls of my colon? What if it was already ripped? Even though the doctor told me I could eat normally, I put myself on a liquid-only diet. Every little discomfort I felt in my abdominal area grabbed my attention.

The very next day, I visited was the urologist. He said my prostate was slightly enlarged and contained hard nodules, which could be cancerous, or they could be calcium deposits, but he wanted to do a prostate ultrasound and biopsy just to be sure. The ultrasound was not a big deal, but the biopsy was painful. The doctor used a highly sophisticated instrument to cut out twelve sections of my prostate gland. Even though he deadened the area, it still felt, and sounded, like he was shooting darts into my prostate. He explained he would have the results in a week.

Life as I knew it had been turned upside down. Before I visited my family doctor, I felt fine. I knew I had a bad back and a sore shoulder, but I assumed both problems could be solved with some type of medication. Thanks to the advances in modern medical technology, I now knew I was walking around with a donut-shaped tumor about the size of a tennis ball in my colon, a group of hard deposits which could be cancerous in my prostate gland, a partially pinched sciatic nerve in my back, and a torn rotator cuff.

With the extent of my medical problems still to be determined, I yearned for stability. I needed something dependable and unchanging in my life. Sleep became very difficult. I generally had to rely on medication for restful sleep.

Food turned into my enemy. I saw every morsel of food as potentially pushing my tumor outward causing my death. Sex was not an option because Sheryl was afraid it would hurt me. What else was there? Any guy will tell you there are only three things that really matter in life--sleep, food, and sex. With nothing else to count on, I again turned to the paper route. The route never changed. I placed my flawed body in my back-up truck and went to work. I thanked God for giving me something I could depend on. I knew Aimee would be in front of my house in about three minutes and the papers would arrive at the substation in about fifteen. There was some certainty in my life.

I didn't share my medical situation with Aimee because I didn't want to upset her. Besides, I didn't actually know if I had cancer. The medication allowed me to continue throwing both sides of the route with limited pain. When she inquired about my medical visits, I just told her the doctors were performing tests.

When she finished rolling the papers and was waiting to get back to my house, she asked, "Do you think you will be able to keep working on the route?"

I thought about the irony of the question. How many times had I asked her the same question? I smiled and said, "As long as I don't have to check-in to the hospital, I'll be on the route."

"Why would you need to go to the hospital?" There was fear in her voice.

I tried to reassure her without telling the whole truth. "I don't know if I will have to go to the hospital or not. If the doctors find something in all of the tests that requires surgery, then I will probably need to have it done. Unless it is life-threatening, I will just take medication. If I'm in the hospital, Brian will probably drive the route for me. He said he could handle the throws as long as he can count on you to do the rolling."

Then she pulled the rug out from under me. "I think I'm going to have to quit."

I am not often at a loss for words, but I was speechless. She could see the surprise on my face and her eyes became glassy. I stopped in front of my house to let her out.

"How much longer are you going to be able to keep working on the route?"

"Mike and I have talked about it a lot and I think I can work up until the baby is born…but…then…I think I'll have to quit. Mike's mother can't help this time and we can't afford to pay for day care. I love helping you on the route and I don't want to quit, but I don't have any choice. I'm sorry. I know you're counting on me."

That was ball four. Ball one, my income. Ball two, my truck. Ball three, my health. Ball four, my helper. It was time for me to take a walk.

Those were the longest seven days of my life. One doctor had taken a sample of the tumor in my colon and another doctor had taken a sample of my prostate to find out if I had cancer. I tried to take my mind off of the potential result, but the thought of cancer permeated every second. For most of my life, the route was my only stability. I needed to accept the fact that it was going to change, also. Aimee was going to leave me. How would I ever find anyone to replace her? If I had cancer, how would I handle it? Could I still run the route? Would I have to take chemo and radiation? How long would I live? My life was full of questions without answers.

I had an appointment with the urologist to discuss the results of the biopsy. He told me the tests had all come back negative and the hard spots in my prostate gland were merely calcium deposits. None of the samples taken were cancerous or even pre-cancerous. If I wanted some medication to reduce the size of my prostate, he would prescribe it, but the side effects could be worse than the problem. He said to make an appointment to see him in one year. Otherwise, I could continue my job as usual.

Aimee was nearing her delivery time and she constantly asked if I had made arrangements for someone to take her place. I hadn't found anyone and I didn't even know if I was going to be able to continue without her. Adam said he would work as much as possible around his schedule at Dick's. Katie had graduated from Northwest Missouri State with a Bachelor's Degree in Elementary Education. She said she would be able to help out until she received a teaching contract. I had talked with Brian and he said he would be able to work two or three mornings a week.

My journey appeared to be coming to an end. I delivered the Star for over fifty years. The paper route had taken me over three million miles, but never more than twenty miles from home. I used nearly a thousand different helpers, but never more than four or five on any one trip. I delivered over thirty million newspapers to more than ten thousand different people, but most of them didn't even know my name.

The route had been the constant in my life. When everything else was uncertain, I always depended on the paper route. But now it let me down. My truck let me down. My help let me down. My body let me down. I always knew someday I would give up the route. Through the good times and the difficult times, the route was my anchor. I figured Sheryl and I would sit down and thrash out the pros and cons of continuing in the business and after a great deal of discussion we would arrive at the agonizing decision to give up this huge part of my entire life. But when all the circumstances came together as they did, it felt like there was no other decision I could make. When I gave notice to the Star, you might think they would throw a big retirement party for me and maybe even give me a gold watch, but they didn't care. I didn't even receive a pat on the back or a thank you.

A few short days before my last day on the route, Aimee went to the hospital and gave birth to a healthy baby girl. Adam helped me on the paper route for the few days I had left. On my way to visit Aimee at the hospital, I received a call from the doctor who had performed the colonoscopy. He told me the lesion in my colon was cancer and recommended I see a surgeon.

In the nursery, I met Aimee's new daughter. Her name was Abigail Marie Jones. The constant in my life came full circle that day. My newspaper delivery journey began with the death and ended with the birth of Abigail Jones.

ACKNOWLEDGEMENT

THIS ACKNOWLEDGEMENT GIVES ME THE OPPORTUNITY TO THANK AND GIVE MENTION TO ALL OF THE TRIBUTARIES THAT HAVE CONTRIBUTED TO THE PRODUCTION OF THIS OCEAN THAT I CALL THE STAR TRUCK. The first person I must mention is Grandmother Parrish. She had faith in me when I didn't deserve it. If I have come close to living up to her expectations in this book, I would consider myself blessed.

The next person I must mention is my English Literature teacher at William Chrisman High School, Dorothy Bierbaum. She made me realize that authors are just people. She frequently referred to William Shakespeare as 'old Willy'. She was the first person, other than family members, who advised me to 'give writing a try'.

In order to have a book, there has to be a story. The Kansas City Star supplied me with the story. I am extremely grateful for the support and friendship I received from the Circulation Department. From the Heads of Circulation, Wilbur Reagan, Del Campbell, Lisa Parks, Roger Minor, and Chris Hammontree to the supporting staff of Bud Guarino, Dermot Hayes, and Ken Batrick, I have always maintained a great relationship with the Corporate Office and I greatly appreciate their help and support in making this book possible. At the local substation, there have been many zone managers, but I could not have lasted as long as I did without the support of Susan Kirwin and Chris Cronk. The district managers are too numerous to mention, but the one who helped me the most was Doug Ingram.

At one point, it was my goal to dedicate this book to all of my former employees. However, there have been over a thousand, so for the sake of brevity I want to take this opportunity to say 'Thank You' to everyone that has worked for me. I want to recognize a few helpers who stayed with me for the long haul. Brian Kibler never thought when he started working when he was 14, he would still be helping me twenty-five years later. James Champ put in many years helping me and is the only helper, besides my son, who actually drove the route for me. Scott Trosper only worked for me for about five years, but he was the answer to a prayer when I needed him. Bill Gardner, David Gardner, and Bobby Jo Gardner (Bill's daughter), managed to work as a team or individually to help me for many years. So, to all of my helpers, let me reiterate, 'Thank You'. I, literally, could not have survived without you.

I started working on this book about twenty years ago. Whenever I mentioned it to Jane Llewellen or Carolyn Smith, their exuberance was intoxicating. They couldn't wait for me to finish it. When I finally concluded the writing, I gave each of them a copy of the rough draft. Their feedback was more positive than it should have been, but greatly appreciated. I know their encouragement kept me going when I wanted to stop. I will love you both til the Sun turns cold.

When my arm gave out, I turned to doctors for help. Dr. Gregg Klosener discovered my colon cancer and directed me to Dr. Christopher Daggett who performed surgery. I thank God for both of them and believe that He guided Dr. Daggett's hand and gave me another shot at life. It was this undeserved second chance that compelled me to complete the book.

Since I was a teenager I have known I wanted to write, but it wasn't until my battle with cancer that the possibility became real to me. After giving up the paper route and dealing with multiple health issues, I found myself reflecting on how my life impacted others and how they impacted me. I thought a paper man's life might be a point of interest, or even a curiosity, to many people. I knew many experiences in my life as a paper man definitely fell out of the range of normal and others might enjoy getting to know the man behind the title. That's when I realized I had a story to tell. A speech teacher once told me the most important facet of communication was the message. I disagreed with her and told her I believed the most important facet was the receiver. No matter how important a message may be, without someone to receive the message, it is pointless. That's where you, the reader, come in. No matter who you are or where you are or when you read this account, you have completed the communication loop. By reading these words you have given them significance. You have my eternal gratitude.

My time on the paper route would probably have been much shorter if it hadn't been for family and friends. There were more times than I would like to count when I called them for help. Sheryl's sister, Terry, never told me 'no'. Even when she moved to Buckner, about thirty minutes away, she showed up when I asked for help. The Brauningers always helped me when I needed it. Either David or Mallory Sasser was always willing to help. Rick Smith was not only was willing to help, but when my 4-wheel drive truck was not running, he let me use his for free. Without a doubt, the ones that I took advantage of the most were Sheryl, Adam, and Katie. As a last resort, I sometimes had to wake one of them up with the words they hated to hear, "Will you help me on the route?" They are relieved to know they will never hear that request again.

After completing Star Truck, it needed to be edited. A long time ago when Sheryl and I were dating, she warned me if I ever did anything wrong, she would tell me. What better person to find my mistakes? She is not only the love of my life, but intelligent and the most capable person I know to do the editing. Besides, her rates were the best. If the finished product is high quality it's her fault. Thank you, Sheryl!

When I finished the actual writing, I never even considered the possibility of creating a cover on my own. There was only one person I considered. I've known Matthew Calfas since he was a small boy. Matt's older brother, Ryan, played on several baseball and soccer teams with my son. Matt's God-given ability is to create artwork. Fortunately, Matt recognized that talent and worked to improve it. Recently, he was involved in a four-wheeler accident that resulted in the amputation of part of his right thumb. God gave him the strength and ability to overcome the setback. Thank you for your help, Matt, and I pray this exposure propels you into the success you deserve.

I have relayed many stories of my life and my ancestors' lives to Adam and Katie. I felt it was important for them to know stories of their parents and extended family. I wanted them to know how I lived my life before they ever came along. I want them to understand why I did what I did and how I became who I am today. I'd like them to experience it through my eyes. To Adam and Katie, I say read this and absorb it and someday, share it with your children. This book is my legacy to you.

I have frequently told Adam and Katie the secret to happiness is to discover the gifts God has given them and then find a way to use those gifts in life. I believe one of the gifts God has given me is the ability to communicate. I have tried to use it in my writing. If this book is good, then thank Him, not me. If not, then I'm still learning.